Business and Politics in Asia's Key Financial Centres

J.J. Woo

Business and Politics in Asia's Key Financial Centres

Hong Kong, Singapore and Shanghai

Springer

J.J. Woo
Nanyang Technological University
Singapore
Singapore

ISBN 978-981-13-5738-1 ISBN 978-981-287-985-1 (eBook)
DOI 10.1007/978-981-287-985-1

Softcover re-print of the Hardcover 1st edition 2016

Printed on acid-free paper

This Springer imprint is published by SpringerNature
The registered company is Springer Science+Business Media Singapore Pte Ltd.

To Debbie,
for providing care, support and inspiration

Preface

The (re)emergence of Asia as an economic power has been accompanied by the rise of Asian cities as the hubs of financial activity. This book focuses on three of these cities: Hong Kong, Singapore and Shanghai. Ranked among the world's most competitive financial centres, these three cities have established themselves as Asia's leading International Financial Centres (IFCs). In acting as intermediaries for global flows of capital, these three cities have effectively become the nexuses of power and finance. This book represents an attempt to understand the ways in which the political-economic context impacts financial sector development and policy-making.

In this book, I argue that each city is characterised by its unique *policy subsystem configuration*, with financial sector development and policy-making "nested" within the political-economic context of the IFC's policy subsystem. In order to provide a conceptual understanding of how the policy subsystem configuration impacts policy-making, I introduce the "nested instrumental approach". As an integrative framework of analysis that draws on the insights of both the policy subsystems and the policy instruments approaches, the nested instrumental approach allows for a more integrated understanding of both political context and policy considerations in the financial policy process. In doing so, it elucidates the causal linkages between context and policy.

This focus on context answers an important question that has driven the research behind this book: How have Hong Kong, Singapore, and Shanghai achieved comparable levels of success despite differences in their political-economic conditions? While much of the existing analysis tends to focus on economic structural variables of IFC development and hence compare and rank the three cities on the assumption of their similarity, the reality is that IFCs differ in many respects. Specifically, Hong Kong, Singapore and Shanghai are characterised by their unique and different political systems, models of financial governance and comparative advantages. Such differences affect the development trajectory of each IFC and determine the policy options available to its policy-makers.

With Asian IFCs becoming increasingly influential and powerful, there is a need to understand the political-economic mechanisms that make these cities "tick". Hopefully, this book provides a useful way for more research into these cities. It also seeks to contribute to ongoing scholarly efforts at theorising the public policy process. Given the increasingly complex policy environment of today, there is an ever-greater need for more integrative and context-sensitive frameworks of policy analysis. The nested instrumental approach presents one such possibility. In addressing the "nested instrumentality" that is inherent in the financial policy process, this book addresses the politics of finance, examining the inter-relations between business and finance in three of the Asia's top financial centres.

Acknowledgments

This book could not have been possible without the support of the Lee Kuan Yew School of Public Policy, National University of Singapore, where it was first developed as my doctoral thesis. I am therefore immensely grateful to the School's Dean, Professor Kishore Mahbubani for his support and encouragement. My thesis advisers, M. Ramesh and Michael Howlett, have also been instrumental in their guidance, having read and commented extensively on earlier versions of this book. I am also indebted to Darryl Jarvis, for having introduced me to the world of financial centres and encouraging my interest in international political economy.

Throughout my research and conception of this book, I have had the privilege of being mentored and guided by a stellar cast of academics. They include Kenneth Paul Tan, Suzaina Kadir, Dodo J. Thampapillai, John Ravenhill and Richard Carney. Their work continues to inspire me in my sojourn into the world of public policy and international political economy, and I am grateful for having had the opportunity to learn from them. I truly stand on the shoulders of giants.

Last but not least, I am extremely thankful to my family and friends for their love and support. To my parents and my sister Huiwen, for their constant presence in my life and the familial love that only they could provide. To Debbie, who has been a wonderful companion and source of inspiration. I am also thankful to Leong Ching and G. Nandhakumar for their friendship and hours of intellectually stimulating conversations. I hope my work does justice to all the support and encouragement I have received from all of you.

Contents

About the Author

J.J. Woo is an assistant professor in the Public Policy and Global Affairs Programme of the School of Humanities and Social Sciences, Nanyang Technological University. He holds a Ph.D. from the Lee Kuan Yew School of Public Policy, National University of Singapore, and a Master of Science in International Political Economy from the S. Rajaratnam School of International Studies, Nanyang Technological University. His research interests include Singapore politics, international financial centres and the political economy of finance.

List of Figures

List of Tables

Acronyms

AFC	Asian Financial Crisis
CBRC	China Banking Regulatory Commission
CIRC	China Insurance Regulatory Commission
CSRC	China Securities Regulatory Commission
DBS	Development Bank of Singapore
FSO	Shanghai Municipality Financial Services Office
FWPC	Shanghai Financial Work Party Committee
GFC	Global Financial Crisis
HKEx	Hong Kong Stock Exchange
HKMA	Hong Kong Monetary Authority
HSBC	Hong Kong Shanghai Banking Corporation
IFC	International Financial Centre
MAS	Monetary Authority of Singapore
PBC	People's Bank of China
SGX	Singapore Stock Exchange
SSE	Shanghai Stock Exchange

Chapter 1
Introduction

Asia has been experiencing rapid economic growth for the past few decades. This rapid economic expansion has been accompanied by an equally precipitous growth in the region's financial markets. As a consequence of this widespread financialization, Asian cities have grown in prominence as International Financial Centres (IFCs). According to the Global Financial Centres Index (GFCI) 17 that was released in March 2015, Hong Kong, Singapore and Tokyo were, respectively, ranked the third, fourth and fifth most competitive financial centres in the world (Yeandle 2015). In other words, three of the world's top five financial centres are from Asia. Other Asian cities ranked within the GFCI's top twenty most competitive financial centres include Seoul (seventh) and Shanghai (sixteenth).

It is also impossible to talk about economic development in Asia without mentioning the rise of China. Asia's economic development has largely been a beneficiary of China and its emergence as an economic superpower. Beginning with the opening up of its economy in 1979 and leveraging on its ample workforce, China has established itself as the world's leading producer of goods and services. With rapid urbanization and an increasingly affluent population, China has also become a burgeoning consumer market for firms, with China's growing domestic demand strengthening Asian supply chains (The Economist 2015). This systematic significance of China's economy is even more pronounced in global finance.

China's financial markets have deepened and grown over the past two decades. Based on its high savings rate and inward foreign direct investments, China has accumulated the world's largest reserves, while outward capital flows have been growing due to foreign direct investments and global lending by its sovereign wealth fund Chinese Investment Corporation (CIC) and Chinese companies, both state-owned and privately held (Dobbs et al. 2013). The Industrial and Commercial Bank of China Limited (ICBC), a state-owned bank, has also been recognized as a global systematically important bank by the Financial Stability Board (FSB) (ICBC 2013).

Among the GFCI's top twenty global financial centres, three cities are strongly affected by and involved in China's financial growth. These three cities are Hong Kong, Singapore and Shanghai. These three cities have experienced economic and financial growth on the back of China's economic rise. More importantly, all three cities are important nodes in China's ongoing efforts to internationalize its currency,

J.J. Woo, *Business and Politics in Asia's Key Financial Centres*,
DOI 10.1007/978-981-287-985-1_1

the Renminbi (RMB). While Hong Kong and Singapore are leading offshore RMB centres, Shanghai is generally recognized as China's main domestic financial centre and hence onshore RMB centre.

Given their systematic significance to Asian financial development, this book focuses on the three IFCs of Hong Kong, Singapore and Shanghai. It addresses the political-economic conditions which have contributed to the success of the three IFCs and emphasizes the importance of sociopolitical context in informing financial policy processes. This contributes to existing studies of IFC development that tend to be based solely on the analysis of economic variables and preconditions for financial sector development. This existing IFC literature is reviewed in the next chapter. Based on case studies of the three IFCs, I argue that political contextual variables are important in determining an IFC's success and defining the nature of its development.

Based on these existing economic studies of IFC development, financial centre rankings such as the GFCI tend to be relatively simplistic and overly reliant on quantifiable measures of competitiveness and connectivity that overstate the homogeneity of factors contributing to IFC success and development. These factors typically include strategic location and time zone, clustering and agglomeration of economic and financial activity, and the presence of transparent and robust regulatory and legal infrastructures. Hierarchies of IFCs have been built based on the prevalence of these factors as well as the size of the financial sector in different IFCs, implying a convergence among financial centres based on the development of these common success factors. These hierarchies continue to inform the IFC rankings that currently hold sway over policy-makers and public opinion on IFC development and success.

In reality, IFCs are vastly differentiated from each other. Each IFC is involved in a unique set of financial activities and follows variegated paths of historical and policy developments. Expectations of regulatory and IFC convergence in the existing literature provide an inadequate basis for understanding IFC development and result in an insufficiently comprehensive understanding of the types of policies required for IFC success. Furthermore, there has been insufficient emphasis on the political-economic context and set within this context, the policy preferences of policy-makers underpinning each IFC's development.

As a result, the existing literature paints an overly homogenous picture of IFC development, without adequately addressing the political-economic and policy differences across different IFCs. This is an important point to note, given that differences exist across the three cases of Hong Kong, Singapore and Shanghai in terms of their political systems and context, models of financial governance, the types of financial markets that each IFC is comparatively advantaged in, and the financial policies used by their respective governments in IFC development.

Singapore's rise as a leading IFC has been driven by its strategic geographic location, political and economic stability, efficient and reliable infrastructure, high regulatory standards and robust legal system. While offering a broad range of financial services, Singapore's financial centre is characterized by its formative role in the Asian Dollar Market, its deep and liquid capital markets, and its emerging role as a leading hub for wealth management and insurance (Monetary Authority of Singapore 2014). Although Singapore's development as an IFC was initially state-driven, with the financial sector recognized by the government as a priority sector contributing to overall economic development, subsequent involvement of the private sector in financial policy through extensive consultation and dialogues has resulted in state–industry "co-creation" of financial policies.

Similarly, Hong Kong's success as an IFC is based on its low taxes, sound legal system and efficient infrastructure. Furthermore, it benefits from its economic and political proximity to rising China. This availability of a Chinese "economic hinterland" has allowed Hong Kong to become China's main offshore financial centre and constitutes the Special Administrative Region's (SAR) main advantage (Wilson 2012). Hong Kong has since capitalized on this "China advantage" by leveraging on the ongoing liberalization of the RMB and positioning itself as the leading offshore RMB centre (Ng 2012).

In contrast to the Singapore government's more proactive financial policy role, Hong Kong largely operates according to free market principles, with state intervention kept to a minimum. However, this means that state–industry linkages are less dense, since the government's non-interventionist stance does not require as much feedback from the industry. While industry consultation does take place, it does not contribute significantly to financial policy-making. Nonetheless, the Hong Kong government has recently played a more active role in developing a market for trade in RMB and RMB-denominated investment products, vigorously promoting itself as the leading offshore RMB centre.

Despite being a relative late comer, Shanghai's rapid rise over the past decade has made it the "domestic financial hub of mainland China" and a centre for a diverse variety of Chinese financial activities (Laurenceson and Tang 2005). It is also slated to become a full IFC by 2020 (Lim 2013) and aims to become a global centre for RMB trading by 2015 (Bloomberg 2012). All this is intricately linked to China's overall national development, with the state "determining the timing, pace and economic and spatial configuration of Shanghai's development" (Lai 2006b). Shanghai's economic reforms are thus linked to national goals of economic development and financialization.

Financial sector development in Shanghai is heavily state-driven, with both central and municipal government agencies actively involved in financial policy-making. Like Hong Kong, financial policy-making lies within the control of the state. However, Shanghai exhibits a much larger extent of state intervention in financial markets than Hong Kong. Given that a majority of the financial institutions operating in Shanghai are state-owned or joint ventures with state-owned enterprises, financial market participation in Shanghai is also state-dominated. Unlike the case of Singapore, there is very little space for private sector industry actors to influence financial policy-making in Shanghai.

In short, Hong Kong, Singapore and Shanghai are each driven by their unique political-economic circumstances, which further feeds into each IFC's unique financial policy practices and preferences. Observers have noted that "Asia's multiple and varied financial centres reflect not only the region's vast geography but also its different economic realities" (The Economist 2007). Despite such distinct differences in political-economic circumstances, all three cities have rapidly risen up the ranks to become the fastest growing IFCs in Asia. A core argument of this book is that such success was achieved through the respective governments' roles in formulating and implementing financial policies that are tailored to each IFC's political-economic circumstances.

This means that each IFC's success is underpinned by a unique set or mix of financial policies. Hong Kong, Singapore and Shanghai have thus attained comparable levels of success as the fastest growing IFCs in Asia based on the implementation of different mixes of financial policies that reflect their unique individual political-economic contexts. This extends the analysis beyond the existing literature's focus on IFC convergence, which does not adequately take into account such differences in political-economic context and the types of financial policies implemented within each IFC but instead overemphasizes commonality in economic structural variables.

In short, this book seeks to provide a clearer understanding of how Hong Kong, Singapore and Shanghai have each risen to their positions as leading Asian IFCs, focusing in particular on the interactions between the political exigencies of policy subsystems and policy considerations in the form of policy instruments and mixes. Given that the existing literature does not provide the analytical tools that allow for such an undertaking, this book develops an analytical framework termed the "nested instrumental approach", which combines the policy subsystem and policy instruments approaches for a more integrated and nuanced analysis of IFC development. This approach is briefly described in the next section and further discussed in Chap. 3.

In combining the policy subsystem and policy instruments approaches, the nested instrumental approach provides an integrated framework for analysis that melds both political context and policy considerations in understanding IFC development and success. While Chap. 3 provides a deeper discussion of the approach by delineating its component parts and describing its inherent logic of "nested instrumentality", this section briefly introduces the nested instrumental approach. Figure 1.1 provides a general illustration of the nested instrumental approach.

As Fig. 1.1 shows, the nested instrumental approach takes the policy subsystem as its basic unit of analysis. A policy subsystem is essentially a set of "actors with sufficient knowledge of a problem area, or a resource at stake, to allow them to

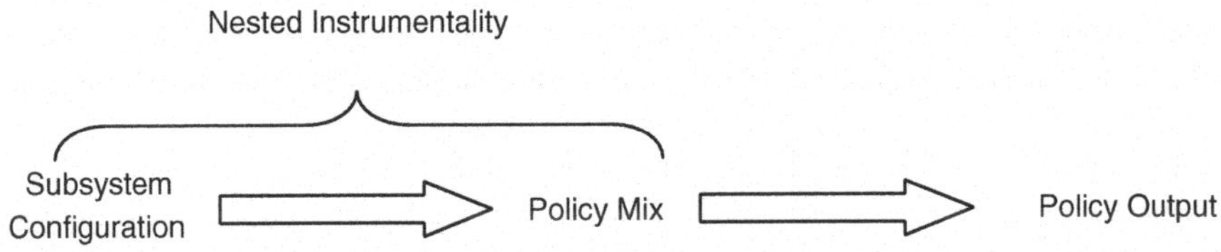

Fig. 1.1 Nested instrumental approach

participate in the process of developing possible alternative courses of action to address the issues raised at the agenda-setting stage" (Howlett et al. 2009). While policy subsystem configuration has been related to the openness of a subsystem to new actors and ideas (Howlett and Ramesh 1998), this book defines policy subsystem configuration around relations of dominance and dependence among subsystem actors. This means that subsystems are configured around a dominant actor or set of actors. This concept of subsystem actor dominance draws from Sabatier's work on advocacy coalitions, which posits the presence of dominant coalitions within a subsystem (Sabatier 1988).

Policy subsystem configurations subsequently define policy mix design, which in turn determines the attainment of desired policy outputs. In other words, a policy mix is "nested" within its policy subsystem, with the design of the policy mix and its component instruments defined by the interests, preferences and beliefs of dominant actors. This use of policy instruments as a means for achieving policy outputs within the political-economic context of the policy subsystem connotes a logic of "nested instrumentality". Furthermore, dominant actors influence policy mix design through two channels: an *instrumental channel* that involves instrumental constituencies and an *ideational channel* involving advocacy coalitions.

Such a logic of nested instrumentality underpins IFC development in Hong Kong, Singapore and Shanghai. As will be discussed in later chapters, all three cases show how individual subsystem configurations have led to the design of unique policy mixes that both reflect and cater to the interests, preferences, and beliefs of dominant subsystem actors and which are implemented for the attainment of desired policy outputs such as financial system stability or IFC development. The nested instrumental approach will be discussed at greater length in Chap. 3.

Based on the nested instrumental approach, I argue that IFC success in all three cases is related to the way in which policy mix design is embedded within each IFC's unique policy subsystem configuration. As discussed in later chapters, financial policy mixes typically comprise stabilizing, developmental and enabling policies in varying weightage, reflecting the interests and preferences of dominant subsystem actors. Specifically, dominant subsystem actors are able to influence policy mix design, in terms of the weightage of these three types of financial policies within a financial policy mix, through two channels: an instrumental channel involving participation in instruments constituencies and an ideational channel involving the formation of advocacy coalitions.

As the rest of this book will show, Hong Kong, Singapore and Shanghai have all attained success as IFCs by nesting policy mix design within the political-economic context of prevailing policy subsystem configurations. The presence of a unique policy subsystem configuration in each IFC has led to the adaptive formulation and implementation of policy mixes tailored to the IFC's subsystem configuration. This is largely achieved through the influence of dominant subsystem actors working through instrumental and ideational channels to exercise and enforce their instrument preferences and policy beliefs in policy mix design.

The nested instrumental approach provides a useful conceptual framework for exploring this causal linkage between subsystem configuration and policy mix design, by combining and integrating the policy instruments and policy subsystems approaches. While the nested instrumental approach contributes theoretically to public policy theory, this book is also an empirical study of Hong Kong, Singapore and Shanghai as IFCs. These three cases are also highly suited for a comparative IFC study, given their similarities and differences.

The three IFCs are highly comparable. Consistently ranked among the top five most competitive IFCs globally, Hong Kong and Singapore are the most successful IFCs to have emerged from Asia. While Shanghai's position in global rankings has fluctuated, it remains ranked among the top IFCs in Asia. Furthermore, the Chinese central government has made clear its intentions to establish Shanghai as a leading IFC by 2020. Taken together, Hong Kong, Singapore and Shanghai are the fastest growing IFCs in Asia. Furthermore, all three IFCs have emerged from similar historical roles as trading entrepot. While Hong Kong and Singapore first started off as trading ports for their British colonial masters, Shanghai has a long history of being a key port for Chinese trade with the rest of the world.

In all three cases, the emergence and development of early financial institutions was predicated upon the presence of substantial trade activity. As a consequence of their positions as global trade and finance hubs, Hong Kong, Singapore and Shanghai are all considered major or "Alpha+" global cities (Sassen 2001; GaWC Research Network 2011). The three cities also share a similar colonial history. Both Hong Kong and Singapore started off as British colonies, while Shanghai experienced occupation by Britain, France, the USA and Japan between the Opium War and the Second World War. The presence of foreign powers in all three cases had stimulated increased cross-border trading activities and the emergence of financial services related to foreign trade.

In terms of governance, all three IFCs are run by highly capable and autonomous governments.[1] Since its independence in 1965, Singapore's People's Action Party (PAP) has retained one-party rule. Given continued popular support for the PAP, the Singapore government possesses an extraordinary amount of policy autonomy and capacity. Although Hong Kong was returned to Chinese rule in 1997, its status as a Special Autonomous Region (SAR) has allowed the Hong Kong government to retain a high level of autonomy in economic policy-making. While Shanghai is neither an independent state nor an autonomous region but a municipality under Chinese central government rule, the Shanghai municipal government enjoys significant autonomy from the centre (Wu 2000; Lai 2006a), bolstered by the presence of a pro-growth coalition led by the local government (Zhang 2002).

However, the three cases are also different in two important ways. These differences provide a useful basis for comparative study. First, political and policy arrangements differ across the three IFCs. The Hong Kong government operates within a highly liberal political environment and plays a minimal role in financial

[1]Hong Kong and Singapore are both ranked highly on government effectiveness by the World Bank's Governance Indicators, http://info.worldbank.org/governance/wgi/index.aspx#reports; for the effectiveness and autonomy of the Shanghai government, see (Wu 2000).

sector development due to its belief in the free markets. In contrast, the Singapore government is much more hands-on in its approach to financial sector development, although industry actors are also heavily involved and influential in the formulation of financial policies. While Shanghai is similarly state-driven in its financial sector development, it does not feature private sector actors in financial policy-making due to the dominance of state-owned banks and financial institutions in its financial markets.

As such, financial policy-making in Shanghai is almost completely state-dominated, while that in Singapore is state-led with strong private sector participation and Hong Kong's laissez-faire approach features minimal government intervention that allows private sector actors to drive financial sector development within the boundaries of the legal and regulatory infrastructure. These differences in political-economic context flow into differences in the types of policies enacted to develop the respective financial sectors. This linkage between political context and the policy process is further discussed in later chapters.

Second, the three IFCs feature distinctly different types of financial markets and activities. This has resulted in the formation of different comparative advantages across the three IFCs. Hong Kong's deep and liquid securities market and proximity to China have allowed it to establish itself as a loan syndication and offshore RMB centre. Based on its first mover advantage in establishing the Asian Development Market and the government's successful efforts at attracting private banking and fund management activities, Singapore is well-established as a Foreign Exchange (Forex) and Wealth Management Centre. Owing to the Chinese government's fiscal policies and the size of Shanghai's primary and secondary sectors, Shanghai has relatively large and active markets for debt and commodities futures (Jao 2003).

While similarities across the three cases make Hong Kong, Singapore and Shanghai comparable as case studies, differences in the three cities' political systems and financial governance models provide useful independent variables for studying IFC success in the three cities. Such differences in political context and financial policy practices are important for illustrating how different financial policy regimes can lead to comparable levels of IFC development and success. Drawing on the example of Hong Kong and Singapore, Tan and Lim note that similar levels of IFC success may be driven by "different philosophies" and different extents of government intervention (Tan and Lim 2007).

Importantly, differences in the financial sector specializations of the three IFCs refute the existing literature's expectations of IFC convergence and suggest the need for a deeper study of how unique comparative advantages are developed as a consequence of different policy instruments and mixes used in IFC development. By delving into the subsystem configurations and policy mixes of each IFC and how these have driven their individual successes, this book addresses existing gaps in current understandings of IFC development and success.

The remainder of this book serve to further elucidate and explicate the points introduced above. A review of the relevant literature is provided in Chap. 2. In this chapter, I first review the literature on financial policy and financial sector regulation in general, followed by the more specialized IFC literature. However, these literatures do not adequately explain the exact means through which governments of IFCs attain success nor do they address the impact of the political-economic context on IFC development. Hence, there is a need for a new theoretical framework based on an amalgamation of the existing work on policy subsystems and policy instruments.

This is provided in Chap. 3, which delves into the theoretical framework and research methodology underlying this book. The theoretical framework that will guide the analysis in the rest of this book is the "nested instrumental approach". This is based on a combination of the policy instruments and policy subsystems approaches, both of which are discussed in this chapter by way of a brief literature review. Having provided an overview of the policy instruments and policy subsystems literature, this chapter will then discuss the theoretical and conceptual foundations of the nested instrumental approach. This is followed by a discussion of the methodology that has informed and guided the research behind this book.

Chapters 4–6 delve into the actual cases, with Chap. 4 focusing on Hong Kong, Chap. 5 on Singapore, and Chap. 6 on Shanghai. These chapters provide a descriptive introduction to each IFC, focusing on aspects related to the components of the nested instrumental approach. Each chapter briefly introduces the IFC and its historical background and describes its unique comparative advantage, model of financial governance, regulatory regime, policy mix and policy subsystem configuration. Taken together, Chaps. 4–6 provide in-depth descriptions of the cases, with an emphasis on the political-economic context of each IFC and the policies enacted to build and develop these IFCs.

Description is naturally followed by analysis. Chapter 7 provides a comparative analysis of the three cases, explaining similarities and differences across the cases in terms of their comparative advantages, financial governance models, regulatory agencies, financial policy mixes and financial policy subsystems. The "nested instrumental approach" is then applied to the analysis of the three cases, providing an integrated comparison that combines both political and policy variables.

Chapter 8 summarizes the findings, insights and core arguments of this book, highlighting in particular its theoretical and empirical contributions to existing IFC studies. Policy implications and recommendations associated with these findings are also discussed, along with other potential avenues for research on IFCs. This chapter will serve as a conclusion for the book.

References

Bloomberg (2012) Shanghai aims to become global Yuan trading center by 2015. Bloom. News

Dobbs R, Leung N, Lund S (2013) China's rising stature in global finance. McKinsey Q

GaWC Research Network (2011) The World according to GaWC 2010. Loughborough University, Leicestershire, UK

Howlett M (2009) Governance modes, policy regimes and operational plans: a multi-level nested model of policy instrument choice and policy design. Policy Sci 42:73–89

Howlett M, Ramesh M (1998) policy subsystem configurations and policy change: operationalizing the postpositivist analysis of the politics of the policy process. Policy Stud J 26:466–481
ICBC (2013) ICBC named global systematically important bank. ICBC, China
Jao YC (2003) Shanghai and Hong Kong as international financial centres: historical perspective and contemporary analysis
Lai H (2006a) Reform and the non-state economy in China: the political economy of liberalization strategies. Palgrave Macmillan, New York
Lai K (2006b) Developing Shanghai as an International Financial Centre: progress and prospects
Laurenceson J, Tang KK (2005) Shanghai's development as an International Financial Center. Rev Pac Basin Financ Mark Policies RPBFMP 08:147–166
Lim K (2013) China's regulators urge for reform of financial sector. In: channelnewsasia.com. http://www.channelnewsasia.com/stories/economicnews/view/1210725/1/.html. Accessed 17 Mar 2013
Monetary Authority of Singapore (2014) Singapore Financial Centre. http://www.mas.gov.sg/singapore-financial-centre/overview.aspx. Accessed 8 June 2015
Ng G (2012) Hong Kong banks on yuan for the future. In: China Daily. http://www.chinadaily.com.cn/china/HK15th/2012-07/01/content_15539890.htm. Accessed 20 Aug 2012
Sabatier PA (1988) An advocacy coalition framework of policy change and the role of policy-oriented learning therein. Policy Sci 21:129–168
Sassen S (2001) Global networks. Linked Cities, Routledge, New York 10001
Tan CH, Lim JYS (2007) Singapore and Hong Kong as competing financial centres. Saw Centre Financial Studies, Singapore
The Economist (2015) Made in China? The Economist
The Economist (2007) All shapes and sizes: Asia's financial centres reflect its vast geography and divergent economies. The Economist
Wilson K (2012) Hong Kong retains edge in region. In: China Daily. http://usa.chinadaily.com.cn/weekly/2012-06/29/content_15533851.htm. Accessed 20 Aug 2012
Wu F (2000) The global and local dimensions of place-making: remaking Shanghai as a World City. Urban Stud 37:1359–1377
Yeandle M (2015) Global financial centres index 17. Z/Yen Group and Qatar Financial Centre Authority, London, UK
Zhang T (2002) Urban development and a socialist pro-growth coalition in Shanghai. Urban Aff Rev 37:475–499

Chapter 2
IFC Studies and the Politics of Finance

The agglomeration and clustering of financial sector activity within cities has resulted in the establishment of the IFC as a subject of research and academic inquiry. IFC studies have also drawn from an existing literature on financial sector development and policy. Policy-makers seeking to develop their cities as financial hubs have long recognized the importance of understanding the nature of financial sector development as well as the financial policies that underpin an IFC's success. A well-established literature on financial sector policy and development provides the analytical tools required for understanding how government policies facilitate or affect IFC development.

Yet, this literature does not adequately take into account contextual and spatial variables, focusing instead on financial policy only at a general level and within the domestic economy. The recognition of these flaws prompted the development of a more specific literature on IFCs that sought to document and understand the rise and success of leading IFCs such as London and New York. Predominantly driven by the work of economists and geographers, these studies contributed to the formation of a specific literature on IFCs that accounts for spatiality and temporality in financial policy. Taken together, the literatures on financial policy and IFCs provide the background information and conceptual knowledge necessary for studying the success of Hong Kong, Singapore and Shanghai as IFCs.

Furthermore, there has been a growing interest in the "politics of finance" among economists and financial experts, with a focus on the influence and implications of politics on financial sector development. However, this emerging strand of research remains at a relatively nascent stage. The remainder of this chapter will provide a critical review of the existing literature on IFCs, financial sector policy and development, as well as emerging studies on the politics of finance. In providing an overview of these literatures, this chapter situates the rest of the book within existing IFC studies and points out the ways in which it contributes to this literature.

J.J. Woo, *Business and Politics in Asia's Key Financial Centres*,
DOI 10.1007/978-981-287-985-1_2

Financial Sector Policy and Development

Given the financial sector's role in generating revenues and supporting real economic growth, research and scholarly work on financial policy have long been related to the impact of the financial sector on the real economy. Financial sector development has been shown to be an important driving force for economic growth through what is known as a "finance–growth nexus" (De Gregorio and Guidotti 1995; Jayaratne and Strahan 1996; Levine 1997; Beck et al. 2000; Levine et al. 2000; Rajan and Zingales 2001a; Calderón and Liu 2003; Demirguc-Kunt and Levine 2008; Zhang and Chen 2013), with financial depth identified as a significant contributing variable to real economic growth (King and Levine 1993). Financial sector development also stimulates growth less directly by boosting manufacturing activities and stimulating trade (Beck 2002). Conversely, real economic growth may also stimulate financial sector expansion via increased savings, suggesting a "reciprocal externality" between the financial and real sectors within an overall process of endogenous growth (Berthelemy and Varoudakis 1996).

Given this important contribution of financial sector development to economic growth, scholarly work in the fields of economics and IPE has largely been focused on understanding how states promote economic growth and competitiveness through financial sector development. However, economists have tended to view financial sector development as a market-driven consequence of burgeoning supply and demand for financial services, while IPE scholars have focused on the active, targeted and often strategic government interventions that drive financial sector development (Cerny 1993a). Nonetheless, economists have since taken a greater interest in the stabilizing role of government interventions in financial markets, especially after the 2008 GFC. This brought a renewed focus on financial policies as both the cause of and potential solution to financial crises (Krugman 2009; Claessens et al. 2010; Stiglitz 2010; Demirgüç-Kunt and Servén 2010; Rötheli 2010; Financial Crisis Inquiry Commission 2011; Rajan 2011; Roubini and Mihm 2011; Peters et al. 2011; Gertler et al. 2012).

However, these studies remained focused on crisis management measures rather than measures geared towards building up and developing new financial markets or sectors. This more developmental focus would be taken up by scholars of IPE, who in the 1990s focused on the role of the state in promulgating policies aimed at financial sector development. This state-centric approach has yielded key theoretical innovations such as the developmental state and competition state models (Cerny 1993a, b; Leftwich 1995; Palan et al. 1996). Other IPE scholars have sought to understand financial sector development in the context of the international system by identifying liberal, realist, pluralist and cognitive models for understanding global finance (Cohen 1996; Dombrowski 1998). However, these IPE studies did not as yet provide a sufficiently clear understanding of the precise measures used by the state to facilitate financial sector development.

This lacuna would be addressed by researchers who focused specifically on the study of financial policies. At the heart of financial sector development is financial policy. According to Polak, financial policies relate to both the domestic financial structure of the economy and the external financial structure, with the latter including exchange rates, and the rules and institutions that guide capital flows (Polak 1989). Polak reaffirms the "finance–growth nexus" by noting that economic development is the "yardstick by which financial flows and financial policies can be made commensurate" (Polak 1989). This necessitates a strong regulatory role of the state, with government interventions focused on reducing market failure (Stiglitz et al. 1993).

Demirguc-Kunt and Levine have emphasized the importance of financial policies in shaping the "structure and functioning of financial systems" by ensuring political and macroeconomic stability, establishing the legal and information infrastructure necessary for financial transactions to take place as well as a regulatory and supervisory infrastructure that "enables" and empowers markets by encouraging financial market competition, liberalization and access (Demirguc-Kunt and Levine 2008). Similarly, the World Bank's recent GFDR report emphasizes the role of the state in better aligning private incentives to private interests, establishing sound regulatory and supervisory frameworks, encouraging financial market contestability and competition, promoting transparency of information and strengthening the governance of state-owned banks (The World Bank 2013).

Hellman, Murdock and Stiglitz have also suggested that a set of "financial restraint" policies form the core of government efforts at financial deepening and financial sector development (Hellman et al. 1997). Financial restraint policies aim to create rents in the financial sector through selective government interventions such as deposit rate controls, regulations on entry and restrictions on competition, in the process reducing opportunistic behaviour and inducing efficiency among private market actors (Hellman et al. 1997; Hellman and Murdock 1997). Financial restraint policies also contribute towards the build-up of 'reputational capital' among private agents and the development of strong governance mechanisms in financial institutions (Hellman and Murdock 1997).

Of particular importance is the policy instruments that contribute to the management and governance of the financial sector. Seen from this instrumental perspective, financial policy involves seeking the "right balance among policy instruments", with financial regulation being part of a set of "complementary financial policy instruments" (OECD 2006). Financial policy involves a wide array of government interventions, with financial regulation representing merely one aspect or type of financial policy. This is particularly the case in East Asia, where the state's role in financial markets has involved creating, regulating and even directing credit to financial institutions, with financial policies serving to both ensure market stability and encourage financial sector growth (Stiglitz et al. 1993). Similarly, Carmichael notes that the public sector participates in the financial sector through its various roles as a regulator of financial institutions, owner of financial institutions, market participant, fiduciary agent and through direct intervention in market operations (Carmichael 2002).

This focus on financial policy instruments has culminated in more recent attempts to provide a typology of financial policy instruments, differentiating between the following: (i) *market-developing policies* that focus on the long-term building of institutions and infrastructure; (ii) *market-enabling policies* that involve regulatory reforms and encouraging greater competition and (iii) *market-stabilizing policies* such as regulatory oversight and macro-prudential management (Barajas et al. 2013). Much of the existing literature has thus far focused on market-stabilizing policies, with efforts at understanding market-developing and market-enabling policies at a relatively nascent stage.

According to mainstream conceptions of financial policy, the *raison d'être* of financial policy is essentially the maintenance of market stability and the prevention of crises. This *stabilizing* aspect and its inherent objectives of market stability and investor protection remain the most commonly held view of financial policy. Under this view, the "core goals" of financial policy are basically the maintenance of financial system stability and integrity, protection of depositors and investors, as well as ensuring that financial intermediaries perform their fiduciary duties to their clients and shareholders (OECD 2006). Financial regulation is a particularly important stabilizing financial policy that exploits the coercive power of the state to ensure market stability and protect investors (Stigler 1988).

However, this exercise of coercive state power is founded on an "essential faith in capitalism" that precludes direct government intervention in markets (Snider 2011). Rather, financial regulation is focused on establishing the systems and rules that ensure the efficient functioning of markets and prevent the occurrence of any market failure that may arise from market distortions or information asymmetry (Vittas 1991).

However, this commonly accepted stabilizing view of financial policy does not take into account the more active and direct roles of financial policy-makers in financial sector development. Due to distributional concerns inherent in the political process, financial regulation has often been used by governments to achieve objectives that may not be related to market stability and consumer protection, such as protecting domestic financial institutions or "supporting specific industrial or regional policies by channelling funds to particular sectors" (OECD 2006). In conflating financial sector development with industrial policy, financial policy may also be "strategic" or "developmental" in nature (Cerny 1993). Such development-oriented financial policies can further be separated into enabling and developmental policies.

Financial policies can be used to build markets through "*enablement*—the creation not merely of incentives but of those conditions that allow activities to take place" (Baldwin et al. 1998). This often involves the allocation of financial resources to targeted sectors (Haggard and Lee 1993). Enabling policies also allow for the establishment and maintenance of "national comparative advantages", by constructing conditions and resources that are favourable or necessary for the efficient functioning of financial markets (Arndt et al. 1988; Porter 1998). In such a way, enabling policies can be used to reach economic and social policy objectives by stimulating growth and productivity as well as enhancing competitiveness through "sectoral liberalization" (International Finance Corporation 2010).

Financial policy also plays a *developmental* role in ensuring that the financial system and infrastructure is geared towards the attainment of developmental goals. Such "development-oriented financial regulation" typically involves the allocation of financial resources towards developmental goals or the appropriate investment projects that contribute towards sustainable and equitable economic development (Chang and Grabel 2004; Murinde and Mlambo 2011). Strategies and policy instruments for doing so include influencing bank lending to key sectors, long-term financing by development banks and managing financial firms' asset holdings through "variable asset-based reserve requirements" (Chang and Grabel 2004).

Such developmental financial policies are therefore used by states in "developmentalist fashion" to favour desired market outcomes (Hira 2006). According to Stiglitz and Uy, financial regulation as a form of development-oriented government intervention contributed to the rapid growth of emerging Asian nations during the "East Asian Miracle" (Stiglitz and Uy 1996). Gordon and Li further note that the Chinese government tends to choose regulations that maximize social welfare objectives and facilitate the collection of revenue from both foreign and domestic investors, by using regulation in place of taxes to extract rents (Gordon and Li 2003).

In short, financial policy comprises three types of policy instruments, namely stabilizing, enabling and developmental instruments. Stabilizing instruments largely include financial regulations that are geared towards ensuring financial sector stability and investor protection; these have traditionally formed the bulk of a financial policy-maker's toolkit. Enabling instruments are typically used to establish or develop the market conditions necessary for financial institutions to operate and thrive and are closely related to industrial policy. Lastly, developmental instruments refer to financial policies that allow policy-makers to directly channel resources towards financial sectors or markets which in turn contribute to the overall economic development of the IFC. As later chapters will show, stabilizing, enabling and developmental instruments are used in varying extents by financial policy-makers in Hong Kong, Singapore and Shanghai, based on the sociopolitical contexts within which these policy-makers are enmeshed.

However, the existing scholarly work on financial sector policy is limited by its assumption of a unitary monolithic state. Almost all the studies reviewed in this section take the "state" or "government" as the basic unit of analysis and agency. In reality, the formulation and implementation of financial policies are carried out by a wide variety of state and non-state actors. These typically include public agencies at all levels of government as well as industry actors, whether exerting their influence over the financial policy process directly or working through industry associations. Litan et al. (2002) provide a more nuanced approach to understanding financial policy by including the entire "range of institutions and practices by which authority is exercised", terming such an approach financial sector *governance* rather than policy. This book takes a similar approach by emphasizing financial governance in its totality of policy subsystems and instruments over a narrow focus on financial policy.

However, the largest shortcoming of this existing literature on financial policy is its neglect of spatiality. These studies tend to locate financial policy-making at the national level, with few attempts to situate this understanding at the level of the city or IFC. This is a weakness that permeates both the work of economists and IPE scholars alike. While studies of financial policy by economists have tended to focus on the national government, IPE scholars have tended to focus on the international financial system, similarly taking the state as the basic unit of analysis. In reality, financial policy-making takes place at the level of the IFC, with city or local governments playing a particularly important role. Furthermore, the IFC is itself an intersection between domestic policy-making and international systemic pressures. A small but significant literature on IFCs, driven by scholars of economics and geography, has sought to understand financial policy-making in the context of the IFC. This literature is crucial for the direction which this book has taken.

International Financial Centres

The origins of the IFC literature can be traced back to early studies by economists on financial centres, which were largely based on a desire to understand the emergence of financial centres as centralized locations of financial and economic activity in the 1950s. These studies allowed scholars to establish clear definitions of what a financial centre is and understand the factors which have contributed to the emergence of major successful IFCs such as London and New York. An oft-cited and succinct definition of a financial centre is provided by Kindleberger, who defines a financial centre as "a single worldwide center with the highly specialized functions of lending abroad and serving as a clearinghouse for payments among countries" (Kindleberger 1974). This means that financial centres typically perform "medium-of-exchange" and "interspatial store-of-value" functions (Kindleberger 1974).

According to Reed (1981), a "financial center is an urban area which contains a concentration of specialized institutions that possess, at least marginally, the international skills and capabilities necessary to facilitate the flow of goods, services, information and capital between its own national economy and the other national economies of the world". Park (1982) provides a more nuanced approach by differentiating between "primary, booking, funding and collecting" financial centres, with each type of centre based on the range and type of international financial transactions that take place within it.

Aside from providing broad general definitions of financial centres, these early IFC scholars also sought to delve deeper into the exact characteristics which make a particular location a financial centre. An important characteristic is the size, liquidity and complexity of financial markets as measured by the number of financial institutions and mobility of capital or funds (Kindleberger 1974; Giddy 1983; Choi et al. 1986; Pagano et al. 1990). Reflecting the international nature of financial centres, a related characteristic is the presence of foreign financial institutions and non-resident market participants (Dufey and Giddy 1978; Choi et al. 1986; O'Brien 1992).

Early scholars also noted the importance of favourable policies that define a location's role as an IFC, with such policies including the maintenance of currency convertibility (Nadler et al. 1955), favourable regulations and taxes (McRae and Cairncross 1973; Choi et al. 1986) and active efforts by the government to attract foreign financial institutions (Johns 1983). Another less direct role of policy is human capital development, with IFCs typically characterized by the presence of skilled financial sector specialists (Nadler et al. 1955; McRae and Cairncross 1973; Kindleberger 1974). These laid the foundation for subsequent efforts to empirically test the validity of such policy and socio-economic factors in contributing to IFC development through the use of quantitative models (Sagaram and Wickramanayake 2012).

Another important aspect of such early scholarly work on IFCs involved identifying and studying the various factors which contribute to the formation of IFCs. According to Kindleberger's "staple theory", the development of banking from its initial roles in serving "sovereigns and nobles" to subsequently serving commerce and government and finally acting as financial intermediaries resulted in the formation of national financial centres which eventually become IFCs (Kindleberger 1974). The concentration of financial activities within IFCs is also explained by the need for face-to-face interaction among market participants, the ability of localization to overcome the costs of information and the dislocation of cross-boundary trades due to time zone differences (Kindleberger 1974).

Goldberg et al. (1988) attribute the development of IFCs to international trade, international financial intermediation and industrial organization factors. The development of these factors stimulates the emergence and growth of a financial services sector, which in turn contributes to the financial market depth and breadth necessary for the development of an IFC. Other more specific factors that have been positively associated with the growth in size of the financial sector include imports, economic development, the number and size of multinational companies present and the significance of the city within the country and time zone, while exports and financial regulation are negatively associated with the financial sector development (Goldberg et al. 1988). The importance of trade in IFC development is underscored by the role that IFCs play in balancing out the surplus and deficits of countries that trade with each other, resulting in the development of an assortment of financial instruments for this very purpose (Economists Advisory Group 1984).

Furthermore, once financial firms within an IFC have achieved external economies of scale and economies of agglomeration, the IFC tends to attain a form of self-perpetuating' growth, even if the initial motivations that had led to the development of the IFC no longer apply (Davis 1990). In other words, a greater number of firms locating to a IFC can result in financial sector growth due to the enlargement of markets, availability of contacts, skilled labour and auxiliary services such as accountants, lawyers and actuaries (Davis 1990). This further led to the view that once IFCs are formed, they show "remarkable powers of survival" in a cumulative process that "concentrate financial markets in a small number of centres" (Economists Advisory Group 1984).

While such early studies have provided definitions of IFC's, delineated the characteristics which qualify a city or location as an IFC and yielded important insights into the factors which have facilitated the emergence of an IFC, they were nonetheless limited by their over-reliance on economics. In particular, these studies focus on quantifiable IFC development variables such as financial market size or the number of financial institutions, which do not reveal much about relations between regulators, financial institutions and other financial sector actors. This means that issues of financial policy actor agency and sociopolitical context were largely under-explored.

As a consequence, these early IFC studies tended to take a passive view of the state in IFC development. According to such early studies, the growth and development of an IFC are typically associated with increased flows of global financial capital and agglomeration of economic activity. The market thus took precedence in these explanations of IFC development. Recognizing this neglect of context, subsequent IFC studies by economic geographers have sought to incorporate spatiality and its inherent sociopolitical assemblages into the study of IFCs. This began with efforts at developing more geographically informed definitions of IFCs, such as Jones' (1992) typology of IFCs as *sub-regional* (involving bilateral trade between the IFC's host country and other economies), *regional* (providing financial services to a specified geographical location) or *global centres* (providing an extensive range of financial services to the whole world). Similarly, Gehrig (2000) defined IFCs as "geographical locations with agglomerations of branches or subsidiaries of banks and other financial intermediaries in narrowly defined regions".

An important theoretical development within this geographically driven study of IFCs is the global cities movement, which studies how a select group of cities tend to dominate the global economy due to their "higher-order functions of control and coordination of economic flows" (Poon 2003). Global cities are therefore "used by global capital as 'basing points' in the spatial organization and articulation of production and markets" (Friedman 2002). While globalization and advances in communications technology have resulted in a "spatial dispersal of economic activities at the metropolitan, national and global level", there is also a "territorial centralization" of management and control over these dispersed economic activities (Sassen 1996).

This centralization means that despite the spatial dispersal of economic activities associated with globalization and technological advancements, global cities continue to serve as sites for the facilitation of global economic transactions by functioning as "command centers in a global economy" (Sassen 1996). Such territorial centralization of global economic activity is in turn associated with two important factors that contribute to IFC formation: national consolidation and market liberalization (Sassen 1999). As such, cities that contain higher concentrations of "major institutional equity holdings" such as banks and investment houses are more likely to become successful IFCs (Sassen 1999). IFC formation and success, according to the global cities literature, is thus based on a simultaneous centralization of financial activities in IFCs and technologically driven dispersal of economic activities globally.

According to Gehrig, this paradox of simultaneous dispersal and centralization of financial activities can be explained by assessing the informational content of financial activities. In particular, IFCs facilitate trade in securities that are "informationally sensitive" and require geographical concentration for communication while securities that are more standardized flow more freely across borders in response to regulatory differences (Gehrig 2000). Information, or access to it, has also been seen as an important factor in determining the functional distribution of roles and services among IFCs (Porteous 1995; Zhao 2013). Such concentration of communication based on the need for information sharing among major market actors results in the formation of an IFC's "social infrastructure" (Sassen 1999). This growing awareness of such a "social infrastructure" has driven subsequent work by economic geographers who sought to achieve a greater awareness of both the spatial and sociopolitical contexts.

For instance, Clark and Wojcick (2007) argue that global finance is deeply influenced by place-specific financial institutions, with the language of finance serving to culturally and ideologically reinforce state–market–societal relations. This prompted a cultural economy approach that sought to understand how social relations constitute and define financial and economic activities (Clark and Thrift 2005; Hall 2006, 2010). Of particular interest is the role of knowledge networks in connecting financial actors and imbuing their activities with market meanings (Sidaway and Bryson 2002; Lai 2006, 2011). This focus on knowledge networks and the role of socio-technical assemblages in determining the nature of financial practices and subjectivities derives from earlier work by economic geographers on financialization.

This strand of work had sought to understand how financial knowledge production and performativity affect financial market development as well as financial policies (Pryke 1991; Langley 2006, 2009; Pryke and Gay 2007). As a major actor within these networks, states play a crucial role in producing financial subjectivity among its citizens, directing the financial practices of such financialized subjected towards developmental goals (Lai and Tan 2015). Yet at the same time, private sector financial actors are equally able to determine the nature of financial sector development through the diffusion of specific market rationalisms (Carroll and Jarvis 2014), favouring specific locations as investment destinations (Wojcik 2013), or proliferating an increasingly complex array of financial instruments (Christophers 2009).

Through this work on financialization, economic geographers have sought to provide an understanding of how sociopolitical relations and interactions, particularly those involving state and financial elites, influence the development of IFCs as well as the nature of their financial markets and subjects (Aalbers 2008; Hall 2012). This has provided a much-needed focus on the spatial and social context and its impact on IFC development. However, IFC scholars from the public policy and political economy perspectives have been slow to pick up on these insights. This book will draw on this emerging interest in the socio-economic context of IFC development among economic geographers, although its does so from the public policy perspective.

Studies of global cities have also often taken a comparative inter-IFC approach, focusing in particular on the reputational factors and perceptions of IFCs among various financial market participants (GaWC Research Network 2014). This has prompted a more agentic view of IFCs is presented in the work of IFC scholars who sought to study inter-IFC competition. Such efforts have largely been focused on the study of a "hierarchy of international financial centres" and how IFCs compete to reach the upper echelons of this hierarchy (Lee and Schmidt-Marwede 1993; Poon 2003; Poon et al. 2004). Financial policies and regulation have therefore become means through which IFCs may explore and enhance existing comparative advantages in order to gain a competitive edge over other IFCs.

Competition has been seen as an important determinant of IFC development, since it stimulates financial sector growth and encourages greater efficiency and competitiveness among both firms and policy-makers (Choi et al. 2009). Scholars have subsequently sought to study the impacts of history, policy, institutions and geography in determining inter-IFC competition, particularly among emerging Asian IFCs (Jao 2003a; Zhao et al. 2004; Tan and Lim 2007; Ho 2009; Cassis 2010; Jarvis 2011; Lai 2012). However, inter-IFC competition may also foster cooperation among IFCs and contribute to regional integration (Choi et al. 2009). This may arise from a collective desire to avoid costly disadvantageous situations such as bank failures (Cohen 1996). Regardless, global financial integration impacts state–market relations by defining the institutions of production, capitalism and state social welfare at the national level (Dixon 2014).

Mid-level international relations concepts such as the hegemonic stability theory, regime theory, epistemic communities and capital mobility hypothesis have been found to be useful in explaining cooperation among states in global financial markets (Dombrowski 1998). Such complex relations of competition and cooperation have contributed to increased interdependency and a tendency towards "functional specialization" or "differentiation", particularly among Chinese financial centres such as Hong Kong, Shanghai and Beijing (Lai 2012; Zhao 2013). Inter-IFC cooperation has also been studied in terms of regulatory or policy convergence, particularly among states that wish to reduce the competitive *dis*advantages arising from financial globalization (Lütz 2004).

Subsequent scholarly work has sought to develop a deeper understanding of such competitive or cooperative dynamics among IFCs, placing particular attention on sociopolitical relations or linkages. These include studying how IFCs act as "public–private coalitions" that strategize against other IFCs by relying on locational advantages in financial production (Lee and Schmidt-Marwede 1993) as well as the "strategic alliances" formed among IFCs in a bid to improve the individual comparative advantages (Budd 1995). Inter-IFC relations and competition are also influenced and constituted by "socio-geographical practices" arising from the interaction of financial actors (Pryke and Lee 1995). In particular, interactions between investors, providers of financial services and intermediaries tend to result in an uneven distribution of stock exchanges (and IFCs), hence stimulating inter-IFC competition (Wojcik 2013).

Aside from these studies of major financial centres, studies focused on tax havens have also sought to delve into the international and domestic sociopolitical aspects of financial sector development and policy, particularly in terms of the strategic nature of state financial policy in establishing tax-friendly jurisdictions (Johns 1983; Palan et al. 1996; Palan 1998, 2002; Hudson 2000; Morriss 2010) or the role of tax havens in regulatory cooperation (Eden and Kudrle 2005; Dean 2006). While studies of tax havens provide a more qualitative and contextualized understanding of financial sector development, they remain largely focused on small island economies and hence not able to connect easily with other existing IFC studies.

Despite emerging attempts to provide more qualitative and contextual accounts of IFC development such as the global cities approach and studies on tax havens, there remains a need to focus on the sociopolitical aspects of IFC development. These include exploring the relations among financial sector actors, both state and non-state, *within* IFCs and the impact of such relations on financial policy-making. This means moving beyond existing state-centric and under-conceptualized studies of IFCs (Ng 1998). However, recent work by scholars from the fields of finance, economics and IPE has sought to address this shortcoming by focusing sociopolitical relations in economic and financial policy, showing a deeper appreciation of political processes and relations in financial policy. These are discussed next.

The Politics of Finance

There has of late been an increasing recognition of the influence and implications of sociopolitical variables in financial policy-making. According to an OECD study, financial regulation influences and is at the same time affected by the existing political and social structures in a society as well as the relations between the government, industry and society that form these structures The rapid globalization and proliferation of financial markets has also made private actors more powerful in their ability to shape and set rules, with the result being an alignment of financial governance with private sector preferences (Underhill and Zhang 2008). This has led scholars to take a more "politically sensitive approach" to understanding financial crisis (Pempel 1999), with one such study focusing on the varying influence which property sector wielded on the Hong Kong and Singapore governments' response to the AFC (Lim 1999).

This growing clout of politically motivated actors in finance is closely aligned to interest groups and lobbying activities by these groups. In their "interest group theory of financial development", Rajan and Zingales (2001b) show how private sector influence may hinder financial sector development, especially when powerful industry actors are focused on their narrow self-interests. While this focus on private sector authority in financial and economic policy had previously received attention in the work of key IPE scholars who focused on state–industry relations and the policy role of industry actors (Strange 1996; Cutler et al. 1999; Haufler 2001; Cutler 2003), this more recent wave of scholarly work on the politics of finance is more focused on domestic politics and the various systemic, institutional and actor-centric drivers of this politicization of finance.

For instance, a state's domestic political system has been seen as an important channel through which inter-actor relations may impact financial policy. Carney (2010) has studied how financial institutions and arrangements are often defined by a priori political contestations between labour, owners of capital and landed interests. More accountable political systems are also positively related to better investor protection and lower costs of entry, thereby stimulating the financial sector development (Perotti and Volpin 2007). Politics also affects corporate ownership in East Asia, with the state becoming a more significant owner of companies over the past few decades and changes in company ownership becoming increasingly dependent upon political change at the national level (Carney and Child 2013).

Scholars have further sought to understand complex inter-actor relations in financial policy through the lens of the policy subsystems approach. While this approach is discussed at greater length in the next chapter, it is necessary to discuss the contributions of subsystem scholars in their studies of sociopolitical relations among financial sector actors. Within the context of US commercial bank regulation, Krause has found that strategic behaviour is prevalent among financial sector actors, who typically engage in a complex mix of cooperative and competitive behaviour in reaction to the behaviour of other actors (Krause 1997). As Worsham (1997) has noted, variations in political arrangements have a significant impact on financial policy subsystems and the policy roles of these subsystems.

Inter-actor relations within a financial policy subsystem also affect how financial sector actors respond to change. Williams (2009) has found that subsystems facilitate endogenous change or policy adjustments in response to exogenous shock, dependent upon the goals and strategies of key actors within the subsystem. However, the dominance of a coalition deeply imbued with a set of strong policy beliefs is also likely to expose a financial system to risk and contagion through "groupthink" and a lack of effective policy coordination (Gieve and Provost 2012). More recently, Woo (2015a, b) has shown how the strength of "policy relations" between state and non-state actors facilitates the "co-creation" of financial policies, particularly in Asian IFCs.

Studies that seek to understand inter-actor relations in the financial sector have also taken on an international approach, focusing on relations between financial sector actors across national boundaries. For instance, scholars have found that regulators and other state actors are increasingly connected to their foreign counterparts, often operating within transnational networks of regulators and central bankers (Kapstein 1992; Cerny 1993b). This increasing recognition of inter-actor relations in global financial markets has resulted in the emergence of a network approach to studying global financial markets. Specifically, Oatley et al. argue from an IPE standpoint that the international financial system has become a system of economic and political relationships between public and private actors (Oatley et al.

2013). Similar efforts can be found in Knoke's work on "economic networks", which takes a more sociological approach to understanding social relations and social capital in the global economic system (Knoke 2012).

While this growing interest in the politics of finance has brought forth useful new insights into the sociopolitical basis of financial sector policy, there remain several issues that have yet to be addressed. First, a vast majority of these studies are based on the context of developed Western economies. Given differences in political systems and state–industry relations between these developed Western economies and emerging Asian economies, there is a need for more extensive research into the political-economic context within which Asian financial policy-makers and regulators operate. Furthermore, existing studies do not sufficiently delineate the precise means or mechanisms through which different combinations of financial policy actors, state or non-state, are involved in financial policy-making. There is thus a need to further explore and explicate politics–policy or subsystem–instruments linkages. This book attempts to achieve these.

Conclusion

This chapter has provided a comprehensive review of the literatures on financial policy and IFCs. Both literatures have made significant contributions to the study of financial sector development. In particular, the financial policy literature has provided a systematic description of the means and mechanisms through which governments are able to develop and regulate financial markets. The IFC literature has further built on this by studying financial policy through a more international systemic lens. This has allowed IFC scholars to identify the factors and processes which have contributed to IFC success. More importantly, these scholars have shifted the study of financial policy to the city or local level of government.

However, these two bodies of work remain insufficient in addressing several key questions that this book will seek to address. First, while the financial policy literature describes ways in which governments have managed to achieve financial sector development, it does not sufficiently address the issues of context and spatiality. Rather, financial policy-making is assumed to take place at the national level, with the state taken as a unitary monolithic financial policymaking unit. In reality, the bulk of financial policy-making is carried out by local or city governments who actually run the IFCs.

While the IFC literature addresses some of these shortcomings by situating financial policy processes spatially and temporally within the globally connected IFC, it does not sufficiently account for the political-economic context within which IFCs exist or the sociopolitical relations which connect policy-makers and other significant financial sector actors. Instead, much of the IFC literature focuses on structural and locational factors contributing to IFC success and overemphasizes a convergence of IFC development models based on these factors. While qualitative

IFC studies on tax havens and global cities have sought to overcome the limitations of such quantitative approaches, these studies have yet to adequately delineate and provide a clearer understanding of the sociopolitical relations which underpin IFC development.

In response to these limitations, scholars have begun to address these shortcomings by taking a network or subsystems approach to studying financial policy and focusing on the "politics of finance". However, these studies remain at a rudimentary stage and are unable to provide a sufficiently clear or in-depth understanding of how such inter-actor relations affect financial policy-making and contribute to IFC success. In other words, the politics–policy linkage in finance is insufficiently explored. Furthermore, the Western-centric nature of these studies raises questions over their applicability to the study of Asian IFCs which operate within markedly different political systems.

These shortcomings in the financial policy and IFC literatures point towards a need to reconceptualize the existing understandings of IFC development. In particular, two clear issues need to be addressed. First, there is a need to develop a comprehensive understanding of the exact means or policies through which governments drive or stimulate IFC development. Second, there is a need to situate these policies within the milieu of the political-economic context. These two areas will be addressed in the remainder of this book. However, this book does not propose to address these issues completely. Rather, it merely constitutes useful first step towards addressing some of these issues and providing a more conceptualized understanding of the politics of finance in Asia.

References

Aalbers MB (2008) The Financialization of home and the mortgage market crisis. Compet Change 12:148–166

Arndt HW, Australia-Japan Research Centre, Australian National University (1988) Comparative advantage in trade in financial services. Research School of Pacific Studies, Australian National University], Canberra, Australia

Baldwin R, Scott C, Hood C (eds) (1998) A reader on regulation. Oxford University Press, Oxford

Barajas A, Beck T, Dabla-Norris E, Yousefi R (2013) Too cold, too hot, or just right? Assessing Financial Sector Development Across the Globe. International Monetary Fund

Beck T (2002) Financial development and international trade: Is there a link? J Int Econ 57: 107–131

Beck T, Levine R, Loayza N (2000) Finance and the sources of growth. J Financ Econ 58:261–300

Berthelemy JC, Varoudakis A (1996) Economic growth, convergence clubs, and the role of financial development. Oxf Econ Pap 48:300–328

Budd L (1995) Globalisation, territory and strategic alliances in different financial centres. Urban Stud 32:345–360

Calderón C, Liu L (2003) The direction of causality between financial development and economic growth. J Dev Econ 72:321–334

Carmichael J (2002) Public sector governance and the finance sector. In: Litan RE, Pomerleano M, Sundararajan V (eds) Financial sector governance: the roles of the public and private sectors. Brookings Institution Press, Washington, pp 121–162

Carney RW (2010) Contested capitalism: the political origins of financial institutions. Routledge, London

Carney RW, Child TB (2013) Changes to the ownership and control of East Asian corporations between 1996 and 2008: the primacy of politics. J Financ Econ 107:494–513

Carroll T, Jarvis DSL (2014) Introduction: financialisation and development in Asia under late capitalism. Asian Stud Rev 38:533–543

Cassis Y (2010) Capitals of capital: the rise and fall of international financial centres 1780–2009. Cambridge University Press, Cambridge

Cerny PG (1993) The political economy of international finance. In: Cerny PG (ed) Finance and world politics: markets, regimes and states in the post-hegemonic era. Edward Elgar Publishing Limited, Aldershot, pp 3–19

Chang H-J, Grabel I (2004) Reclaiming development: an alternative economic policy manual. Zed Books Ltd., London

Choi S-R, Tschoegl A, Yu C-M (1986) Banks and the world's major financial centers, 1970–1980. Rev World Econ Weltwirtschaftliches Arch 122:48–64

Choi D, Seade J, Shirai S, Young S (2009) Competition among financial centres in Asia-Pacific: Prospects, benefits, risks and policy challenges. competition and financial centres in Asian Pacific. Institute of Southeast Asian Studies, Singapore, pp 3–57

Christophers B (2009) Complexity, finance, and progress in human geography. Prog Hum Geogr 33:807–824

Claessens S, Dell'Ariccia G, Igan D, Laeven L (2010) Cross-country experiences and policy implications from the global financial crisis. Econ Policy 25:267–293

Clark GL, Thrift N (2005) The return of bureaucracy: managing dispersed knowledge in global finance. In: Knorr K, Preda A (eds) The sociology of financial markets. Oxford University Press, Oxford, pp 229–249

Clark GL, Wojcik D (2007) The geography of finance: corporate governance in a global marketplace. Oxford University Press, New York

Cohen BJ (1996) Phoenix risen: the resurrection of global finance. World Polit 48:268–296

Cutler AC (2003) Private power and global authority: transnational merchant law in the global political economy. Cambridge University Press, Cambridge

Cutler AC, Haufler V, Porter T (1999) Private authority and international affairs. State University of New York Press, Albany

Davis EP (1990) International financial centres—an industrial analysis

De Gregorio J, Guidotti PE (1995) Financial development and economic growth. World Dev 23:433–448

Dean SA (2006) Philosopher kings and international tax: a new approach to tax havens, tax flight, and international tax cooperation. Hastings Law J 58:911

Demirguc-Kunt A, Levine R (2008) Finance, financial sector policies, and long-run growth. Res Work Pap 1:1–82

Demirgüç-Kunt A, Servén L (2010) Are All the sacred cows dead? Implications of the financial crisis for macro- and financial policies. World Bank Res Obs 25:91–124

Dixon AD (2014) The new geography of capitalism: firms, finance, and society. Oxford University Press, Oxford

Dombrowski P (1998) Haute finance and high theory: recent scholarship on global financial relations. Mershon Int Stud Rev 42:1

Dufey G, Giddy IH (1978) The international money market. Prentice Hall International, New Jersey

Economists Advisory Group (1984) City 2000: the future of London as an international financial centre. Lafferty Publications, London

Eden L, Kudrle RT (2005) Tax havens: renegade states in the international tax regime?. Law Policy 27:100–127

Financial Crisis Inquiry Commission (2011) The financial crisis inquiry report: final report of the National Commission on the Causes of the Financial and Economic Crisis in the United States. Public Affairs, New York

Friedman J (2002) The world city hypothesis. In: Pacione M (ed) The city: the city in global context. Routledge, London, pp 151–163
GaWC Research Network (2014) What GaWC is about. http://www.lboro.ac.uk/gawc/group.html. Accessed 16 Apr 2014
Gehrig T (2000) Cities and the geography of financial centers. In: Huriot J-M, Thiesse J-F (eds) Economies of cities: theoretical perspectives. Cambridge University Press, Cambridge, pp 415–446
Gertler M, Kiyotaki N, Queralto A (2012) Financial crises, bank risk exposure and government financial policy. J Monet Econ 59(Supplement):S17–S34
Giddy IH (1983) The theory and industrial organization of international banking. In: Hawkins RG, Levich RM, Wihlborg CG (eds) The internationalization of financial markets and national economic policy. JAI Press, Greenwich, pp 195–243
Gieve J, Provost C (2012) Ideas and coordination in policymaking: the financial crisis of 2007–2009. Governance 25:61–77
Goldberg MA, Helsley RW, Levi MD (1988) On the development of international financial centers. Ann Reg Sci 22:81–94
Gordon RH, Li W (2003) Government as a discriminating monopolist in the financial market: the case of China. J Public Econ 87:283–312
Haggard S, Lee CH (1993) The political dimension of finance in economic development. In: Haggard S, Lee CH, Maxfield S (eds) The politics of finance in developing countries. Cornell University Press, New York, pp 3–20
Hall S (2006) What counts? Exploring the production of quantitative financial narratives in London's corporate finance industry. J Econ Geogr 6:661–678
Hall S (2010) Geographies of money and finance I: cultural economy, politics and place
Hall S (2012) Geographies of money and finance II: financialization and financial subjects. Prog Hum Geogr 36:403–411
Haufler V (2001) A public role for the private sector: industry self-regulation in a global economy. Carnegie Endowment for International Peace, Washington
Hellman T, Murdock K (1997) Financial sector development policy: the importance of reputational capital and governacne. In: Szekely IP, Sabot R (eds) Development strategy and management of the market economy. Oxford University Press, Oxford, pp 269–324
Hellman T, Murdock K, Stiglitz JE (1997) Financial restraint: towards a new paradigm. In: Aoki M, Kim H-K, Okuno-Fujiwara M (eds) The role of government in East Asian economic development comparative institutional analysis. Clarendon Press, Oxford, pp 163–207
Hira A (2006) Governance crisis in Asia: developing a responsive regulation. In: Ramesh M, Howlett M (eds) Deregulation and its discontents: rewriting the rules in Asia. Edward Elgar Publishing Limited, Cheltenham, pp 13–28
Ho KC (2009) Competitive urban economic policies in global cities: Shanghai through the lens of Singapore. In: Chen X (ed) Rising Shanghai: state power and local transformations in a global megacity. University of Minnesota Press, Minneapolis, pp 73–91
Hudson A (2000) Offshoreness, globalization and sovereignty: a postmodern geo-political economy? Trans Inst Br Geogr 25:269–283
International Finance Corporation (2010) Regulating governance in developing countries. World Bank, Washington
Jao YC (2003a) Shanghai and Hong Kong as international financial centres: historical perspective and contemporary analysis
Jarvis DSL (2011) Race for the money: international financial centres in Asia. J Int Relat Dev 14:60–95
Jayaratne J, Strahan PE (1996) The finance-growth nexus: evidence from bank branch deregulation. Q J Econ 111:639–670
Johns RA (1983) Tax havens and offshore finance: a study of transnational economic development. St Martin's Press, New York

Jones G (1992) International financial centres in Asia, the Middle East and Australia: a historical perspective. In: Cassis Y (ed) Finance and financiers in European history. Cambridge University Press, Cambridge, pp 405–428

Kapstein EB (1992) Between power and purpose: central bankers and the politics of regulatory convergence. Int Organ 46:265–287

Kindleberger CP (1974) The formation of financial centers: a study in comparative economic history (Princeton Studies in International Finance No. 36), 1st edn. Princeton University Press, New Jersey

King RG, Levine R (1993) Finance and growth: Schumpeter might be right. Q J Econ 108: 717–737

Knoke D (2012) Economic networks. Polity Press, Cambridge

Krause GA (1997) Policy preference formation and subsystem behaviour: the case of commercial bank regulation. Br J Polit Sci 27:525–550

Krugman PR (2009) The return of depression economics and the crisis of 2008. W. Norton & Co., New York

Lai KPY (2006) "Imagineering" asian emerging markets: financial knowledge networks in the fund management industry. Geoforum 37:627–642

Lai KPY (2011) Marketization through contestation: reconfiguring China's financial markets through knowledge networks. J Econ Geogr 11:87–117

Lai K (2012) Differentiated markets: Shanghai, Beijing and Hong Kong in China's financial centre network. Urban Stud 49:1275–1296

Lai KPY, Tan CH (2015) "Neighbours first, bankers second": mobilising financial citizenship in Singapore. Geoforum 64:65–77

Langley P (2006) The making of investor subjects in Anglo-American pensions. Environ Plan Soc Space 24:919–934

Langley P (2009) The everyday life of global finance: saving and borrowing in Anglo-America. Oxford University Press, Oxford, U.K

Lee R, Schmidt-Marwede U (1993) Interurban competition? Financial centres and the geography of financial production. Int J Urban Reg Res 17:492–515

Leftwich A (1995) Bringing politics back in: towards a model of the developmental state. J Dev Stud 31:400–427

Levine R (1997) Financial development and economic growth: views and agenda. J Econ Lit 35:688–726

Levine R, Loayza N, Beck T (2000) Financial intermediation and growth: causality and causes. J Monet Econ 46:31–77

Lim LYC (1999) Free market fancies: Hong Kong, Singapore, and the Asian financial crisis. In: Pempel TJ (ed) The politics of the Asian economic crisis. Cornell University Press, Ithaca, pp 101–115

Litan RE, Pomerleano M, Sundararajan V (2002) Strengthening financial sector governance in emerging markets. In: Litan RE, Pomerleano M, Sundararajan V (eds) Financial sector governance: the roles of the public and private sectors. Brookings Institution Press, Washington, D.C

Lütz S (2004) Convergence within national diversity: the regulatory state in finance. J Public Policy 24:169–197

McRae H, Cairncross F (1973) Capital city: London as a financial centre. Magnum Books, London

Morriss AP (2010) Offshore financial centers and regulatory competition. AEI Press, Washington D C

Murinde V, Mlambo K (2011) Development-oriented financial regulation

Nadler M, Heller S, Shipman SS (1955) The money market and its institutions. Ronald Press Company, New York

Ng BK (1998) Hong Kong and Singapore as international financial centres: a comparative functional perspective. Nanyang Technological University, Singapore

O'Brien R (1992) Global financial integration: the end of geography. Council on Foreign Relations Press, Washington

Oatley T, Winecoff WK, Pennock A, Danzman SB (2013) The political economy of global finance: a network model. Perspect Polit 11:133–153
OECD (2006) The financial policy landscape: a conceptual overview. Finance Mark Trends 2006:61–109
Pagano M, Roell A, Danthine J-P, Schaefer SM (1990) Trading systems in european stock exchanges: current performance and policy options. Econ Policy 5:63
Palan R (1998) Trying to have your cake and eating it: how and why the state system has created offshore. Int Stud Q 42:625–643
Palan R (2002) Tax havens and the commercialization of state sovereignty. Int Organ 56:151–176
Palan R, Abbott J, Deans P (1996) State strategies in the global political economy. Pinter, London
Park YS (1982) The economics of offshore financial centers. Columbia J World Bus 17:31–35
Pempel TJ (1999) The politics of the Asian economic crisis. Cornell University Press, Ithaca and London
Perotti E, Volpin P (2007) Investor protection and entry. Tinbergen Institute, Amsterdam
Peters BG, Pierre J, Randma-Liiv T (2011) Global financial crisis, public administration and governance: do new problems require new solutions? Public Organ Rev 11:13–27
Polak JJ (1989) Financial policies and development. OECD Publishing, Paris
Poon JPH (2003) Hierarchical tendencies of capital markets among international financial centers. Growth Change 34:135–156
Poon JPH, Eldredge B, Yeung D (2004) Rank size distribution of international financial centers. Int Reg Sci Rev 27:411–430
Porteous DJ (1995) The geography of finance: spatial dimensions of intermediary behaviour. Avebury, Aldershot
Porter ME (1998) Competitive advantage of nations. Free Press, New York
Pryke M (1991) An international city going "global": spatial change in the City of London. Environ Plan Soc Space 9:197–222
Pryke M, du Gay P (2007) Take an issue: cultural economy and finance. Econ Soc 36:339–354
Pryke M, Lee R (1995) Place your bets: towards an understanding of globalisation, socio-financial engineering and competition within a financial centre. Urban Stud 32:329–344
Rajan R (2011) Fault lines: how hidden fractures still threaten the world economy. Princeton University Press, New Jersey
Rajan RG, Zingales L (2001a) Financial systems, industrial structure, and growth. Oxf Rev Econ Policy 17:467–482
Rajan RG, Zingales L (2001b) The great reversals: the politics of finanical development in the 20th century. National Bureau of Economic Research, Massachusetts
Reed HC (1981) The preeminence of international financial centers. Praeger, New York
Rötheli TF (2010) Causes of the financial crisis: risk misperception, policy mistakes, and banks' bounded rationality. J Socio-Econ 39:119–126
Roubini N, Mihm S (2011) Crisis economics: a crash course in the future of finance. Penguin Books, New York
Sagaram JPA, Wickramanayake J (2012) Financial centers in the Asia-pacific region: an empirical study on Australia, Hong Kong, Japan and Singapore. PSL Q Rev 58:21–50
Sassen S (1996) Whose city is it? Globalization and the formation of new claims. Public Cult 8:205–223
Sassen S (1999) Global financial centers. Foreign Aff 78:75–87
Sidaway JD, Bryson JR (2002) Constructing knowledges of "emerging markets": UK-based investment managers and their overseas connections. Environ Plan A 34:401–416
Snider L (2011) The conundrum of financial regulation: origins, controversies, and prospects. Annu Rev Law Soc Sci 7:121–137
Stigler GJ (1988) The theory of economic regulation. University of Chicago Press, Chicago
Stiglitz JE (2010) Freefall: America, free markets, and the sinking of the world economy. W. W. Norton & Company, New York
Stiglitz JE, Uy M (1996) Financial markets, public policy, and the East Asian miracle. World Bank Res Obs 11:249–276

Stiglitz JE, Jaramillo-Vallejo J, Park YC (1993) The role of the state in financial markets. World Bank, Washington

Strange S (1996) The retreat of the state: the diffusion of power in the world economy. Cambridge University Press, Cambridge

Tan CH, Lim JYS (2007) Singapore and Hong Kong as competing financial centres. Saw Centre Financial Studies, Singapore

The World Bank (2013) Rethinking the role of the state in finance. The World Bank, Washington DC

Underhill GRD, Zhang X (2008) Setting the rules: private power, political underpinnings, and legitimacy in global monetary and financial governance. Int Aff 84:535–554

Vittas D (1991) The impact of regulation on financial intermediation. The World Bank

Williams RA (2009) Exogenous shocks in subsystem adjustment and policy change: the credit crunch and canadian banking regulation. J Public Policy 29:29–53

Wojcik D (2013) The global stock market: issuers, investors, and intermediaries in an uneven world, 1st edn. Oxford University Press, Oxford, U.K

Woo JJ (2015a) Policy relations and policy subsystems: financial policy in Hong Kong and Singapore

Woo JJ (2015b) Beyond the neoliberal orthodoxy: alternative financial policy regimes in Asia's financial centres

Worsham J (1997) Other people's money: policy change, congress, and bank regulation. Westview Press, Boulder, C.O

Zhang X, Chen D (2013) The influence of financial industry cluster on economic growth: three economic zones in China. Account Finance Res. doi:10.5430/afr.v2n4p69

Zhao SXB (2013) Information exchange, headquarters economy and financial centers development: Shanghai, Beijing and Hong Kong. J Contemp China 22:1006–1027

Zhao SXB, Zhang L, Wang DT (2004) Determining factors of the development of a national financial center: the case of China. Geoforum 35:577–592. doi:10.1016/j.geoforum.2004.01.004

Chapter 3
Taking a Public Policy Theoretical Approach

As cities vie to become top financial centres and policy-makers seek to establish the conditions and factors necessary for the establishment of a successful financial services sector, there is an increasing need to take a policy-oriented approach to understanding IFC development. Furthermore, policies associated with IFC development are often enmeshed within an overarching financial policy subsystem with its inherent sociopolitical institutions, norms and logic. Yet as the previous chapter has shown, existing studies on IFCs do not always take a sufficiently policy-oriented approach, nor do they sufficiently address the sociopolitical context within which IFCs exist in sufficient depth.

In seeking to address this lacuna in the existing literature, this book situates the financial policy process within its sociopolitical context and assesses the impacts of both policy and politics in IFC development. This requires a "mid-level" framework of analysis that addresses both the macro-level sociopolitical context and micro-level policies. This book seeks to provide such a framework in the form of the "nested instrumental approach", which draws from the policy subsystems and policy instruments approaches. While insights drawn from the policy instruments literature provide a clear and tool-based understanding of the types of financial policies implemented and the mechanisms through which they operate, the policy subsystems approach facilitates the delineation and analysis of policy actors, their interrelations and the impact of these relations on financial policy.

By drawing on and combining the policy instruments and policy subsystems approaches, the nested instrumental approach addresses both the policy and politics of IFC development, in the process embedding policy mix design within the sociopolitical context of the policy subsystem configuration. This chapter will provide the theoretical foundations of the nested instrumental approach by providing a critical overview of the policy instruments and policy subsystems literatures, in the process situating it within existing public policy theory. This is followed by an in-depth discussion of the nested instrumental approach, its components and the logic of "nested instrumentality" that drives it. This chapter will also discuss the research methodology and design that underpins the findings of this book.

J.J. Woo, *Business and Politics in Asia's Key Financial Centres*,
DOI 10.1007/978-981-287-985-1_3

Policy Instruments and the Design Process

Given the ambiguities of defining what exactly constitutes a "policy" and the need to identify, isolate and analyse causal linkages between a specific policy and its effects, scholars of policy instruments have sought to provide a more precise understanding of policy design by taking an instrument or tool-based approach. This involves understanding individual policies as tools within a policy-maker's toolkit of policies. The concept of policy instruments can be traced back to 1936, when Harold Lasswell first distinguished between policy means and policy goals (Lasswell 1936; Howlett 2011) and categorized policy means as symbols, violence, goods or practice (Lasswell 1936).

While Lasswell's approach also emphasized context, his greatest contribution was to reorientate policy analysis to focus on the availability and use of policy instruments (Lasswell 1951; Torgerson 1985). The study of such policy means has since evolved in comprehensiveness and sophistication, with Lasswell's means-ends differentiation continuing to permeate the policy instruments literature. This is exemplified in other early attempts to study and categorize policy instruments, such as Dahl and Lindblom's (1953) analysis of "politico-economic techniques" in economic and social policy or Kirschen's (1964) comprehensive list of policy instruments used in economic policy.

However, such economics-focused attempts at studying policy instruments tended to oversimplify instrument use and selection, providing little more than comprehensive lists of instruments with insufficient analytical depth (Howlett 2004). A deluge of scholarly work subsequently attempted to address this shortcoming. For instance, Lowi's (1972) typology of policy instruments sought to differentiate between "regulatory", "distributive", "redistributive" and "constituent" policies, based on whether the instrument is strongly or weakly sanctioned and whether it targets individuals or the collective. Hood's (1986) "NATO" model provides more nuance and depth, categorizing instruments according to the type of "governing resource" used by the government, namely "nodality" (information), "authority", "treasure" and "organization" policy instruments. The NATO model has since become one of the most influential approaches to studying policy instruments.

In another study, Elmore (1987) categorized policy instruments into the four types: mandates, inducements, capacity-building and system-changing. In their attempt to consolidate existing typologies of policy instruments, Linder and Peters (1989) have classified policy instruments into the seven classes: direct provision, subsidy, tax, contract, authority, regulation, and exhortation. Salamon and Lund (1989) further sough to classify policy instruments according to the four main "tool dimensions" of government activity, structure of delivery system, degree of centralization, and degree of automaticity. This then allowed them to categorize policy instruments into four broad categories: money payment, provision of goods or services, legal protection or guarantees and prohibition or restriction. Vedung (1998) provides a more parsimonious typology by classifying policy instruments into economic means (carrots), regulations (sticks) and information (sermons), based on the amount of "authoritative force" that the government is prepared to use.

Other early studies of policy instruments can also be found in the literature on "statecraft", which refers to the "science of government" (Anderson 1977) or "art of conducting state affairs" (Baldwin 1985). Although the term statecraft has since been appropriated by IR scholars and lost traction in public policy studies, it nonetheless retains an instrument orientation, with statecraft defined as the "selection of means for the pursuit of foreign policy goals" (Baldwin 1985). Based on Lasswell's (1945) "fourfold division of policy instruments", Baldwin (1985) has also devised a taxonomy of policy instruments used in statecraft; this includes propaganda, diplomacy, economic statecraft and military statecraft.

The policy instruments literature has further benefited from the contributions of a group of Canadian public policy scholars (Phidd and Doern 1978; Trebilcock and Hartle 1982; Doern and Phidd 1992), with much of their work focusing on how policy instrument choice and governments' capacity for policy instrument implementation affect policy goal attainment and influence the policy-making process (Woodside 1986). This literature yielded the key insight that given the technical substitutability of most policy instruments, policy instrument choice is mostly influenced by degree of government coercion (Doern 1981; Tupper and Doern 1981; Doern and Phidd 1992). These scholars then classified policy instruments on a continuum, rather than on rigid categories of mutual exclusion, according to the level of governmental coercion involved in the use of each instrument (Doern and Phidd 1992).

However, such classifications of policy instruments by degree of coercion have been shown to be analytically limited, given that "each policy instrument can be used in a wide range of ways that involve differing degrees of coercion" (Woodside 1986). This difficulty in operationalizing "coercion" is avoided in Howlett and Ramesh's taxonomy of policy instruments, which is based on the level of state involvement required in the use of each instrument (Howlett and Ramesh 1995). This typology identifies ten types of policy instruments categorized into three major groups: Voluntary Instruments (low state involvement) comprising family and community, voluntary organizations and private markets; Compulsory Instruments (high state involvement) that include regulation, public enterprises and direct provision; and Mixed Instruments (varying levels of state involvement) that comprise information and exhortation, subsidies, auction of property rights and tax and user charges (Howlett and Ramesh 1995).

While providing significant insight into the policy instruments that governments have at their disposal and the sorts of resources or levels of intervention required in the use of these instruments, such "first-generation" studies of policy instruments were analytically limited in several ways. Specifically, they did not differentiate between substantive and procedural policy instruments or the different levels at which policy instruments exist, were overly focused on single instruments without addressing policy mixes and did not deal with the "micro-level" aspects of specific instrument selection within a general policy instrument category (Howlett 2011). These limitations have since been addressed by advances in the policy instruments literature, sparking off "second-generation" theories of policy instruments (Howlett 2004) that have since evolved into a "new policy design orientation" (Howlett et al. 2014).

One of the key contributions of such "second-generation" policy instruments studies is the focus from single instrument studies to studies of policy mixes, based on the recognition that policy-makers in the real world tend to utilize a combination of various instruments rather than one instrument at a time. These second-generation studies have yielded various ways of describing and classifying such combinations of instruments. For instance, Elmore (1987) classified combinations of policy instruments aimed at a broad set of policy goals as "strategies", while van der Doelen (1998) discussed how seemingly conflicting stimulative and repressive instruments may complement each other when combined within "policy packages". In their seminal study on environmental regulatory policy, Gunningham et al. (1998) note how multiple instruments can be used in policy-making through the "design of efficient and effective 'optimal' policy mixes" that allow the deficiencies of each individual instrument to be compensated for with the strengths of another.

This recognition that policy instruments are utilized by governments as part of a larger policy mix adds a significant dose of nuance and realism to the study of policy instruments. Scholars of policy design have subsequently sought to understand the internal workings of the policy mix, studying complementarities and interactions between policy instruments within a mix, and emphasizing how processes of policy patching or layering can result in greater consistency, coherence and congruence in a policy mix (van der Heijden 2011; Rayner 2013; Howlett and Rayner 2013b, 2014; Howlett et al. 2014).

Addressing another major analytical deficit in the existing policy instruments literature, Howlett (2000, 2011) distinguishes between substantive and procedural policy instruments. While substantive policy instruments directly affect society's production, distribution and consumption of goods and services, procedural policy instruments alter "political or policy behaviour in the *process* of the articulation of implementation goals and means" (Howlett 2011). It is, however, important to note that the idea of procedural instruments had already received prior attention in the works of various scholars who sought to understand how policy instruments may affect the policy process or even reshape the international political and economic order (Baldwin 1985; Bressers and Klok 1988).

Furthermore, procedural policy instruments may also affect the subjective perceptions of actors, with instruments both influencing and becoming influenced by individual perceptions (Linder and Peters 1989; Schneider and Ingram 1990a, 1990b, 1993, 1994, 1997). However, it was only in the early 2000s that a clearer understanding of procedural policy instruments emerged. Based on Hood's NATO model, Howlett (2000, 2011) has sought to typologise procedural policy instruments and subsequently developed an extensive catalogue of substantive and procedural policy instruments based on the type of governing resources associated with the use of each instrument. Procedural policy instruments have come to permeate "second-generation" policy instrument theorizing, driving the study of policy mixes comprising procedural and substantive instruments (Howlett 2004).

Furthermore, policy instruments do not exist in a vacuum. Policy instrument choice is often influenced by contextual elements such as political or organizational culture and social relations (Linder and Peters 1989, 1990; Salamon 1989; Howlett 2004). This suggests that policy instruments are in reality "nested" within these contextual elements and even within other instruments, with the result being multiple levels of abstraction (Howlett 2011). As John (2011) has noted, policy instruments are in "infinite regress: tools needing to implement tools, meta tools to introduce these guiding tools, meta-meta tools and so on". This recognition of nestedness draws from earlier attempts to identify and understand the various levels at which policy instruments operate and impact policy change.

According to Hall (1993), policy change occurs at three levels, with "first-order" change referring to changes to policy instrument calibrations, "second-order" change referring to changes in type of policy instrument chosen and "third-order" change denoting a paradigmatic change in the policy goal pursued. There are therefore three levels of policy instrumentation: instrument logic, mechanisms and calibrations (Howlett and Cashore 2009). Hence, policy instruments are multi-level and nested in nature, with levels of abstraction "ranging from the most general level of a relatively abstract governance mode, to the level of a policy regime and finally to the level of specific programme settings" (Howlett 2011).

Subsequent studies of policy instruments have sought to incorporate these later advances in policy instruments theorizing. For instance, Howlett et al. (2009) have consolidated a comprehensive typology of substantive and procedural instruments and placed both types of instruments on continuums based on the extent to which the use of these instruments involve the manipulation of the market and network actors. Howlett et al. (2009) have further developed a "model of basic instrument preferences", with policy-makers' preferences for directive, authoritative, subsidy or information instruments dependent upon government capacity (or the level of constraints on the state) and subsystem complexity (number and complexity of subsystem actors).

Developing in tandem with this systematic study of policy instruments is the notion of a policy design process or orientation (Dryzek 1983; Linder and Peters 1984, 1991; May 2003), which has provided a meta-level framework that is heavily reliant on instrumental reasoning and within which policy instrument formulation and choice are situated (Linder and Peters 1988). Although the recognition of a design orientation in the development of policy instruments was recognized only in retrospect by scholars who came to appreciate the design processes that underpinned the formulation and implementation of policy instruments, it has since become a significant aspect of the policy instruments literature.

However, scholarly work on policy design went into decline in the 1990s and 2000s with the dominance of the globalization and governance literatures (Howlett and Lejano 2013). The globalization literature's focus on the meta-level and its downplaying of the government's role in policy design (Howlett 2011) nonetheless led to renewed efforts at re-establishing the central role of government and the importance of policy design, resulting in a revival of the policy design orientation in the process (Considine 2012; Craft and Howlett 2012; Howlett and Lejano 2013). This "new" policy design orientation dealt with complexity in the design of multi-instrument policy mixes over time and space (Howlett and Rayner 2007, 2013a; van der Heijden 2011; Howlett 2011; Considine 2012).

In sum, the policy instruments literature has provided a clear understanding of how policy instruments work, allowing for the development of comprehensive instrument typologies that match different instruments to specific goals and objectives. Furthermore, the reinvigorated policy design orientation has addressed the various shortcomings of the policy instruments approach by addressing issues of complexity, multiple instruments, time and spatiality in design processes. This book draws on some of these insights by taking an instruments-focused and design-oriented approach to understanding financial policy in the three IFCs. However, attempts by policy instruments and design scholars to incorporate context into the policy design process remain insufficient to capture the complexity and contextual layers of financial policy-making in modern IFC's.

In particular, the design orientation places the policy designer, i.e. government policy-makers, centre stage in public policy-making. In reality, financial policy-making involves a plethora of state and powerful non-state actors operating within the political-economic milieu of each IFC. This is especially so in the context of Asia, where state authority tends to diffuse into the private sector through state ownership and/or informal influence, and conversely, powerful non-state actors often also wield an inordinate amount of influence over the government. The design orientation's limited attention to policy actor interactions and dynamics can be overcome by considering insights drawn from the policy subsystems approach. The following section provides an overview of the policy subsystems literature.

Policy Subsystems

Scholarly work on policy actors and their interrelations have taken on many forms within the public policy theoretical literature, with conceptual innovations such as subgovernments, policy networks, policy communities and policy regimes seeking to provide a clearer understanding of how groups of policy actors converge and persist over time to influence, or even dominate, the policy process. Political scientists focusing on domestic politics have also noted the role of interest groups or civil society in influencing policy. However, this diversity of conceptual frameworks and labels does not facilitate parsimony in understanding the role(s) of different actors in the policy process.

The policy subsystems approach presents a potentially useful way to consolidate these various concepts and provides a broader understanding of actor groupings and their impacts on policy. This book therefore draws on the policy subsystems approach to address the sociopolitical context within which the three IFCs exist, with insights drawn from subsystems studies, along with policy design, forming one of the theoretical pillars of this book's framework of analysis: nested instrumental approach. This section will therefore provide a critical review of the policy subsystems literature and briefly discuss the steps required for its application to the cases in the rest of the book.

Identifying policy subsystems with the policy formulation and implementation processes, Howlett et al. (2009) have defined a policy subsystem as comprising of "actors with sufficient knowledge of a problem area, or a resource at stake, to allow them to participate in the process of developing possible alternative courses of action to address the issues raised at the agenda-setting stage". Importantly, policy subsystems represent the arena within which actors, institutions and ideas come together in the public policy-making process within an issue area (Howlett et al. 2009).

Various attempts have been made to identify and characterize the various types of policy subsystems in existence. The earliest such attempt was Cater's (1964) identification and conceptualization of "iron triangles" comprising government agencies, congressional committees and interest groups. This was followed by Heclo's (1978) criticism that the concept of iron triangles is "not so much wrong as it is disastrously incomplete". Instead, he suggested that policy-making involves "issue networks" made up of a large number of constantly changing participants (Heclo 1978). Heclo and Widlavsky (1974) subsequently introduced the idea of "policy communities" to describe policy subsystems formed around a set of shared understandings. This concept of policy communities would come to gain traction with later scholars (Maloney et al. 1994).

An important development in the study of subsystems is the introduction of "policy networks" through the work of scholars such as Rhodes, Wilks and Wright (Rhodes 1981; Wilks and Wright 1987). The policy network concept allowed for the identification of a large variety of subsystem types according to their level of "integration", insulation from external influence, membership stability and restrictiveness, and control over resources (Rhodes 1984, 1990, 1997; Howlett et al. 2009). It also underpinned the emergence of the "governance" movement, which placed greater emphasis on the policy influence of non-state actors working through closely-knit policy networks (Rhodes 1996). However, these early studies on policy networks did not adequately account for the interests and beliefs of subsystem actors, which arguably form the "glue" holding networks together.

Reflecting the emergence of constructivist approaches in political science in the 1980s and early 1990s, the advocacy coalition framework first developed by Sabatier in 1988 represents a major attempt to address this deficit. Sabatier's approach identifies subsets of policy subsystems formed around the shared beliefs of its members as "advocacy coalitions", with coalition members coming from all levels of government (Sabatier 1988). The central role of ideas in defining and driving policy subsystems would be further explored in the literature on "epistemic communities" (Fischer 1993; Hajer 1993). Advocacy coalitions can further be categorized into dominant coalitions, transitory coalitions and competing coalitions (Worsham 1997). Baumgartner and Jones have also found that the entrenchment of particular ideas results in the formation of stable "policy monopolies", whereby powerful subsystem actors dominate interpretations of policy issues to form enduring "policy images" (Baumgartner and Jones 1991, 1993; Jones et al. 1998; Jones and Baumgartner 2005).

While advocacy coalitions, epistemic communities and policy monopolies are driven by the prevalence of a set of beliefs or ideas and earlier concepts such as iron triangles and issue networks are focused on interests and issues, more recent research has found that policy subsystems may also be defined around a set of preferred policies. Voss and Simons (2013) have shown that networks may be formed around a preferred policy instrument, with such networks known as "instrument constituencies". An instrument constituency is basically formed around the preference and advocacy of particular policy instruments by a group of subsystem actors who may form a subset of the subsystem or even dominate the entire subsystem. This means that an instrument constituency may become a policy monopoly through its dominance of a subsystem, or an advocacy coalition through its belief in the efficacy of a particular instrument type and its inherent normative beliefs. Boundaries between instruments constituencies, advocacy coalitions and policy monopolies therefore often overlap in practice.

Having provided characterizations and typologies of policy subsystems, policy scholars next sought to understand the dynamics through which subsystems evolve or change, whether through endogenous processes or in response to exogenous stimuli. Howlett and Ramesh (2002) have proposed that policy subsystems adjust to the exogenous forces of globalization through policy learning, venue change, systemic perturbations and subsystem spillovers. While policy learning and venue change are *endogenously* driven by subsystem actors, systemic perturbations and subsystem spillovers represent the response of subsystem actors to *exogenous* shocks and stimuli (Howlett and Ramesh 2002; Williams 2009). This draws on existing studies on endogenous policy learning (Sabatier 1988; May 1992; Bennett and Howlett 1992; Rose 1993; Hall 1993) and exogenous motivations for learning that often involve the entrance of new actors and ideas into a subsystem (Heclo 1974; Williams 2009).

Subsystem formation and dynamics have also received attention in the IPE and comparative politics literatures. Bryson (2011) has noted that strategy formulation and adoption often require establishing a "winning coalition", with strategy formulation involving intense dialogue and deliberation and strategy adoption rife with politics and bargaining. According to Gilpin (1981), the objectives of states are determined by the "interests of the dominant members of the ruling coalitions". Palan et al. (1996) further argue that state competitive strategies are often defined by a "commingling" of public and private actors. Aside from industry actors, other non-state actors such as academics and think tank researchers may also play an important role in informing and even influencing public policies through their participation in transnational "knowledge networks" or epistemic communities (Stone 2000, 2002, 2008, 2013; Stone and Maxwell 2013).

Yet, the policy subsystems approach does not on its own serve as a sufficiently comprehensive framework for policy analysis. While it accounts for the sociopolitical context and actor interrelations within which policy-making takes place, it does so at the neglect of the exact policy means used by policy-makers within a given subsystem. A key reason for this is that subsystems studies tend to be carried out at a relatively high level of abstraction that focuses on subsystem membership and configuration rather than the precise ways in which policies are formulated, chosen and implemented. Causal linkages between subsystems and policy means remain relatively unexplored. This stands in stark contrast to the policy instruments literature reviewed above, which focuses on precise policy means but does not adequately account for the sociopolitical relations and context within which policy designers are embedded. A logical solution would therefore be to merge the two approaches.

Analytical Framework: The Nested Instrumental Approach

The nested instrumental approach merges the policy subsystems and policy instruments approaches to provide an integrated framework of analysis that addresses both policy instruments and the subsystemic context within which these instruments are designed and used. It is this book's framework of analysis for understanding IFC development in Asia. By merging the two public policy theoretical approaches, the nested instrumental approach seeks to overcome their individual weaknesses and at the same time draw on the insights of both. This allows for an integrated understanding of policy *and* politics in IFC development.

While the policy instruments approach provides a rigorous understanding of the design and implementation of policies as tools for the attainment of desired policy outputs, the policy subsystems approach brings with it an in-depth understanding of the sociopolitical context within which policy-making takes place. Melding the two therefore provides a more realistic approach to understanding how policy design is embedded within the sociopolitical milieu of the policy subsystem. Certainly, the impact of politics on policy-making has been alluded to in existing institutional studies such as the Varieties of Capitalism (VOC) approach or the Institutional Analysis and Design (IAD) framework (Ostrom 1990; Hall and Soskice 2001), although these approaches remain at an overly general level of abstraction and do not provide a sufficiently granular understanding of inter-actor relations and policy preferences.

This section provides an in-depth discussion of the nested instrumental approach, discussing the logic of "nested instrumentality" that drives the approach and delineating its constituent components. This in-depth understanding of the nested instrumental approach and its inner workings will facilitate and considerably simplify the application of the approach to the study of Hong Kong, Singapore and Shanghai in Chap. 7. A diagrammatic representation of the nested instrumental approach is illustrated in Fig. 3.1.

A key aspect of policy-making is the formulation and implementation of policy instruments. It is through these instruments that policy-makers are able to effect change and influence the behaviour of citizens and other market participants.

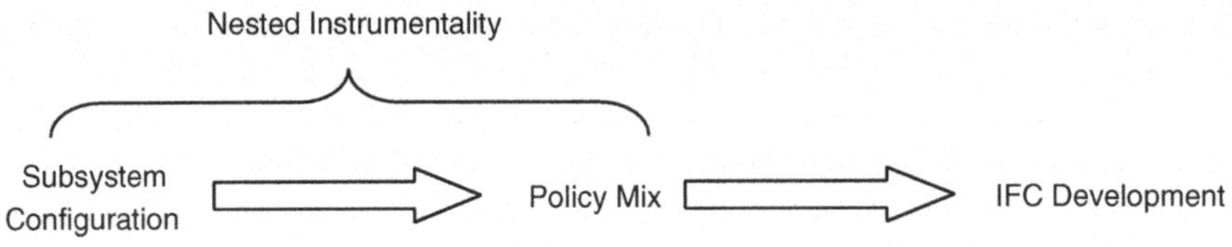

Fig. 3.1 Nested instrumental approach

Furthermore and as the second-generation policy instruments studies discussed above show, each government has at its disposal a combination or mix of policy instruments that can be used to develop the financial sector and hence influence the development of its city as an IFC. These instruments directly determine the attainment of a government's desired policy output, in this case IFC development. This represents the instrumental aspect of policy-making.

However, policy instruments do not exist in a vacuum. They are "nested" within a political-economic milieu that is made up of the interactions between a variety of state and non-state policy actors. "Nestedness" is no doubt a concept that carries considerable baggage in the public policy literature, particular in Ostrom's work on common pool resources (Ostrom 1990, 1994). Notions of the embeddedness of policy within the social context further predate Ostrom, particularly in the work of Granovetter (1985). Similarly, Hollingsworth (1998) has attempted to study the different institutional mechanisms that coordinate inter-actor relationships and which result in different governance and institutional arrangements, although he does not discuss how these different arrangements influence or affect the form and substance of policies.

More relevant to the purposes of this book is Howlett's work on the multi-level "nesting" of policy instruments within the context of established governance modes and regime logics (Howlett 2009, 2011; Howlett and Cashore 2009). This has led to the recognition that financial policies are often jointly formulated and implemented by actors, both state and non-state, operating within dense webs of policy relations (Woo 2014, 2015a). In applying the nested instrumental approach to the analysis of the three IFCs, this book builds on such recent research, further conceptualizing and developing a clearer understanding of how policy design is nested within policy subsystems.

A more important, and easily understated, point to note is that policy subsystems are often comprised both state and non-state actors. While the government is the official policy-maker in most instances, non-state actors are also often able to influence the policy process through their participation and membership in policy subsystems. Configurations of state and non-state actors within any given policy subsystem differ across jurisdictions. While policy subsystem configurations have been related to the openness of a subsystem to new actors and ideas (Howlett and Ramesh 1998), this book further explores how policy subsystem configurations are defined by relations of dominance and dependence among subsystem actors, taking into account both the interests and ideological underpinnings of dominant subsystem actors.

As scholars of the advocacy coalition framework have shown, the dominance of a political actor or set of political actors tends to result in the formation of specific policy-making arrangements or coalitions (Sabatier 1988; Worsham 1997; Weible 2007; Carney 2010). Yet there is also a need to understand the dominance of particular actors within a dominant coalition, an aspect which the advocacy coalition framework has not sufficiently addressed. This requires studying individual actor dominance within the overall context of the subsystem, and how dominant individual actors or organizations determine policy subsystem configuration and influence policy mix design. The nested instrumental approach facilitates the study of this causal link between subsystem configuration and policy mix design.

As with the concept of "nestedness", prior attempts have been made by public policy scholars to understand the causal linkages between policy context and instrument choice. In particular, scholars of policy learning have noted that policy instrument choice is made by subsystem actors, based on lessons learned by these actors and influenced by the membership and norms of a subsystem (Hall 1989; Kenis and Schneider 1991; Haas 1992; Howlett and Ramesh 1993). Policy instrument choice has also been related to national policy styles (Howlett 1991) and policy networks (Bressers and Jr 1998), with the latter focusing on the relationship between policy network attributes and instrument choice. Studies have also focused on the how policy subsystem configurations are related to instrument choice (Howlett and Ramesh 1995) and policy change (Howlett and Ramesh 1998, 2002; Howlett 2002).

This book builds on such existing attempts to conceptualize and study the linkages between policy subsystems and instrument choice by integrating insights drawn from them into the nested instrumental approach and applying it to the study of nested financial policy processes in Hong Kong, Singapore and Shanghai. In the process, it further conceptualizes the subsystem-design link and tests it empirically on the three cases. This requires a dual focus on the macro-level subsystem and micro-level individual subsystem actors. This book therefore takes the policy subsystem as the unit of analysis and at the same time focuses on political relations and dynamics among individual subsystem actors.

Given this need to refocus the attention on subsystems configuration and inter-subsystem actor dynamics, the nested instrumental approach takes the policy subsystem as its analytical starting point and studies the impact of policy subsystem configuration on policy mix design. This "nesting" of the policy mix within the political-economic context of the policy subsystem means that the policy process is driven by a logic of "nested instrumentality". While understanding policies as instruments used for the attainment of policy outputs provides an instrumental approach to understanding policy, studying policy instruments within the context of the subsystem "nests" instrumentality within the context of the political-economic drivers of policy.

As illustrated in Fig. 3.1, a logic of "nested instrumentality" is exhibited when subsystem configurations inform and influence the formulation and implementation of policy mixes and instruments used by policy-makers in the pursuit of specified policy outputs. "Nested instrumentality" also defines the causal linkage between subsystem configuration and policy mix. In particular, dominant subsystem actors are able to influence and define policy mix design through ideational and/or instrumental channels, by forming or participating in advocacy coalitions and instruments constituencies, respectively. These two channels are further discussed below.

Having described the theoretical foundations of the nested instrumental approach, there is a further need to delineate the individual components that make up the approach. Figure 3.2 provides a more detailed overview of the nested instrumental approach.

In general, the three main components of the nested instrumental approach are defined by parameters which define the dynamics operating within each component. First, policy subsystem configuration is defined by positions of *dominance versus dependence* held by subsystem actors. Dominance in this context is defined as the ability of an actor to affect or influence the policy-making process, with other subsystem actors dependent upon these policies for their survival or success. This draws on Sabatier's (1988) work on advocacy coalitions, whereby policies in a subsystem are made by a dominant coalition. Dominant subsystem actors invariably include state actors such as government agencies and departments, although non-state actors such as large firms and industry associations can also influence policy by operating as dominant or co-dominant actors.

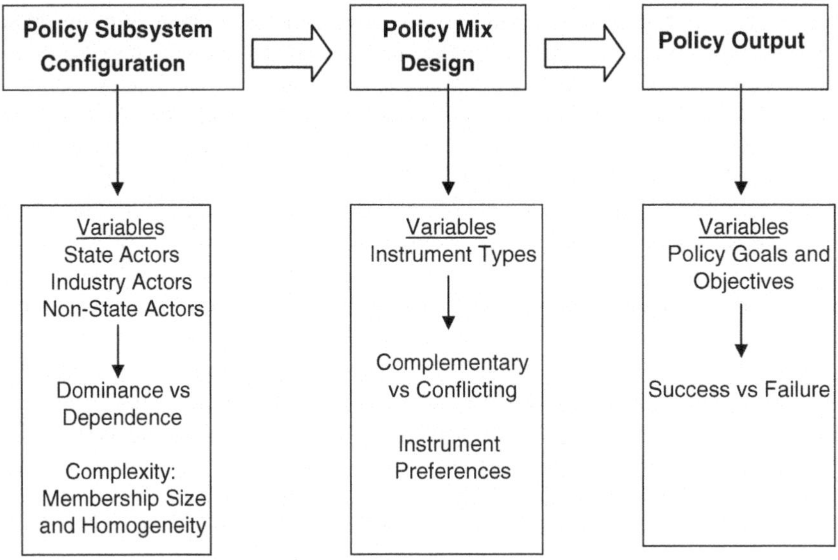

Fig. 3.2 Nested instrumental approach (detailed)

A second parameter that defines policy subsystem configuration is complexity. Subsystem complexity has been related to the "existing range of policy actors present in the policy subsystem" (Howlett et al. 2009), with scholars of policy networks further defining subsystem complexity by the size, type and stability of subsystem membership as well as the varied roles of state and non-state actors within a subsystem (Rhodes 1984, 1996; Smith 1993; Coleman and Perl 1999; Howlett et al. 2009). This book defines policy complexity by the number and homogeneity of subsystem membership. Specifically, a complex policy subsystem features a large number of actors and low homogeneity in the types of actors involved. Low homogeneity is in turn associated with a high degree of diversity in subsystem actors, with subsystem membership fluid and frequently changing. Conversely, subsystems which are homogenous typically comprise a relatively uniform and unchanging set of actors.

Importantly, policy subsystem configurations subsequently influence and define policy mix design through the actions of dominant subsystem actors. Specifically, dominant subsystem actors are able to influence policy mix design by exercising their authority over instrument choice and influencing the instrument preferences of other subsystem actors. Direct influence over instrument choice represents an overt expression of the instrument preferences of dominant actors, while less direct attempts to influence the instruments preferences of other subsystem actors entail the advocacy or promotion of dominant actors' policy beliefs. These two channels through which dominant subsystem actors are able to influence policy mix design are further discussed below.

Within a given subsystem configuration, policy mixes typically comprise a set of policy instruments, with combinations of the various types of instruments within each mix varying across cases. A policy mix is defined by the *complementary versus conflicting* relations among policy instruments. Instruments within each policy mix may complement each other and result in a more integrated policy mix; they may also be in conflict with each other, with instruments working at cross purposes or worse, negating each other's impacts on the policy output. Complementary relations between instruments contribute to a policy mix's consistency, coherence and congruence (Howlett and Rayner 2014).

Furthermore, the choice of policy instruments which make up a mix is also affected by the instrument preferences of policy actors, in particular dominant subsystem actors. Such preferences are dependent upon whether instruments allow dominant actors to pursue their interests and in the process perpetuate their dominance as well as the ideological predispositions of actors towards particular instruments. These are further discussed below in the segment on channels of policy mix nesting. Policy mixes in turn affect the attainment of policy outputs, which are typically defined in terms of *policy success versus policy failure*.

In short, policy subsystem configurations affect and define policy mix design through the influence of dominant subsystem actors. Based on their positions within the policy subsystem, dominant subsystem actors are able to shape policy mix design through their participation in instrument constituencies which favour and advocate particular instruments or by shaping the beliefs and norms of other

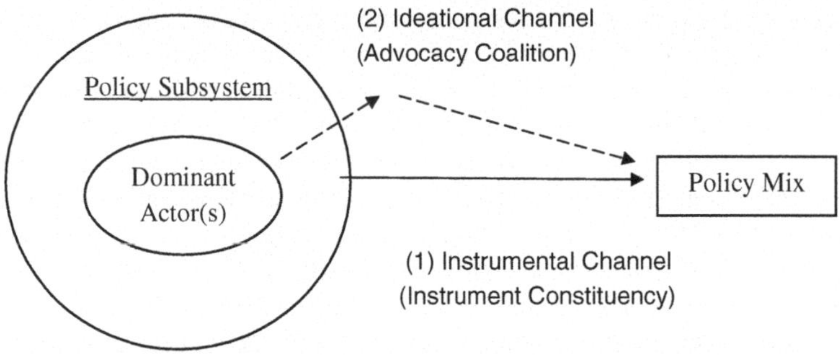

Fig. 3.3 Two channels of policy mix nesting

subsystem actors through advocacy coalitions. These two means or channels through which subsystem configuration affects policy mix design are nested as illustrated in Fig. 3.3.

First, dominant actors determine the types of instruments that make up a policy mix based on their dominance over instrument choice through an *instrumental channel*. Voss and Simons (2013) have defined the subset of a policy subsystem that determines policy instrument choice through the articulation of a preferred instrument as an "instruments constituency". Given that instruments constituencies are formed around a shared preference among its members for a particular set or type of instruments, dominant actors who belong to an instrument constituency are likely to promote an instrument choice that is favourable to the interests and preferences of the constituency. However, policy instrument choice may not necessarily be driven by instrument preferences.

There is a second *ideational channel* through which dominant actors influence policy mix design. This channel involves advocating dominant norms and beliefs through the actions of dominant actors. At a fundamental level, this involves promoting the achievement of particular policy objectives or outputs and favouring the instruments which allow these outputs to be achieved, in the process influencing the belief structure and normative instruments preferences of other subsystem actors. According to Sabatier (1988), dominant subsystem actors or coalitions are defined by their adherence to a set of shared beliefs. This means that the choice of policy instruments by these dominant actors tends to reflect their beliefs and preferences.

As such, dominant actors are able to define policy subsystem configurations by shaping the subsystem around their interests, preferences and beliefs. They do not simply represent or reflect these norms and beliefs; they actively propagate them as well. Given that norms and beliefs provide the normative basis for instrument choice and increase the acceptability of particular instruments, dominant actors exercise an indirect influence over policy mix design through this ideational channel. It is also important to note that the ideational channel presupposes a prioritization of policy outputs over instrument preferences as the basis for driving policy design processes.

In sum, dominant actors within a given policy subsystem configuration define and determine policy mix design and instrument choice through two channels: (i) an instrumental channel that articulates the instrument preferences of instrument constituencies and (ii) an ideational channel that involves the shaping of a subsystem's belief structure by an advocacy coalition. However, it should also be noted that in reality, these two channels tend to overlap and are often hard to distinguish from each other. In other words, dominant actors may influence policy mix design through *both* instrumental and ideational channels, with the dominance of either channel often unclear.

As such, these two channels are not always clear-cut and mutually distinguishable. In reality, dominant actors are likely to belong to both instrument constituencies and advocacy coalitions, with policy mix design often goal-driven and instruments designed or chosen based on their efficacy in achieving desired policy outputs. This suggests that while instrument constituencies may exert an influence over instrument choice, the implementation of instruments by goal-oriented policy-makers may instead be geared towards policy output achievement rather than instrument constituency preferences. Hence, while Fig. 3.3 separates between the instrumental and ideational channels, this is purely for heuristic purposes. The reality is that both channels tend to overlap in practice.

Nonetheless, both instruments constituencies and advocacy coalitions are accounted for in the nested instrumental approach. This addresses the myriad ways in which subsystem actors interact with each other, and the impacts of such inter-actor relations on policy mix design. In combining the policy subsystems and policy instruments approaches, the nested instrumental approach addresses both political context and policy considerations. This will allow for a deeper understanding of how policy mixes are designed and used within the political-economic context of the policy subsystem. While the development of the nested instrumental approach allows this book to contribute to public policy theory, its application to the three cases in Chap. 7 paves the way for a more systematic and empirically driven understanding of IFC development. The next section discusses the research design and methodological issues that underpin the empirical aspects of this book.

Research Design and Methodology

These findings of this book are based on extensive research conducted over the course of a year, which includes the collection of primary and secondary data. This section provides a brief discussion of the research design and methodology that underpins this book. Given the need for a contextually nuanced and in-depth understanding of IFC development, this book relies on the case study method and the collection of qualitative data to achieve a greater depth of understanding. This is particularly important, given this book's focus on the political context of policy-making, which can only be studied qualitatively. These points are further elaborated below.

Case Study Method

A comparative case study approach was taken to describe and analyse the development of Hong Kong, Singapore and Shanghai as successful IFCs. The case study method was chosen as case studies provide depth and sensitivity to context in the study of contemporary phenomenon (Yin 2009, 2014; Neuman 2011). Case studies also allow for a closer examination of linkages between the micro-level of the individual and the macro-level of structure and process (Vaughan 1992; Neuman 2011). Case studies are therefore useful for answering explanatory questions that typically involve the tracing of "operational links over time" (Yin 2014).

Taking a case study approach has therefore allowed this book to provide a deeper understanding of how financial policy decisions are embedded within the political-economic context of the policy subsystem. This enmeshment of policy within politics suggests that phenomena (policy instruments used) and context (policy subsystem configuration) are highly intertwined and difficult to separate, precluding the applicability of quantitative methodologies. Specifically, this book has relied on an "embedded multiple-case" design (Yin 2012) to analyse data collected from different groups of financial sector actors and from different sources across the three cases.

The strengths of case study research are well noted. Case study research provides conceptual validity by identifying and conceptualizing core variables, captures complex events succinctly, permits process tracing over time and space, allows for the calibration of abstract concepts to concrete real-life experiences, incorporates multiple perspectives in a holistic manner and, most importantly, permits the identification of causal mechanisms (George and Bennett 2005; Gerring 2007; Ragin 2008; Neuman 2011). Importantly, case studies yield valid causal inferences, with thick descriptive data layered around a causal question or explanation (King et al. 1994). This typically requires the collection and analysis of qualitative data.

Qualitative Data

Given this book's focus on sociopolitical context and financial policy preferences, it was necessary to collect and analyse qualitative data from a range of sources. Primary data were drawn from in-depth interviews with senior financial policy-makers, private sector professionals and experts in the financial industry, while secondary data comprised official speeches, documents and reports published by relevant government agencies and major financial institutions.

Interviews were carried out between April and November 2013 with policy-makers at the ministerial and directorial levels, senior financial sector professionals and independent experts. However, several respondents also requested for anonymity, whether to protect themselves from the consequences of disclosing sensitive or confidential information or due to an unwillingness to be publicly associated with unsuccessful or unpopular policies. In these instances, respondents are referred to by their job titles. Nonetheless, providing anonymity ensures candour in responses. Interview data were also triangulated with secondary data for greater accuracy.

In terms of interview design, questions were designed to address three different groups of interviewees, namely financial regulatory officials, financial sector professionals, and independent experts or the “interested public”. Separate questions were designed for each group of interviewees, tailored to their specific fields. The interview questions can be found in Appendix 1. While the interview was largely structured by the interview questions, there were inadvertently instances where interviewees brought up issues or subjects that were of interest or potentially useful. Such responses were also recorded and analysed.

Archival data in the form of official reports, speeches and documents were mostly obtained from the Websites of regulatory agencies and online databases. In particular, the Websites of the relevant financial regulatory agencies were perused for official documents, policy announcements and publications. The MAS, HKMA and CSRC Websites proved particularly comprehensive in maintaining databases of past policy reports and publications. However, many of these Websites do not provide copies of archival data that were published before the 1990s. For documents published before the 1990s, hard copies were obtained from various university and public libraries, where available. Relevant private sector reports and publications were also perused.

Qualitative data analysis allows this book to: (1) provide detailed descriptions based on both observable and non-observable information and (2) draw and explicate causal relations between variables. This means making both descriptive and causal inferences (King et al. 1994). Through analyses of archival and interview data, important causal inferences were derived with regard to how a specific subsystem configuration resulted in the formulation of a policy mix tailored to that configuration in the three IFC’s. In-depth interviews allowed for the collection of less observable data, as these high-level interviewees possess valuable experience and access to the financial policy process, both of which are not always publicly available.

Triangulation of data is achieved by drawing on different sources of data and interviewing different groups of respondents. The first round of triangulation involved using both interview data and official publications to analyse and assess financial policies enacted in each IFC. This is complemented by a second round of triangulation that involved collecting interview data from a variety of financial policy actors such as financial regulatory policy-makers, private sector professionals and independent experts such as academics and researchers. Drawing on the views of financial regulators and private sector professionals who are often the target of regulations allows for a more balanced understanding of the nature and impacts of financial policies enacted within each case.

Conclusion

This chapter has provided a detailed description of the theoretical and methodological foundations that underpin this book, both of which have allowed this book to make key theoretical and empirical contributions to the field. Through a discussion of the policy instruments and policy subsystems approaches, it is clear that neither of these two approaches is sufficient for the development of an integrative and nuanced approach to studying IFC development in Asia. Rather, they are both limited in their scope of analysis.

While the policy instruments literature provides a comprehensive understanding of the tools that policy-makers have at their disposal and how these tools have been designed for achieving various policy goals, it has not sufficiently addressed the wider sociopolitical context within which policy instruments are designed and implemented. Conversely, the policy subsystems literature has yielded important insights on the different combinations of state and non-state actors within a given policy area. However, it does not adequately address the specific policies used by policy-makers within subsystems.

The nested instrumental approach seeks to address these limitations by drawing on the insights of both approaches. This allows for a more integrative approach to understanding IFC development, taking into account both political context and policy processes. This chapter has provided an in-depth discussion of the development, components and theoretical foundations of the nested instrumental approach. The approach will subsequently be applied to the three cases in Chap. 7. Furthermore, the use of qualitative data and case study methods allows this book to provide a contextually driven and in-depth analysis of IFC development and hence incorporating contextual elements into the study of financial policy. Such nuance and depth of analysis is largely missing in the existing IFC literature, which draws heavily on quantitative methods.

References

Anderson CW (1977) Statecraft: introduction to political choice and judgment. Wiley, California

Baldwin DA (1985) Economic statecraft. Princeton University Press, New Jersey

Baumgartner FR, Jones BD (1991) Agenda dynamics and policy subsystems. J Polit 53:1044–1074

Baumgartner FR, Jones BD (1993) Agendas and instability in American politics. University of Chicago Press, Chicago

Bennett CJ, Howlett M (1992) The lessons of learning: Reconciling theories of policy learning and policy change. Policy Sci 25:275–294

Bressers H, Klok P-J (1988) Fundamentals for a theory of policy instruments. Int J Soc Econ 15:22–41

Bressers HTA, LJO Jr (1998) The selection of policy instruments: a network-based perspective. J Public Policy 18:213–239

Bryson JM (2011) Strategic planning for public and non-profit organizations: a guide to strengthening and sustaining organizational achievement, 4th edn. Jossey-Bass, California

Carney RW (2010) Contested capitalism: the political origins of financial institutions. Routledge, London

Cater D (1964) Power in Washington: a critical look at today's struggle to govern in the nation's capital. Random House, New York

Coleman WD, Perl A (1999) Internationalized policy environments and policy network analysis. Polit Stud 47:691–709

Considine M (2012) Thinking outside the box? Applying design theory to public policy. Polit Policy 40:704–724

Craft J, Howlett M (2012) Policy formulation, governance shifts and policy influence: location and content in policy advisory systems. J Public Policy 32:79–98

Dahl RA, Lindblom CE (1953) Politics, economics and welfare planning and politico-economics systems resolved into basic social processes. Harper & Brothers, New York

Doern GB (1981) The peripheral nature of scientific and technological controversy in federal policy formation. Science Council of Canada

Doern GB, Phidd RW (1992) Canadian public policy: ideas, structure, process. University of Michigan Press, Michigan

Dryzek JS (1983) Don't toss coins in garbage cans: a prologue to policy design. J Public Policy 3:345–367

Elmore RF (1987) Instruments and strategy in public policy. Rev Policy Res 7:174–186

Fischer F (1993) Policy discourses and the politics of Washington think tanks. In: Fischer F, Forester J (eds) The argumentative turn in policy analysis and planning. Duke University Press, Durham, pp 21–42

George AL, Bennett A (2005) Case studies and theory development in the social sciences. MIT Press, Massachusetts

Gerring J (2007) Case study research: principles and practices. Cambridge University Press, New York

Gilpin R (1981) War and change in world politics. Cambridge University Press, Cambridge

Granovetter M (1985) Economic action and social structure: the problem of embeddedness. Am J Sociol 91:481–510

Gunningham N, Grabosky P, Sinclair D (1998) Smart regulation: designing environmental policy. Oxford University Press, New York

Haas PM (1992) Introduction: epistemic communities and international policy coordination. Int Organ 46:1–35

Hajer MA (1993) Discourse coalitions and the institutionalization of practice: the case of acid rain in Britain. In: Fischer F, Forester J (eds) The argumentative turn in policy analysis and planning. Duke University Press, Durham, pp 43–76

Hall PA (ed) (1989) The political power of economic ideas: Keynesianisrn across nations. Princeton University Press, Princeton

Hall PA (1993) Policy paradigms, social learning, and the state: the case of economic policymaking in Britain. Comp Polit 25:275–296

Hall PA, Soskice D (2001) Varieties of capitalism: the institutional foundations of comparative advantage: the institutional foundations of comparative advantage. OUP Oxford

Heclo H (1974) Modern social politics in britain: from relief to income maintenance. Yale University Press, New Haven

Heclo H (1978) "Issue networks and the executive establishment. In: Anthony K (ed) The new American political System. American Enterprise Institute, Washington DC, pp 87–124

Heclo H, Wildavsky AB (1974) The private government of public money: community and policy inside British politics. Macmillan, London

Hollingsworth RJ (1998) Territoriality in modern societies: the spatial and institutional nestedness of national economies. In: Immerfall PDS (ed) Territoriality in the globalizing society. Springer, Berlin, pp 17–37
Hood C (1986) The tools of government. Chatham House Publishers, London
Howlett M (1991) Policy instruments, policy styles, and policy implementation. Policy Stud J 19:1–21
Howlett M (2000) Managing the "hollow state": procedural policy instruments and modern governance. Can Public Adm 43:412–431
Howlett M (2002) Do networks matter? linking policy network structure to policy outcomes: evidence from four canadian policy sectors 1990-2000. Can J Polit Sci Can Sci Polit 35:235–267
Howlett M (2004) Beyond good and evil in policy implementation: instrument mixes, implementation styles, and second generation theories of policy instrument choice. Policy Soc 23:1–17
Howlett M (2009) Governance modes, policy regimes and operational plans: a multi-level nested model of policy instrument choice and policy design. Policy Sci 42:73–89
Howlett M (2011) Designing public policies: principles and instruments, 1st edn. Routledge, London
Howlett M, Cashore B (2009) The dependent variable problem in the study of policy change: understanding policy change as a methodological problem. J Comp Policy Anal Res Pract 11:33–46
Howlett M, Lejano RP (2013) Tales from the crypt the rise and fall (and rebirth?) of policy design. Adm Soc 45:357–381
Howlett M, Ramesh M (1993) Patterns of policy instrument choice: policy styles, policy learning and the privatization experience. Rev Policy Res 12:3–24
Howlett M, Ramesh M (1995) Studying public policy: policy cycles and policy subsystems, 1st edn. Oxford University Press, Oxford
Howlett M, Ramesh M (1998) Policy subsystem configurations and policy change: operationalizing the postpositivist analysis of the politics of the policy process. Policy Stud J 26:466–481
Howlett M, Ramesh M (2002) The Policy effects of internationalization: a subsystem adjustment analysis of policy change. J Comp Policy Anal 4:31–50
Howlett M, Rayner J (2007) Design principles for policy mixes: cohesion and coherence in "new governance arrangements". Policy Soc 26:1–18
Howlett MP, Rayner J (2013a) Patching vs packaging: complementary effects, goodness of fit, degrees of freedom and intentionality in policy portfolio design. Social Science Research Network, Rochester, NY
Howlett M, Rayner J (2013b) Patching vs packaging: complementary effects, goodness of fit, degrees of freedom and intentionality in policy portfolio design
Howlett M, Rayner J (2014) Patching vs packaging in policy formulation: complementary effects, goodness of fit, degrees of freedom and feasibility in policy portfolio design
Howlett M, Ramesh M, Perl A (2009) Studying public policy: policy cycles and policy subsystems, 3rd edn. Oxford University Press, Oxford
Howlett M, Mukherjee I, Woo JJ (2014) From tools to toolkits in policy design studies: the new design orientation and policy formulation research. Policy Polit 43:291–311
John P (2011) Making policy work. Routledge, New York
Jones BD, Baumgartner FR (2005) The politics of attention: how government prioritizes problems. University of Chicago Press, Chicago
Jones BD, Baumgartner FR, True JL (1998) Policy punctuations: U.S. budget authority, 1947–1995. J Polit 60:1–33
Kenis P, Schneider V (1991) Policy networks and policy analysis: scrutinizing a new analytical toolbox. In: Marin B, Mayntz R (eds) Policy networks: empirical evidence and theoretical considerations. Westview Press, Boulder, pp 25–62
King G, Keohane RO, Verba S (1994) Designing social inquiry: scientific inference in qualitative research. Princeton University Press, New Jersey

Kirschen ES (ed) (1964) Economic policy in our time. Rand McNally, Chicago
Lasswell HD (1936) Politics; who gets what, when, how. Whittlesey House, Michigan
Lasswell HD (1945) World politics faces economics: with special reference to the future relations of the United States and Russia. McGraw-Hill, New York
Lasswell HD (1951) The Policy Orientation. In: Lerner D, Lasswell HD (eds) The policy sciences: recent developments in scope and method. Stanford University Press, California, pp 3–15
Linder SH, Peters BG (1984) From social theory to policy design. J Public Policy 4:237–259
Linder SH, Peters BG (1988) The analysis of design or the design of analysis? Rev Policy Res 7:738–750
Linder SH, Peters BG (1989) Instruments of government: perceptions and contexts. J Public Policy 9:35–58
Linder SH, Peters BG (1990) Policy formulation and the challenge of conscious design. Eval Program Plann 13:303–311
Linder SH, Peters BG (1991) The logic of public policy design: linking policy actors and plausible instruments. Knowl Policy 4:125–151
Lowi TJ (1972) Four systems of policy, politics, and choice. Public Adm Rev 32:298
Maloney WA, Jordan G, McLaughlin AM (1994) Interest groups and public policy: the insider/outsider model revisited. J Public Policy 14:17–38
May PJ (1992) Policy Learning and Failure. J Public Policy 12:331–354
May PJ (2003) Policy design and implementation. In: Peters BG, Pierre J (eds) Handbook of public administration. SAGE Publications Ltd., London, pp 223–233
Neuman WL (2011) Social research methods: qualitative and quantitative approaches. Allyn & Bacon, Boston
Ostrom E (1990) Governing the commons: the evolution of institutions for collective action. Cambridge University Press, Cambridge
Ostrom E (1994) Rules games and common—pool resources. University of Michigan Press, Michigan
Palan R, Abbott J, Deans P (1996) State strategies in the global political economy. Pinter, London
Phidd RW, Doern GB (1978) The politics and management of Canadian economic policy. Macmillan of Canada, Ontario
Ragin CC (2008) Redesigning social inquiry: fuzzy sets and beyond. University of Chicago Press, Chicago
Rayner J (2013) On smart layering as policy design: tackling the biofuels policy mess in Canada and the United Kingdom
Rhodes RAW (1981) Control and power in central-local government relations. Allen and Unwin, London
Rhodes RAW (1984) Power-dependence, policy communities and intergovernmental networks. Public Adm Bull 49:4–31
Rhodes RAW (1990) Policy networks a british perspective. J Theor Polit 2:293–317
Rhodes RAW (1996) The new governance: governing without government. Polit Stud 44:652–667
Rhodes RAW (1997) Understanding governance: policy networks, governance, reflexivity, and accountability. Open University Press, London
Rose R (1993) Lesson-drawing in public policy: a guide to learning across time and space. Chatham House Publishers, London
Sabatier PA (1988) An advocacy coalition framework of policy change and the role of policy-oriented learning therein. Policy Sci 21:129–168
Salamon LM (1989) Beyond privatization: the tools of government action. The Urban Institute Press, Washington
Salamon LM, Lund MS (1989) The tools approach: basic analytics. In: Salamon LM (ed) Beyond privatization: the tools of government action. The Urban Institute Press, Washington, pp 23–49
Schneider A, Ingram H (1990a) Policy design: elements, premises and strategies. In: Nagel SS (ed) Policy Theory and policy evaluation: concepts, knowledge, causes and norms. Greenwood, New York, pp 77–102
Schneider A, Ingram H (1990b) Behavioral assumptions of policy tools. J Polit 52:510–529

Schneider A, Ingram H (1993) Social construction of target populations: implications for politics and policy. Am Polit Sci Rev 87:334
Schneider A, Ingram H (1994) Social constructions and policy design: implications for public administration. Res Public Adm 3:137–173
Schneider AL, Ingram HM (1997) Policy design for democracy. University Press of Kansas, Kansas
Smith MJ (1993) Pressure, power, and policy: state autonomy and policy networks in Britain and the United States. Harvester Wheatsheaf, Aldershot
Stone D (2000) Think tank transnationalisation and non-profit analysis, advice and advocacy. Glob Soc 14:153–172
Stone D (2002) Introduction: global knowledge and advocacy networks. Glob Netw 2:1–12
Stone D (2008) Global public policy, transnational policy communities, and their networks. Policy Stud J 36:19–38
Stone D (2013) Knowledge actors and transnational governance: the private-public policy nexus in the global agora. Palgrave Macmillan, London
Stone D, Maxwell S (2013) Global knowledge networks and international development. Routledge, London
Torgerson D (1985) Contextual orientation in policy analysis: the contribution of Harold D. Lasswell. Policy Sci 18:241–261
Trebilcock MJ, Hartle DG (1982) The choice of governing instrument. Int Rev Law Econ 2:29–46
Tupper A, Doern GB (1981) Public corporations and public policy in Canada. Institute for Research on Public Policy
van der Doelen FCJ (1998) The "give-and-take" packaging of policy instruments: optimizing legitimacy and effectiveness. In: Bemelmans-Videc M-L, Rist RC, Vedung E (eds) Carrots, sticks & sermons: policy instruments & their evaluation. Transaction Publishers, New Jersey, pp 129–146
van der Heijden J (2011) Institutional layering: a review of the use of the concept. Politics 31:9–18
Vaughan D (1992) Theory elaboration: the heuristics of case analysis. In: Ragin CC, Becker HS (eds) What is a case?. Cambridge University Press, Cambridge, Exploring the foundations of social inquiry, pp 173–202
Vedung E (1998) Policy instruments: typologies and theories. In: Bemelmans-Videc M-L, Rist RC, Vedung E (eds) Carrots, sticks & sermons: policy instruments & their evaluation. Transaction Publishers, New Jersey, pp 21–58
Voss J-P, Simons A (2013) Instrument constituencies and the supply-side of policy innovation. Lee Kuan Yew School of Public Policy. National University of Singapore, Singapore
Weible CM (2007) An advocacy coalition framework approach to stakeholder analysis: understanding the political context of california marine protected area policy. J Public Adm Res Theory 17:95–117
Wilks S, Wright M (1987) Comparative government-industry relations: Western Europe, the United States, and Japan. Clarendon Press, Oxford
Williams RA (2009) Exogenous shocks in subsystem adjustment and policy change: the credit crunch and Canadian Banking Regulation. J Public Policy 29:29–53
Woo JJ (2014) Singapore's policy style: statutory boards as policymaking units. J Asian Public Policy 8:120–133
Woo JJ (2015a) Policy relations and policy subsystems: financial policy in Hong Kong and Singapore
Woodside K (1986) Policy instruments and the study of public policy. Can J Polit Sci 19:775–794
Worsham J (1997) Other people's money: policy change, congress, and bank regulation. Westview Press, Boulder
Yin RK (2009) Case study research: design and methods. Sage Publications, Los Angeles
Yin RK (2012) Applications of case study research. SAGE Publications, California
Yin RK (2014) Case study research: design and methods. Sage Publications, Los Angeles

Chapter 4
Hong Kong

Hong Kong is currently Asia's leading IFC. As the GFCI shows, the city is ranked third in the world and continues to rank ahead of Singapore. As of 2014, Hong Kong is host to 203 authorized financial institutions and 63 representative offices and the financial services sector makes up 16.5 % of its GDP (Hong Kong Trade Development Council 2015). More importantly, Hong Kong's success as an IFC has been predicated upon its low taxes, sound legal system, efficient regulatory regime and proximity to China. The Hong Kong government's commitment to free market principles, a laissez-faire model of financial governance and general political freedom has also contributed to the city's attractiveness as a location for doing business and expatriate living. However, there is a need to take a "deep dive" approach to understanding these policy and political drivers of Hong Kong's success.

From a policy perspective, Hong Kong's development as an IFC has thus far been based on a financial policy mix that largely comprises stabilizing financial policy instruments which reflects and perpetuates a laissez-faire approach that minimizes government intervention in markets. This means limited use of enabling or developmental instruments. Such an approach is reflected in the government's "big market, small government" doctrine that largely employs stabilizing policies to ensure market stability, eschewing more interventionist developmental and enabling policies. It goes without saying that this financial policy mix is designed and utilized within the sociopolitical milieu of Hong Kong's financial policy subsystem.

Specifically, the Hong Kong Monetary Authority (HKMA) is enmeshed within a web of financial sector relations that include industry and other non-state actors operating within institutionalized channels of engagement. However, these actors do not factor heavily into the HKMA's financial policies. Rather, financial policy-making remains largely state-driven, although paradoxically this dominance over policy is not always obvious, given the government's laissez-faire approach. Hong Kong's financial governance model, financial policy mix and subsystem are discussed in greater depth below. It is also important to note that Hong Kong's financial governance model is a function of history as much as it is a result of active government efforts.

J.J. Woo, *Business and Politics in Asia's Key Financial Centres*,
DOI 10.1007/978-981-287-985-1_4

Hong Kong's beginnings as an IFC can be traced as far back as 1842, when Hong Kong had first become a British colony and thriving entrepot for the region (Schenk 2001). Its transformation from a trading entrepot to an IFC was largely the result of a "natural process", as such extensive trading activity stimulated the formation and agglomeration of trade-related financial services in the territory (Schenk 2001; Cartland 2013; Chong 2013. The financial services sector would subsequently grow to become a self-sustaining industry, as a post-war decline in international trade prompted banks to shift from commercial activities to purely financial activities (Schenk 2001; Cartland 2013). By the 1970s, Hong Kong had truly taken off as an IFC, with the rapid internationalization of banking and financial activities in the territory (Jao 1980).

Importantly, the early emergence and subsequent success of Hong Kong's financial services sector was a result of the government's liberal economic policy, which allowed the territory to leverage on its strategic location and proximity to China by internationalizing its financial markets and catering to a growing demand for multinational banking services (Jao 1980; Lee and Jao 1982). This laid the foundation for the rapid securitization and financial innovation that characterized Hong Kong's financial sector development in the 1980s and 1990s (Mak 1993; Jao 1997). A key policy development that contributed immensely to Hong Kong's development as an IFC was the establishment of the HKMA in 1993 (Pauly 2011).

While the 1997 handover saw a transfer of Hong Kong's sovereignty to the People's Republic of China (PRC), the government of Hong Kong nonetheless retained independent authority to "formulate monetary and financial policies, safeguard the free operation of financial business and financial markets, and regulate and supervise them in accordance with law".[1] As such, Hong Kong retained laissez-faire approach to financial governance despite changes in its political situation with the handover. This allowed the city to enjoy intense growth and innovation in its financial markets well into the 2000s, with intense competitive prompting banks to expand their businesses and offer other financial products and services such as personal finance and wealth management products in 2000 (Hong Kong Monetary Authority 2000).

Hong Kong also leveraged on its advantageous proximity to China by signing the Closer Economic Partnership Arrangement (CEPA) with China in 2003 and transforming itself into world's leading offshore Renminbi (RMB) centre. Along with the establishment of the Renminbi Qualified Foreign Institutional Investor (RQFII) scheme in December 2011, Hong Kong has firmly established itself as the financial gateway into China. However, this proximity to China represents but one source of Hong Kong's competitive advantage. Domestic policy and political factors play an important role in driving Hong Kong's competitive advantage in various key financial sectors. These determinants of competitive advantage are discussed next.

[1]The Basic Law of the Hong Kong Special Administrative Region of the People's Republic of China, Chapter V, Sect. 1, Article 110.

Determinants of Competitive Advantage

In all three cases, financial sector growth has been predicated upon economic openness. While Hong Kong and Singapore have always featured relatively open economies by virtue of their history as trading entrepots, Shanghai has also benefitted from the Chinese government's moves to open up and liberalize the Chinese economy in the late 1970s. However, there are both internal and external drivers of competitive advantage in the case of Hong Kong's, with both presenting policy implications that are discussed in later sections. Internal drivers are typically policy-based and include political and social stability, economic freedom, adherence to GATT National Treatment principles, a robust legal system, accountable and responsive governing style, favourable tax regime, skilled workforce, modern and efficient infrastructure, low costs from regulation, free flows of information and the use of English as an official language (Jao 1997).

These internal drivers correspond to what Schenk (2001) refers to as the "classic attributes of an IFC: political stability, infrastructure and regulatory freedom". More specific factors have thus far been identified. Enright et al. 1997 suggests that underlying Hong Kong's competitive advantages are the "favourable institutional structures that set and enforce clear rules of the game on a level playing field; motivated and hardworking individuals who continually strive for success; and a prevailing ethos that has fostered and stimulated economic development". Mak (1993) has identified factors such as having a free economic system, government policies aimed at financial liberalization, equal "National Treatment" of foreign and domestic banks, relatively low transaction costs, an advanced telecommunication system, availability of electronic banking services, an advantageous location and the presence of a skilled workforce with good industrial relations.

Of particular significance to Hong Kong's success as an IFC is the city's adherence to a common law system that ensures transparent laws and a reliable judiciary; this common law system is also seen as an important driver of success for other IFCs such as London and Singapore (Tsang 2013). As McCauley and Chan (2009) have also noted, Hong Kong's advantage as an IFC lies in its legal system, regulatory framework, and clearing and settlement systems. Another significant advantage that Hong Kong enjoys is its wholly convertible currency, the Hong Kong dollar that is pegged to the US dollar (Chong 2013; Sheng 2013; Tsang 2013). Hong Kong's transparent and trusted financial infrastructure with its "multi-currency, multi-dimensional platform" is a key defining competitive advantage that sets it apart from other IFCs (Hong Kong Monetary Authority 2006a).

However, Hong Kong would not have emerged as an IFC in the first place if not for a confluence of external factors. Such external drivers of success are associated with the spatio-temporal aspects of Hong Kong's position within the regional and global economy, such as strategic location and time zone, proximity to a rapidly liberalizing Chinese economy (the "China factor"), strong growth among Asia-Pacific economies and the globalization or internationalization of banking and finance (Jao 1997). These external factors had previously bolstered Hong Kong's competitive advantage as a trade entrepot, and with the development of its financial sector, Hong Kong was able to transfer its advantages as a trading entrepot into its new role as a "financial entrepot" (Jao 1974), as "industrial capitalism on a national scale developed into financial capitalism on a global scale" (Pauly 2011).

However, Hong Kong's most significant external driver is its proximity to China, or the "China factor" (Subacchi et al. 2012). This is a unique advantage which, according to deputy chief executive of the HKMA Eddie Yue, is "difficult for other financial centres to replicate" (Yue 2011). As one of China's leading IFCs, Hong Kong has been able to benefit from China's phenomenal rise over the past few decades by tapping into China's financial liberalization process and becoming a leading offshore RMB centre amidst increasing external use of China's currency (Yue 2011). Hong Kong has also found a niche in managing initial public offerings by firms seeking to raise capital in Hong Kong (Pauly 2011). More recently, Hong Kong has established mutual stock market access with Shanghai and gained access to China's capital markets, providing the city with a strategic position within China's economic and financial reforms (Hong Kong Trade Development Council 2015).

Hong Kong's linkages to the Mainland and its "deep knowledge of business cultures and practices on the Mainland" (Pauly 2011) thus augment its other existing advantages, allowing the SAR to become "embedded in China's grander national marketization and globalization project … becoming a *Chinese* global city" (Lui and Chiu 2009). Based on such linkages, Hong Kong's business and financial services sectors have also become "honed to the needs of … business on the Chinese Mainland" (Enright et al. 1997). This makes Hong Kong a "privileged zone where arbitrage can thrive between open global markets and a massive and internally focused Chinese economy" (Pauly 2011), allowing the SAR to act as a key gateway into China. Furthermore, Hong Kong's diverse set of local and foreign firms are able to "pack and integrate" international financial activity and use Hong Kong as a platform from which to invest in China (Enright et al. 1997).

A succinct summary of Hong Kong's drivers of success factors is provided by Lee and Vertinsky (1988) who attribute Hong Kong's success as an IFC to: "(1) its British legal traditions and legal and financial expertise, (2) its less constraining levels of regulation and disclosure, (3) its role in the investment in and trade flows to and from the PRC … (4) its role as a prime financial centre for overseas Chinese … and (5) opportunities for abnormal profits resulting from the structure of the domestic banking market". This can further be condensed into three key drivers of success. These are (i) economic freedom based on a laissez-faire limited government approach to economic governance, (ii) a robust legal and regulatory infrastructure and (iii) proximity to an increasingly affluent and powerful China.

However, these factors are merely a descriptive account of what makes Hong Kong successful and attractive as an IFC. They do not explain the exact means through which Hong Kong was able to attain its pre-eminence as an IFC. These are discussed in the following sections on Hong Kong's financial governance model, regulatory regime and its financial policy mix.

Financial Governance

Hong Kong's model of financial governance is characterized by two fundamental tenets: commitment to economic freedom and adherence to the rule of law. First, the economic freedom that underpins Hong Kong's financial governance approach flows from its "laissez-faire" style of economic policy, which has boosted the SAR's competitiveness by endowing it with "freedom from onerous regulation" (Schenk 2002). Li situates Hong Kong's economic freedom within a growth-oriented "paradigm of economism" that involves an indirect yet active role of government in maintaining the conditions necessary for laissez-faire (Li 2012).

Such adherence to a "neoclassical principle of limited government" has provided Hong Kong with a measure of economic resilience and flexibility that is conducive to financial sector development (Sung 1989). As former HKMA Chief Joseph Yam has noted, Hong Kong's success as an IFC is based on its adherence to "sound principles of the free market with minimal governmental intervention" (Yam 1995). This fundamentally means that in terms of financial governance, there is "no intervention from the government unless market failure occurs" (Chong 2013). Jao (1980) similarly notes that the Hong Kong government generally adopts a "permissive or accommodating posture: it merely aims to provide a stable framework for the development of the city as a financial centre, but does not, however, offer specific concessions or incentives to encourage such a trend".

Hong Kong thus represents the extreme exemplification of self-regulation and has been described as the "paradigm case of a laissez-faire economy" (Gunningham 1990), especially when compared with more state-driven IFCs such as Shanghai and Singapore. Paradoxically, this lack of direct government action is in itself a means to promote the territory as an IFC, since Hong Kong's attractiveness as an IFC lies in its business-friendly, laissez-faire economic environment. In other words, businesses are attracted to Hong Kong precisely because it features minimal state intervention in the market. Hong Kong's economic openness has thus been used as an "instrument for attracting inward capital in the form of foreign investment and external demand in the form of manufactured goods and services exports" (Li 2012).

As such, it is important to note that Hong Kong's "laissez-faire" image belies an *active* role played by the government in Hong Kong's success. This means that Hong Kong's laissez-faire economic policy is a "deliberate policy choice rather than merely an absence of policy" (Schenk 2002). This is a policy choice that is "guided by a liberal economic ideology" (Tang 1999) and hence requires considerable governmental restraint from market intervention. Former Financial Secretary John J. Cowperthwaite has described Hong Kong's unique brand of economic policy-making as "positive non-interventionism" (Schenk 2002), with the "positive" aspect suggesting an active coordinative role of government and "non-intervention" denoting the favouring of laissez-faire capitalism (Li 2012).

Hong Kong's financial governance model has since evolved from "positive non-intervention" to what former Chief Executive Donald Tsang has termed "big market, small government" (Tsang 2006, 2013). The central belief of "big market, small government" is that "government will only do the things which the market does not do" (Tsang 2013). This means "highly selective intervention by the government on the basis of necessity, especially during crises or in the face of market failure" (Glassburner and Riedel 1972). Hong Kong's financial governance model is therefore predicated upon the need to maintain the efficient functioning of its free markets and minimize state intervention in the markets, in order to attract foreign financial institutions and firms.

Pauly characterizes Hong Kong's government as a "facilitator" that intervenes in the economy only in reaction to crises, enabling the formation of a "strong society" capable of functioning with minimal government direction (Pauly 2011). This means that industry actors are able to drive financial sector growth with little government interference, although they still operate within the regulatory oversight of the government. Hence, there is a "clear separation in Hong Kong between the role of government as referee and the role of private companies as active players in the economy" (Enright et al. 1997). This entails "combining industrial entrepreneurship with access to financial and land resources directly or indirectly sustained and steered by government policies" (Pauly 2011). However, more recent efforts by the government to promote Hong Kong as an IFC and financial gateway to China suggest a certain extent of state intervention (China Economic Review 2010).

The second major aspect of Hong Kong's financial governance model is the SAR's adherence to the rule of law. Hong Kong's robust legal system is essentially based on the English common law that it had been endowed with as a British colony, prior to the 1997 handover. The British administration had in fact ensured that the "tradition of judicial independence and the rule of law has been transplanted and firmly entrenched in Hong Kong" (Jao 1997). This legal system ensures the protection of property rights and civil liberties, effectively preventing the government of the day from violating these rights and liberties (Jao 1997). Former Chief Executive Donald Tsang has noted that Hong Kong's common law system provides a significant measure of flexibility or adaptability to rapid changes in global financial markets (Tsang 2013).

The importance of Hong Kong's legal system to its financial and economic development has led Lee to consider it the "bedrock of its (Hong Kong's) economic success" (Lee 1995). Transparency, predictability of rules and availability of investor protection define the business fundamentals upon which the SAR's reputation as a world-class IFC depends (Lee 1995). Although initially inherited from the British administration, Hong Kong's legal system has since been adapted and developed to meet its current needs in financial development (Norton and Arner 2000). This reflects the government's attempts to keep its legal framework relevant to constantly evolving financial markets, while at the same time ensure its transparency and efficiency. Hong Kong's legal system can thus be seen as complementary to the government's commitment to positive non-intervention, providing a legal safeguard against excessive government intervention and facilitating the smooth functioning of Hong Kong's free markets.

With regard to the latter, Hong Kong's Western-styled legal system underpins its free markets by "providing a level playing field, due process, protection of property rights and legal contracts" (Lee 1995). As Li (1995) has noted, Hong Kong's "principles of free enterprise, and the supporting legal framework, are enshrined in the Basic Law". Hong Kong's legal system thus provides the legal basis and foundation for the SAR's key competitive advantage of economic freedom, even as it remains a competitive advantage in its own right. An important consequence of Hong Kong's commonwealth legal system is its acceptability by other developed nations and its adaptability to international standards.

In sum, Hong Kong's economy remains free and open, driven by the government's doctrine of "big market, small government". This is complimented by a robust legal system that limits government intervention in financial markets through an adherence to due process and the rule of law, providing investor protection through transparent predictable rules. As such, economic freedom in the form of the "big market, small government" doctrine and the rule of law make up the two foundational pillars upon which financial governance in Hong Kong is built. It is also evident that the Hong Kong government plays an important role in maintaining this economic freedom and robust legal system, particularly through the formulation and implementation of sound regulations through a transparent and reliable regulatory infrastructure.

Regulatory Regime

In Hong Kong, the Financial Secretary is tasked with "overseeing policy formulation and implementation in financial, monetary, economic, trade and employment matters" (Hong Kong Financial Secretary 2009). Specifically, the Financial Secretary is responsible for (Hong Kong Monetary Authority 2006b):

1. The money system (including formulating monetary policy objectives and determining Hong Kong's monetary system),
2. The exchange fund,
3. Public finance,
4. The financial system,
5. Hong Kong's status as an IFC.

With regard to (3), (4) and (5), the Financial Secretary is only responsible for formulating macro-policy objectives, while the Secretary for Financial Services and the Treasury formulates more specific policy objectives and ensures effective implementation through the various regulatory agencies (Hong Kong Monetary Authority 2006b). While financial policy-making is generally carried out by the Financial Secretary, the Financial Services Bureau (FSB) is in charge of "translating policy into regulation" and other specialist regulatory agencies tasked with the actual regulation and supervision of financial services (International Monetary Fund 1999; Norton and Arner 2000). These specialist regulatory agencies include the

Hong Kong Monetary Authority (HKMA), Securities and Futures Commission (SFC) and the Office of the Commissioner of Insurance (OCI) (Norton and Arner 2000).

Established on 1 April 1993 through a merger between the Office of the Exchange Fund and the Office of the Commissioner of banking, the HKMA is the Hong Kong government's chief financial regulatory agency. The responsibilities, authorities and functions of the HKMA are largely spelt out in the Exchange Fund Ordnance, Banking Ordnance and Clearing and Settlement Systems Ordnance, with Legislative Council amendments to the Exchange Fund Ordinance in 1992 granting the Financial Secretary full authority in appointing the Chief Executive of the HKMA (Hong Kong Monetary Authority 2011). Although the HKMA is tasked with implementing the broad financial and monetary policy objectives set by the Financial Secretary, it nonetheless possesses significant autonomy in terms of "determining the strategy, instruments and operational means" for achieving these policy objectives (Hong Kong Monetary Authority 2011).

In general, the HKMA performs the four main functions of ensuring monetary or currency stability, maintaining financial system stability, managing the exchange fund and maintaining Hong Kong's position as an IFC (Hong Kong Monetary Authority 2012a). The mandates of the HKMA include maintaining open and efficient markets with an appropriate regulatory and legal system, playing a larger role in international financial intermediation, ensuring an efficient financial infrastructure for safer cross-border transactions, raising standards of corporate governance to increase investor confidence and attracting foreign capital (Hong Kong Monetary Authority 2006b).

More specifically, the HKMA's responsibilities are comprised of: "promoting the general stability and effective working of the banking system; promoting the development of the debt market, in cooperation with other relevant bodies; matters relating to the issuance and circulation of legal tender notes and coins; promoting the safety and efficiency of the financial infrastructure through the development of payment, clearing and settlement systems and, where appropriate, the operation of these systems; seeking to promote, in cooperation with other relevant bodies, confidence in Hong Kong's monetary and financial systems, and market development initiatives to help strengthen the international competitiveness of Hong Kong's financial services" (Hong Kong Monetary Authority 2011).

These responsibilities reflect the Financial Secretary's dual focus on ensuring the stability of Hong Kong's financial markets and promoting the city as an IFC. Other agencies are also involved in regulating Hong Kong's financial markets, although the HKMA remains the chief regulator coordinating the activities of all other regulatory agencies. While the SFC is tasked with regulating Hong Kong's securities and futures markets through the Securities and Futures Ordinance (Securities and Futures Commission 2012), the publicly listed HKEx regulates frontline issuers who list in the stock and futures exchanges it operates (HKEx 2010). The OCI is a government department that is independent in regulating the insurance industry, under the Insurance Companies Ordnance (International Monetary Fund 1999).

Recognizing the increasingly dense cross-sector linkages in financial markets and its implications for financial regulation, the Hong Kong government has sought to improve cross-sector policy coordination through the establishment of the Council of Financial Regulators (CFR) and the Financial Stability Committee (FSC). While the CFR deals with cross-sector regulatory issues, the FSC monitors and ensures financial system stability (Hong Kong Monetary Authority 2006b). In addition, the HKMA has signed several Memorandums of Understanding (MOUs) with other financial regulatory authorities. These include the MOUs signed with the SFC in December 2002 and the OCI in September 2003 as well an MOU among the HKMA, OCI, SFC and the Mandatory Provident Fund Schemes Authority that was signed in October 1999 and revised in December 2003. These MOUs serve to foster greater cooperation among financial regulatory authorities, improve regulatory policy consistence, as well as reduce regulatory duplication and gaps (Hong Kong Monetary Authority 2006b).

Having addressed Hong Kong's model of financial governance as well as its regulatory regime, the next section discusses the financial policy mix used by the Hong Kong government, in particular the HKMA, in regulating and developing Hong Kong as an IFC.

Financial Policy Mix

Given its position as a leading IFC and the contribution of its financial sector to its GDP,[2] policy-makers in Hong Kong place significant priority on financial sector development. However, Hong Kong's approach to financial sector development differs from that of Singapore and Shanghai, particularly in terms of financial policy instrument preferences. The government's laissez-faire approach has resulted in a preference for stabilizing financial policy instruments that aim to maintain stable and functioning markets, in contrast to the presence of development-oriented and interventionist instruments in Singapore's and Shanghai's financial policy mixes. This section discusses the financial policy mix used by the Hong Kong government in governing and guiding the SAR's development as an IFC.

As enshrined in its basic laws, the Hong Kong government is committed to providing "an appropriate economic and legal environment for the maintenance of the status of Hong Kong as an international financial centre".[3] Upholding Hong Kong's status as an IFC is a key macro-policy objective for the Financial Secretary, along with maintaining stability and efficiency in the financial system and public

---

[2]Financial services represent one of Hong Kong's four "pillar economic sectors" and account for approximately 16.5 % of GDP value added. HKTDC Research, *Economic and Trade Information on Hong Kong*, 2 June 2015 http://hong-kong-economy-research.hktdc.com/business-news/article/Market-Environment/Economic-and-Trade-Information-on-Hong-Kong/etihk/en/1/1X000000/1X09OVUL.htm.

[3]Hong Kong *Basic Law*, Article 109.

finance (Hong Kong Monetary Authority 2006b). The Financial Secretary's policy objectives concerning the maintenance of a sound and efficient financial system are also geared towards enhancing Hong Kong's status as an IFC, especially given the SAR's externally oriented economy and open financial markets (Hong Kong Monetary Authority 2006b).

Evidently, ensuring a sound and stable financial system contributes towards further expansion in Hong Kong's financial markets, by allowing existing financial actors to operate securely within the SAR's free markets and attracting more foreign financial institutions. Given Hong Kong's reputational advantages as a stable IFC and its government's commitment to free markets, stabilizing financial policies have traditionally been an important part of the HKMA's policy toolkit. According to former HKMA Executive Director Simon Topping, the HKMA's supervisory policies are mostly aimed at maintaining financial market stability and protecting depositors or investors (Topping 2013). Furthermore, the implementation of "free and liberal policies" works towards reducing regulatory or business costs and upholding investor confidence (Yam 1995).

At a fundamental level, the HKMA is officially tasked with enhancing the SAR's competitiveness in international financial markets, fostering confidence in its financial system as well as developing and maintaining its financial infrastructure (Hong Kong Monetary Authority 2012b). Financial regulation represents an important stabilizing financial policy instrument used by the HKMA to ensure market stability and, through such market stability, further enhance Hong Kong's status as an IFC. According to the Financial Secretary's policy objective 3(c), the "regulatory regime should aim to provide a regulatory framework that promotes the stability of the financial system, provides an appropriate measure of protection to users of financial services and facilitates competition, and is consistent with the standards and practices of major international financial centres" (Hong Kong Monetary Authority 2006b).

As Hong Kong's chief financial regulator, the role of the HKMA in promoting Hong Kong as an IFC cannot be understated. The HKMA's specific roles have been spelt out in a letter from the Financial Secretary to the Monetary Authority, and they include ensuring safe and efficient cross-border transactions through a sound financial infrastructure, participation in international forums to increase confidence in Hong Kong's financial system and "appropriate market development initiatives that help strengthen the international competitiveness of Hong Kong's financial services" (Leung 2003). Stabilizing instruments are therefore a significant part of the HKMA's toolkit. An important part of the HKMA's efforts at promoting financial market stability is the maintenance of a sound and stable financial infrastructure. As noted by Yam (1995), Hong Kong's financial infrastructure is a key competitive advantage driving its success as an IFC.

The Hong Kong financial infrastructure's "multi-currency, multi-dimensional platform … helps maintain the stability and integrity of the monetary and financial systems, and consolidate Hong Kong's position as an international financial centre" (Hong Kong Monetary Authority 2006a). Having such a "multi-currency, multi-dimensional platform" facilitates multi-currency transfers, payments and settlements in the financial markets through diverse channels of financial intermediation, maintaining currency stability, enhancing Hong Kong's position as a regional hub for fund transfers and debt settlements, and reducing overall systemic risk (Hong Kong Monetary Authority 2006a). This ensures the stability of Hong Kong's financial markets by providing a significant measure of transparency and predictability to capital flows.

However, the HKMA's policies extend beyond achieving market stability. Given the importance of the financial services sector as a key source of revenue for the government, developmental financial policy instruments have on occasion been used to develop potential streams of revenue from new and burgeoning financial sectors. For instance, recent reforms to the financial infrastructure were targeted at encouraging the formation of new financial market niches and increasing transactions in these niches. Specifically, the launch of the Renminbi Settlement System on March 2006 has allowed Hong Kong to "cater for the settlement needs arising from expanded renminbi business" (Hong Kong Monetary Authority 2006a) and leverage on China's rapidly expanding economic clout.

Recent plans by the HKMA to establish a local repository for trade in over-the-counter (OTC) derivatives (Hong Kong Monetary Authority 2010) also aimed to "make Hong Kong a relatively more attractive centre than its regional competitors" (Pauly 2011) for OTC derivatives trading. Such reforms are part of the HKMA's "market development initiatives" (Leung 2003), aimed at enhancing Hong Kong's competitiveness and contributing directly to its revenue stream. The HKMA has also enacted policies that are enabling in nature, targeting specific market sectors or niches and establishing the necessary conditions for their development. For instance, the upgrade of licensed DTCs to restricted license banks in 1990 was part of the government's moves to promote Hong Kong as an international financial centre (Jao 2003).

This reform was particularly advantageous to foreign and merchant banks that wished to establish a presence in Hong Kong, providing them with the regulatory space to develop their businesses in the SAR. The HKMA also launched the CMU in the same year, as part of its efforts to "strengthen and deepen Hong Kong's financial markets" (Li 1995) and develop the market for Hong Kong dollar debt. More recently, the HKMA has been aggressively driving the development of the SAR as an offshore RMB centre and participating in various international financial fora and committees (Hong Kong Monetary Authority 2011). The development of RMB business in Hong Kong has involved significant reductions in restrictions to RMB trade and the promotion of greater cooperation among banks and other financial institutions across the Hong Kong–Mainland border.

Given its highly internationalized markets, Hong Kong's financial policy mix is also defined by domestic–international dynamics. The result is an "optimal policy mix" that sustains confidence in Hong Kong as an IFC through internal improvements to the financial infrastructure and external collaboration with other governments (Pauly 2011). According to Pauly, less direct regulatory instruments aimed at a stable financial infrastructure are used in the domestic sphere, while more aggressive lobbying efforts are employed in the international sphere to create an international environment that allows the Hong Kong to thrive as an international banking and finance hub. This means the use of stabilizing policies domestically and the promulgation of development-oriented financial policies internationally.

However, interviews with senior policy-makers and analysts show that Hong Kong's financial policy mix remains heavily skewed towards stabilizing policy instruments. In general, there is a belief that the Hong Kong government regulates and governs the financial sector in a laissez-faire style and that Hong Kong's development as a financial centre has more or less been a natural process thus far, i.e. free from direct state intervention (Chong 2013; Sheng 2013). According to former Chief Executive Donald Tsang, Hong Kong practises a "totally free market economy", with government interventions maintained only in areas which are absolutely necessary (Tsang 2013). Instances of "absolute necessity" typically include bank failures or even market failures (Cartland 2013).

As such, the HKMA's banking supervisory policy is primarily aimed at banking sector stability and depositor protection, with monetary stability, effective working of the financial system and promotion of Hong Kong as an IFC taken to be secondary objectives (Topping 2013). Furthermore, the government's heavy reliance on stabilizing instruments provides a measure of political stability. It has been noted that the Hong Kong government's stable and transparent financial management policies play a big part in gaining the trust of investors and attracting them to the city (Tsang 2013). Even the HKMA's efforts at developing the banking sector in the late 1990s were based on stabilizing instruments such as promoting competition or measures to enhance the regulatory infrastructure (Tan and Lim 2007).

However, it is important to note that stabilizing policy instruments can also be used for developmental purposes. Stabilizing policy instruments allow the HKMA to contribute to Hong Kong's overall development as an IFC by ensuring market efficiency and stability, "making Hong Kong an attractive place to do business" (Topping 2013). The Hong Kong government's role in developing the financial sector is therefore based on the development of the necessary "software" such as human capital, an English-speaking environment, a robust judicial system and the rule of law and accounting systems (Chong 2013), rather than direct financial investments or incentives. In short, stabilizing financial policy instruments that aim to establish the necessary conditions for the proper functioning of financial markets may inadvertently contribute towards developmental goals, given that international financial institutions tend to be attracted to Hong Kong's stable markets and hence establish themselves in the SAR, contributing to Hong Kong's financial sector development and growth.

Furthermore, interview respondents also acknowledged that recent events have prompted the HKMA to take a more development-oriented approach. In particular, the emergence of Hong Kong as an offshore RMB centre has necessitated the fulfilment of two new objectives by the HKMA: developing market depth and "trying to provide revenue for the institutions", particularly through the payment system (Topping 2013). Both objectives are aimed at attracting more RMB business, by creating favourable market conditions and ensuring a potential stream of revenues, respectively. However, it has been noted that Hong Kong's approach differs from that of Singapore.

According to former HKMA Executive Director Simon Topping, the HKMA promotes Hong Kong largely through "appropriate supervision and infrastructure… there's no financial incentives, tax incentives, or promissory government bond issues" (Topping 2013). This differs markedly from the case of Singapore, which is discussed in the next chapter. As such, development-oriented regulations promulgated for the purpose of developing Hong Kong's RMB market are typically of the enabling type. These regulations create conditions that are conducive for RMB business to take root and flourish. As former Secretary of Financial Services Michael Cartland has noted, the Hong Kong government's job was to "provide an environment in which market players can succeed" (Cartland 2013).

As this section has shown, Hong Kong's financial policy mix largely comprises stabilizing financial policy instruments, although the authorities have on occasion relied on enabling and developmental policy instruments to facilitate the development of specific financial markets or niches. Nonetheless, Hong Kong's financial policy mix remains largely skewed towards stabilizing financial policy instruments, with such instruments inadvertently contributing to financial sector development by establishing the stable market conditions that are attractive to international financial institutions. The next section describes Hong Kong's financial policy subsystem.

Financial Policy Subsystem

Hong Kong's financial governance model of "big market, small government" suggests a financial policy system that involves strong industry actors and limited government intervention. The existing literature and official government publications suggest as much. However, interviews with senior policy-makers paint a different picture of Hong Kong's financial policy subsystem. Rather, the government retains significant control over financial policy-making, with limited financial policy participation or influence by industry and other non-state actors. This differs from the case of Singapore, where almost all financial policies and regulations are informed by industry input. However, this state dominance of the financial policy process is not always obvious, due to the Hong Kong government's commitment to a laissez-faire approach to financial governance.

This means a strong reliance on a stabilizing financial policy mix in financial sector development, with the government's commitment to economic freedom resulting in the exclusion of industry actors from the policy process. While such commitment to free market principles suggests that Hong Kong's dominant state actors are part of an advocacy coalition formed around laissez-faire policy beliefs, the preference for stabilizing financial policy instruments also suggests that these state actors are further part of a stabilizing instrument constituency. This suggests overlapping dominant actor membership in a stabilizing instrument constituency and a free market-oriented advocacy coalition. These are further discussed below.

Existing studies of Hong Kong's financial policy processes tend to highlight the involvement of both a strong state and strong society. For instance, Tang (1999) notes that Hong Kong's "limited government" approach is underwritten by a "strong state in terms of its institutional capacity and political dominance", with the state's "political dominance" shared among the government, business community and prominent individuals. While Hong Kong's early adherence to "positive non-intervention" had ensured a "separation of interests of public servants and business people" (Enright et al. 1997), observers have often noted that the relationship between government and business remains close and "characterized by consultation rather than confrontation" (Enright et al. 1997).

Scholars have further noted that such consultation has permitted the formation of "opaque linkages between public and private sectors that, relatively speaking, permitted deep interaction between domestic and international markets" (Pauly 2011). This close collaborative relationship between the government and private sector has since become institutionalized in financial law, with the modernization of financial law after 1987 resulting in the "relationship between government, business and the financial system becoming increasingly rule-based and transparent" (Norton and Arner 2000). Given the limited role of the state in the economy, private actors in Hong Kong play a "leadership role in business and economic development" (Enright et al. 1997) through their representation in the Executive and Legislative Councils. Industry interests from the finance and insurance sectors are typically represented in the Legislative Council's "functional constituencies" (Loh 2006).

Furthermore, commercial banks such as the Hong Kong and Shanghai Bank (HSBC) play a significant developmental role by financing local companies and industrial projects, "operating almost as a development bank" (Enright et al. 1997). As such, Hong Kong's laissez-faire approach to economic governance has culminated in the evolution of "production organization based on social networks" revolving around manufacturers, traders and financiers (Meyer 2000). This is not to suggest the insignificance of the government in Hong Kong's financial sector development. Just as private actors can influence the policy-making process, the Hong Kong government also influences private actors "through a complex of committees and commissions" (Glassburner and Riedel 1972). As Tang has noted, Hong Kong's "administration ruled in coalition with the major business corporations with the support of prominent local Chinese" (Tang 1999).

Such state–industry interactions have been institutionalized in the form of the government's various consultative and advisory committees. For instance, the Financial Secretary and HKMA receive advice and guidance from several advisory committees, with the Exchange Fund Advisory Committee (EFAC) and its subcommittees being the most significant in carrying out the various functions of a management board (Hong Kong Monetary Authority 2006b). Under Sect. 3(1) of the Exchange Fund Ordnance, the Financial Secretary chairs the EFAC and is required to consult the committee with regard to his control of the exchange fund (Hong Kong Monetary Authority 2006b). Members of the EFAC are appointed by the Financial Secretary and currently include representatives from the HKMA, banks, investments and holdings companies, legal and auditing firms, as well as academia (Hong Kong Monetary Authority 2012c).

The EFAC also consists of governance, audit, currency board, investment and financial infrastructure subcommittees which "monitor specific areas of the HKMA's work and report and make recommendations to the Financial Secretary through the EFAC" (Hong Kong Monetary Authority 2006b). Other advisory committees include the Banking Advisory Committee (BAC) chaired by the Financial Secretary and which includes the Secretary for Financial Services and the Treasury, as well as representatives from the HKMA, SFC and banks, providing advice to the Chief Executive on issues related to the Banking Ordnance (Hong Kong Monetary Authority 2012d) and the Deposit-Taking Companies Advisory Committee (DTCAC), which advises the Chief Executive on issues related to deposit-taking companies as well as restricted license banks (Hong Kong Monetary Authority 2006b).

The DTCAC is also chaired by the Financial Secretary and includes the Secretary for Financial Services and the Treasury and representatives from the HKMA, consumer council, association of restricted license banks and deposit-taking companies, banks, auditors and legislative council (Hong Kong Monetary Authority 2012e). In addition, the Insurance Advisory Committee provides advice on the insurance industry, under the chairmanship of the Secretary for Financial Services and the Treasury (Office of the Commissioner of Insurance 2012). Appendix 2 provides a list of the current members of the EFAC, BAC and DTCAC. While all three committees are chaired by the financial secretary and include regulatory agencies such as the HKMA and SFC, major banks such as HSBC, Bank of China, Citibank and Standard Chartered feature heavily in these committees.

Furthermore, these banks have enjoyed membership in the BAC over a long period of time. Appendix 3 provides a list of BAC members from 1993 to 2012. As shown in Appendix 3, BAC participation by HSBC, Standard Chartered and Bank of China has been consistent over the two decades covered in these data. Other banks such as Citibank, the Bank of East Asia, DBS, BNP Paribas and the Bank of Tokyo-Mitsubishi have also become mainstays of the BAC, attaining membership at different points in time. While individuals representing these banks have changed over time, the banks themselves have remained heavily involved in their advisory roles. The BAC also includes consultants such as Arthur Andersen and Deloitte Touche Tohmatsu, industry associations and experts drawn from academia.

Financial and regulatory policy-making in Hong Kong also involves non-state actors in less formal capacities. Consultant firm KPMG Barents was commissioned by the HKMA in March 1998 to review the banking sector of Hong Kong as well as provide recommendations, with the government accepting most of the recommendations pertaining to deregulation and clarifying the HKMA's role as lender of last resort (Jao 2003). Independent non-governmental experts have also been included in consultative organizations such as the Hong Kong government's Central Policy Unit, which draws its members from academia, industry and elites

(Chong 2013) as well as the Hong Kong Economic Development Commission, which includes local and foreign experts (Independent Expert 2013).

However, interviews with senior policy-makers suggest that the role of the private sector and other non-state actors in financial policy-making is often overstated. As noted by former HKMA executive director Simon Topping, HKMA consultation is effectively "taking the views of the people, and then making up your mind on what you want to do. It doesn't mean taking accountable the views of people or coming to a compromise" (Topping 2013). As noted by Mr. Topping, the HKMA has often pushed through policies that are unfavourable to banks, such as the implementation of a minimum risk weight of 15 % on residential mortgages, despite industry resistance during consultation (Topping 2013).

Having participated in government consultations as an independent expert through the Hong Kong government's Central Policy Unit, Professor Chong Tai Leung notes that "consultation (in Hong Kong) is only a procedure, it is a way for the government to inform the industry about what kind of policy it plans to do, rather than take in policy advice from the industry" (Chong 2013). Consultation is therefore focused on disseminating policy outputs and outcomes rather than collecting industry inputs. In the words of Glassburner and Reidel, there is "far more centralization of economic activity in Hong Kong than meets the eye" (Glassburner and Riedel 1972).

In other words, government agencies remain the dominant financial policy subsystem actors in Hong Kong. Such a view is not completely new. Scholars have noted this state-driven aspect of Hong Kong's economic and financial development, characterized by a state-centred policy process and the insulation of policy-makers from political and societal forces (Harris 1988; Painter 2005). This dominance of state policy-making bodies amidst the government's continued commitment to laissez-faire principles has allowed the government to effectively implement policies and manage crises, even as Hong Kong continues to enjoy the benefits of free market-driven economic growth (Scott 1989).

Although Lim has attempted to show how the Hong Kong government's response to the AFC was motivated by the interests of a "property cartel" that comprised powerful property market interests (Lim 1999), her account is based on secondary information gleaned from newspapers and other journalistic sources. Rather, and as former HKMA Deputy Chief Executive Andrew Sheng notes, the Hong Kong government's move to intervene in the stock markets during the AFC was "instinctive action against speculation" taken to prevent a liquidity squeeze and in its focus on maintaining financial market stability, "did not go against Hong Kong's laissez-faire approach" (Sheng 2013).

Post-handover Hong Kong's financial subsystem has also come to involve Mainland actors such as the Chinese central government, state banks and regulatory authorities. Hong Kong's linkages with the Mainland have existed since the 1870s, forming a "social network of capital" that is attractive to foreign banks and financial institutions seeking to ply their trade in the East Asian region (Meyer 2000). Indeed, Hong Kong's status as an IFC is dependent on the "relationship between the local government, mainland interests and local financial institutions" (Schenk 2001).

With Mainland firms becoming more active in Hong Kong, financial governance in the territory will see greater involvement of major Chinese banks and financial institutions. One instance of this is their greater representation on corporate boards as well as public institutions such as advisory boards (Tang 1999).

However, this does not mean a dominance of Chinese interests. Rather, Hong Kong's financial subsystem will continue to be characterized by a "diverse economic structure and fragmentation of business and pro-China interests as well as resistance within the administration" (Tang 1999). Given the significance of Hong Kong's open markets and economic stability in attracting foreign financial institutions, the government has retained its commitment to economic freedom and rule of law despite the entry of powerful Mainland financial interests. The city has retained strong positions within IFC rankings that tend to factor in regulatory and legal transparency in their assessment of IFC competitiveness. The fact that Hong Kong remains well regarded by these rankings is testimony of the HKMA's ability to maintain economic freedom and rule of law through its stabilizing policy instruments.

Hong Kong's financial subsystem also involves regional and international actors, by virtue of the SAR's involvement in international forums and organizations. For instance, HKMA is a member of the ASEAN Plus Three Macroeconomic Research Office (AMRO). This is a regional macroeconomic surveillance unit set up under the aegis of the ASEAN Plus Three (APT) grouping's Chiang Mai Initiative Multilateralization (CIMM) programme, aimed at monitoring risk among member economies as well as facilitating remedial actions upon detection of risk (ASEAN + 3 Macroeconomic Research Office 2012).

The CIMM is a multilateral currency swap agreement established among APT members in 2010 for the purpose of addressing "balance of payment and short-term liquidity difficulties in the region" (ASEAN + 3 Macroeconomic Research Office 2012). As a regional surveillance unit, the AMRO ensures regional economic stability by providing early warning of potential risks and hazards. Hong Kong's participation in the AMRO and the CIMM initiative is important for ensuring the territory's status and stability as an IFC, given the vulnerability of its open markets to crises and contagion effects.

While Hong Kong's financial policy subsystem includes government actors of all levels as well as both domestic and international industry and other non-state organizations, interviews with senior policy-makers and independent experts involved in Hong Kong's financial policy process are unanimously in favour of the view that the Hong Kong government retains significant authority over financial policy. In other words, government actors such as the HKMA remain dominant in financial policy-making. Yet the government's dominance over financial policy is balanced by its adherence to a laissez-faire approach that involves limited government intervention. As such, state agencies such as the HKMA are members of an advocacy coalition formed around a long-standing belief in free market principles and a laissez-faire approach to financial governance.

Furthermore, while the HKMA occupies a dominant policy role in Hong Kong's policy subsystem, it limits its direct influence over financial sector development and focuses instead on maintaining financial market stability and investor protection. The consequent reliance on and preference for a stabilizing financial policy mix, as discussed in the previous section, further suggests that dominant state actors are part of a stabilizing instrument constituency. Importantly, the participation of Hong Kong's dominant state actors in a free market-oriented advocacy coalition and a stabilizing instrument constituency allows policy-makers to exercise their influence on financial policy mix design through both ideational and instrumental channels. This is discussed in Chap. 7.

Hong Kong's success as an IFC is thus underpinned by a "balance" struck by the state and industry. While financial institutions are allowed to operate and flourish in a free and open market, the state's dominance over financial policies and its commitment to free market principles ensure both market and political stability. In contrast to the more proactive and interventionist role of the state in Singapore's financial markets, the development of financial markets in Hong Kong is largely "market-driven" and has "relied on efforts of firms rather than government sponsorship" (Harrison 2003; Tan and Lim 2007).

Conclusion

As this chapter has shown, the Hong Kong government is committed to ensuring economic freedom through a governing doctrine of "big market, small government" that involves minimal government intervention. While Hong Kong's financial policy subsystem includes state actors, private sector industry actors and independent non-state experts, financial policy-making remains well within the purview of the government. Consultation is seen by policy-makers as a means to inform industry actors about intended policies rather than a mechanism for including private sector actors in the policy process.

However, this state dominance over financial policy-making is not always obvious due to the government's commitment to a laissez-faire model of financial governance that limits state intervention in financial markets. Hong Kong's laissez-faire approach to financial policy also flows into its financial policy mix. Stabilizing and enabling instruments are used, respectively, to maintain financial market stability and establish necessary conditions for new financial activities such as RMB businesses to take root. These stabilizing and enabling instruments are thus reflective of the Hong Kong government's preference for policies that enhance Hong Kong's attractiveness to investors, particularly in terms of its free and open markets, transparent regulatory framework and strong rule of law. These factors shield investors from market instabilities as well as industry influence over regulations.

Seen from a broader perspective, Hong Kong's financial governance model defines its financial policy subsystem configuration, in terms of membership and inter-actor relations. This state-dominated financial policy subsystem in turn defines Hong Kong's financial policy mix, which largely comprises stabilizing policy instruments and is geared towards the attainment of financial market stability. These linkages between subsystem configuration, policy mix design and policy output attainment are further explored in Chap. 7.

References

ASEAN + 3 Macroeconomic Research Office (2012) What we do. In: ASEAN 3 Macroecon. Res. Off. Website. http://www.amro-asia.org/about-amro/overview/what-we-do/. Accessed 1 Dec 2012

Cartland M (2013) Interview

China Economic Review (2010) A tale of two cities. China Econ Rev

Chong TL (2013) Interview

Enright M, Scott E, Dodwell D (1997) The Hong Kong advantage, 1st edn. Oxford University Press, Oxford

Glassburner B, Riedel J (1972) Government in the economy of Hong Kong*. Econ Rec 48:58–75

Gunningham N (1990) Moving the goalposts: financial market regulation in Hong Kong and the crash of October 1987. Law Soc Inq 15:1–48

Harris PB (1988) Hong Kong: a study in bureaucratic politics. Macmillan, Hong Kong

Harrison M (2003) Fund management in Hong Kong and Singapore. Securities and Futures Commission, Hong Kong

HKEx (2010) Rules and regulations. In: HKEx website. http://www.hkex.com.hk/eng/rulesreg/regulatory.htm. Accessed 27 Oct 2012

Hong Kong Financial Secretary (2009) Role. In: Financ. Secr. Gov. Hong Kong Spec. Adm. Reg. http://www.fso.gov.hk/eng/role.htm. Accessed 31 Oct 2012

Hong Kong Monetary Authority (2000) Annual report 2000. Hong Kong Monetary Authority, Hong Kong

Hong Kong Monetary Authority (2006a) Financial infrastructure in Hong Kong. Hong Kong Monetary Authority, Hong Kong

Hong Kong Monetary Authority (2006b) Mandate & governance of the Hong Kong Monetary Authority. Hong Kong Monetary Authority, Hong Kong

Hong Kong Monetary Authority (2010) Annual Report 2010. Hong Kong Monetary Authority, Hong Kong

Hong Kong Monetary Authority (2011) Annual report 2011. Hong Kong Monetary Authority, Hong Kong

Hong Kong Monetary Authority (2012a) An introduction to the Hong Kong Monetary Authority. Hong Kong Monetary Authority, Hong Kong

Hong Kong Monetary Authority (2012b) International financial centre. In: Hong Kong Monet. Auth. Website. http://www.hkma.gov.hk/eng/key-functions/international-financial-centre.shtml. Accessed 20 Aug 2012

Hong Kong Monetary Authority (2012c) The Exchange Fund Advisory Committee. In: Hong Kong Monet. Auth. Website. http://www.hkma.gov.hk/eng/about-the-hkma/hkma/advisory-committees/exchange-fund-advisory-committee.shtml. Accessed 30 Oct 2012

Hong Kong Monetary Authority (2012d) The Banking Advisory Committee. In: Hong Kong Monet. Auth. Website. http://www.hkma.gov.hk/eng/about-the-hkma/hkma/advisory-committees/banking-advisory-committee.shtml. Accessed 30 Oct 2012

Hong Kong Monetary Authority (2012e) The Deposit-Taking Companies Advisory Committee. In: Hong Kong Monet. Auth. Website. http://www.hkma.gov.hk/eng/about-the-hkma/hkma/advisory-committees/deposit-taking-companies-advisory-committee.shtml. Accessed 30 Oct 2012

Hong Kong Trade Development Council (2015) Economic and trade information on Hong Kong. Hong Kong
Independent Expert (2013) Interview
International Monetary Fund (1999) People's Republic of China-Hong Kong special administrative region. International Monetary Fund, Washington
Jao YC (1974) Banking and currency in Hong Kong: a study of postwar financial development. Macmillan, London
Jao YC (1980) Hong Kong as a regional financial centre: evolution and prospects. In: Leung C-K, Cushman JW, Wang G (eds) Dilemmas of growth. Australian National University Press, Canberra, pp 161–194
Jao YC (1997) Hong Kong as an international financial centre: evolution, prospects and policies. City University of Hong Kong Press, Hong Kong
Jao YC (2003) Financial reform in Hong Kong. In: Hall MJB (ed) The international handbook on financial reform. Edward Elgar Publishing Limited, Cheltenham, pp 113–133
Lee MQC (1995) Business and the rule of law in Hong Kong. Columbia J World Bus 30:28–32
Lee S-Y, Jao YC (1982) Financial structures and monetary policies in Southeast Asia. Macmillan, London
Lee K-H, Vertinsky I (1988) Strategic adjustment of international financial centres (IFCs) in small economies: a comparative study of Hong Kong and Singapore. J Bus Adm 17:151–172
Leung A (2003) Functions and responsibilities in monetary and financial affairs
Li DKP (1995) Enter the dragon: Hong Kong's growing role in world finance. Columbia J World Bus 30:34–40
Li KW (2012) Economic freedom: lessons of Hong Kong, 1st edn. World Scientific Publishing Company, Singapore
Lim LYC (1999) Free Market Fancies: Hong Kong, Singapore, and the Asian financial crisis. In: Pempel TJ (ed) The politics of the Asian economic crisis. Cornell University Press, Ithaca and London, pp 101–115
Loh C (2006) Functional constituencies: a unique feature of the Hong Kong Legislative Council. Hong Kong University Press, Hong Kong
Lui T, Chiu SWK (2009) Becoming a Chinese global city: Hong Kong (and Shanghai) beyond the global-local duality. In: Chen X (ed) Shanghai rising: state power and local transformations in a global megacity. University Of Minnesota Press, Minneapolis
Mak SH (1993) Hong Kong as a financial centre. Whurr Publishers, London
McCauley RN, Chan E (2009) Hong Kong and Shanghai: yesterday, today and tomorrow. In: Ito T, Rose AK (eds) Financial sector development in the Pacfic rim. University of Chicago Press, Chicago, pp 13–37
Meyer DR (2000) Hong Kong as a global metropolis. Cambridge University Press, Cambridge
Norton JJ, Arner DW (2000) Hong Kong SAR: financial regulation and future as an international financial centre. In: Norton JJ, Li CJ, Huang Yangxin (eds) Financial regulation in the greater China area: mainland China, Taiwan and Hong Kong SAR. Kluwer Law International Ltd, London, pp 255–317
Office of the Commissioner of Insurance (2012) Insurance Advisory Committee. In: Off. Comm. Insur. Website. http://www.oci.gov.hk/framework/index07.html. Accessed 26 Nov 2012
Painter M (2005) Transforming the administrative state: reform in Hong Kong and the future of the developmental state. Public Adm Rev 65:335–346
Pauly LW (2011) Hong Kong's international financial centre: retrospect and prospect. Savantas Policy Institute, Hong Kong
Schenk CR (2001) Hong Kong as an international financial centre: emergence and development 1945–1960. Routledge, New York
Schenk CR (2002) Banks and the emergence of Hong Kong as an international financial center. J Int Financ Mark Inst Money 12:321–340
Scott I (1989) Administration in a small capitalist state: The Hong Kong experience. Public Adm Dev 9:185–199

Securities and Futures Commission (2012) Annual report 2011–2012. Securities and Futures Commission, Hong Kong

Sheng A (2013) Interview

Subacchi P, Huang H, Molajoni A, Varghese R (2012) Shifting capital: the rise of financial centres in greater China. Chatham House, London

Sung Y (1989) The Hong Kong development model and its future evolution: neoclassical economics in a Chinese society. In: Jao YC, Mok V, Ho L (eds) Economic development in Chinese societies: models and experiences. Hong Kong University Press, Hong Kong, pp 155–176

Tan CH, Lim JYS (2007) Singapore and Hong Kong as competing financial centres. Saw Centre Financial Studies, Singapore

Tang JTH (1999) Business as usual: the dynamics of government-business relations in the Hong Kong special administrative region. J Contemp China 8:275–295

Topping S (2013) Interview

Tsang D (2006) Big market, small government. The Government of Hong Kong Special Administrative Region, Hong Kong

Tsang D (2013) Interview

Yam J (1995) Hong Kong as an international financial centre. Hong Kong Monetary Authority, Hong Kong

Yue E (2011) Hong Kong as an international financial center—the China factor

Chapter 5
Singapore

While Singapore is typically ranked behind Hong Kong in most IFC rankings, it is largely seen as a close competitor to the SAR and contender for top IFC in Asia. For instance, Singapore trails Hong Kong by merely 4 rating points in the GFCI 17 (Yeandle 2015). Fifth-placed Tokyo trails Singapore by 32 points, while Hong Kong trails second-placed London by 26 points. Like Hong Kong, Singapore enjoys natural advantages such as a strategic location and favourable time zone. As of 2015, the finance and insurance industry makes up 12.5 % of Singapore's GDP (Department of Statistics Singapore 2015). Singapore also hosts more than 200 banks and is well known as a premier wealth management hub (Monetary Authority of Singapore 2014).

On the surface, Singapore is similar to Hong Kong in terms of its global ranking as an IFC and the size of its financial services sector relative to its economy. However, the similarities end here. While Hong Kong's financial sector development was driven by a laissez-faire approach to financial governance that prioritized free market principles, the development of Singapore's financial sector stems from a post-independence "systematic effort" by the government to develop the then-newly formed republic into an IFC (Cassis 2010). This state-driven approach was based on the government's "conceived vision deliberately nurtured with far-sighted liberal monetary policies … and managed with administrative efficacy" (Tan 1982).

As a result of such early governmental efforts, Singapore established a favourable tax system, robust regulatory regime, strong rule of law and a pool of trained financial professionals. However, government policy only tells half the story. Singapore's success as an IFC is also based on the active participation of industry and other non-state actors in financial policy-making. For instance, the Asian Dollar Market (ADM), which would come to underpin Singapore's early success as an IFC, was first proposed by Professor Albert Winsemius and subsequently established with support from the Bank of America. Financial institutions and academics continue to play significant roles in the Singapore government's financial policy-making today.

This close involvement of industry and academics has resulted in the formation of a financial policy subsystem that features financial policy "co-creation" by a closely knit set of state and non-state actors. This important role of the private sector and other non-state actors in financial policy-making constitutes a

J.J. Woo, *Business and Politics in Asia's Key Financial Centres*,
DOI 10.1007/978-981-287-985-1_5

key-defining feature of Singapore's development as an IFC. As a reflection of the mix of state and non-state actors in Singapore's financial policy subsystem and their varying interests, Singapore's financial policy mix comprises a full spectrum of financial policy instruments, including stabilizing, enabling and developmental instruments. Singapore's financial subsystem and policy mix are discussed in greater depth below. However, there is a need to situate these within the historical context of Singapore's emergence and development as an IFC.

Singapore's development as an IFC formally began with its founding as an independent republic in 1965. As part of a "two-pronged strategy", the government had identified financial services as a key sector that could both support the development of existing industries and become a growth industry in its own right (Montes 1999). This initial intention to develop the financial services sector as an industry in its own right has since made it relatively less dependent on the real sector, compared to many other IFCs (Bryant 1989).

More importantly, Singapore's emergence as an IFC was "a result of orderly stimulation by the Government through legislative measures and administrative monitoring by the MAS" (Tan 1982). The government therefore played an active, even "activist" role in guiding the development of Singapore's financial centre and promoting the city as an IFC (Jao 1974; Yoon 1982). This often involved extensive efforts at identifying and targeting specific financial activities, which were then provided with tax and fiscal incentives to stimulate their growth (Tan 2006). As Austin (2004) has noted, the "success of Singapore as Southeast Asia's premier financial and industrial centre was the product of the State".

A crucial milestone in Singapore's early development as an IFC is the establishment of the ADM in 1968, which was built on Singapore's time zone advantage, allowing it to bridge the "gap between the close of markets in the USA and the reopening of business the next day in Europe" (Tee 2003). Underpinning the ADM's subsequent success was a key move by the government to abolish a withholding tax on interest income from non-resident foreign currency deposits (Hodjera 1978). The government also introduced regulations and incentives that aimed to expand the ADM and encourage the participation of foreign financial institutions in the growing offshore banking sector that had emerged from the ADM (Hodjera 1978; Cassis 2010).

With Singapore's financial industry becoming increasingly complex, the Monetary Authority of Singapore (MAS) was formed on 1 January 1971 under the aegis of the Monetary Authority of Singapore Act (Monetary Authority of Singapore 2012a). The MAS serves as central bank and chief regulator of Singapore's financial markets and has been tasked with promoting Singapore as an IFC. The MAS also represents an institutionalization of then-finance minister Goh Keng Swee's twin philosophies of pragmatism and interventionism (Austin 2004). Importantly, the MAS exists as an important component of Singapore's overall economic governance machinery, rather than a "standalone statutory entity" (Jarvis 2011). The formation of the MAS immediately set the stage for major financial sector reforms that would drive the internationalization of Singapore's financial markets (Tan 2011).

These reforms enabled Singapore's structural transformation from a pure trading economy to a "manufacturing–finance–service and trading economy" (Mochizuki 1985) and facilitated the diversification of Singapore's economy. Singapore's financial markets rapidly deepened, as various exchanges were established and new financial instruments proliferated. A significant milestone was the establishment of the Stock Exchange of Singapore (SES) in 1973, which was subsequently demutualized and merged with the Singapore International Monetary Exchange (SIMEX) to form the Singapore Exchange (SGX) in 1999 (Monetary Authority of Singapore 2000). The SGX has since formed a crucial part of Singapore's financial success, enlarging Singapore's issue base and trade volumes through electronic trading and the formation of strategic alliances with overseas exchanges (Tan 2011).

Singapore's financial sector also experienced an intense period of government-directed internationalization, liberalization and consolidation through the 1980s and 1990s. Internationalization and liberalization were driven in part by the government's desire to tap on new emerging markets, particularly those recognized in its Economic Review Committee report in 1985 (Lessard 1994), and in part by a recognition of the emerging trends of liberalization and deregulation in international financial markets that were beginning to threaten Singapore's traditional market niches (Lee and Vertinsky 1988). As a result of these "positive" and "negative" drivers of internationalization, Singapore's financial sector rapidly expanded and foreign exchange trading expanded (Bryant 1989).

Yet while Singapore's financial sector experienced rapid liberalization, its banking sector was undergoing a government-driven process of "rationalization" and consolidation, driven by a perceived need to increase the size of local banks to ensure their competitiveness (Hamilton-Hart 2002) and align their long-term interests with the local economy (Monetary Authority of Singapore 1999). For the latter, the MAS required local banks to appoint a Nominating Committee which ensures that local banks "act in a manner consistent with the national interest" (Monetary Authority of Singapore 1999). Singapore's domestic banking market is largely dominated by three major local banks: DBS, UOB and OCBC. While DBS remains state-owned, UOB and OCBC continue to include current or former government officials on their boards of directors.

Another state-directed development in Singapore's financial sector was the development of its asset management industry. First identified as a growth sector in the 1980s (Harrison 2003), the asset management industry was developed through deliberate government policies such as grants and tax incentives aimed at attracting fund managers (Tan 1999; Harrison 2003). Singapore has since become the "premier asset management location in Asia", with total assets under management reaching SGD $1.4 trillion (Monetary Authority of Singapore 2012b). Such efforts at developing new financial markets or niches highlights the MAS's dual focus on financial market stability and development, with the formation of its Financial Sector Promotion Department serving to sharpen this distinction by consolidating market promotion activities within this new department (Monetary Authority of

Singapore 1998a). This dual focus on the MAS on stabilizing and promoting markets is further discussed below.

Singapore's simultaneous liberalization and consolidation of its financial markets continues to take place. Even as the MAS seeks to upgrade local banks and promote subsidiarization among more established foreign banks through its the introduction of a "Qualifying Full Bank" (QFB) category (Tan 2002; Monetary Authority of Singapore 2012c), it has also increased the number of restricted banks, granted offshore banks with greater flexibility in SGD wholesale business, lifted a 40 % foreign shareholding limit on local banks (Monetary Authority of Singapore 1999). Singapore's financial markets therefore became increasingly diverse, with consolidation in the banking sector and expansion in the insurance industry and capital markets (Monetary Authority of Singapore 2003).

The continued growth of Singapore's financial sector and the city's resilience in the face of financial crises is testimony to the success of this dual-focus policy approach. For instance, Singapore recovered relatively quickly from the 1997 Asian Financial Crisis (AFC), although it suffered some contagion effects due to its open financial markets (Monetary Authority of Singapore 1998b). Similarly, Singapore recovered from the impacts of the 2007 GFC. This was largely attributed to timely government stimulus, tightened financial supervision by the MAS, increased overall industrial output and improvements in financial market conditions (Monetary Authority of Singapore 2008, 2010a). Singapore's economy would experience a record growth of 14.5 % in 2010, with the financial sector expanding by 12 % in the same year (Monetary Authority of Singapore 2011a).

Importantly, the Asia-driven post-GFC recovery of the global economy had significant impacts for Singapore's financial sector, with "the surge in trade and capital flows, strong growth of Asian corporate activity and increasing wealth accumulation in Asia" (Monetary Authority of Singapore 2011a) driving demands for financial services in the region. As MAS Managing Director Ravi Menon noted in a speech delivered on 13 March 2013, Singapore's "pan-Asian focus" drives the republic's continued development and value proposition as an IFC (Menon 2013a). More recently, Singapore has established itself as an offshore Renminbi (RMB) Centre, leveraging on the growth of RMB-denominated investment in the ASEAN region (Shanmugaratnam 2013).

At the heart of Singapore's development as an IFC, therefore, is a focus on Singapore's value propositions as an IFC and the various ways in which the government, particularly through the MAS's financial policies, can identify, cultivate and develop new and emerging sources of financial sector growth. While these value propositions are themselves important competitive advantages, they also reflect the government's efforts at "niche creation", a process that has driven the formation of these competitive advantages and is therefore itself a factor of Singapore's success. These various sources of competitive advantage are discussed next.

Sources of Competitive Advantage

Given the state's role in driving Singapore's success as an IFC, many of the city-state's competitive advantages are naturally derived from government policy and planning. However, Singapore also benefits from "natural" advantages such as its strategic location and time zone. These two sources of competitive advantage have been recognized by Low, who differentiates between naturally occurring advantages of location and labour availability and state-driven advantages arising from the government's efforts at restructuring the economy and injecting new activities into it (Low 2001). State-driven advantages represent a form of "artificial or acquired comparative advantage" (Low 2001).

Similarly, the MAS differentiates between "tangible" advantages such as a favourable time zone and good communications and payments networks, and "intangible" advantages including rule of law, currency stability and "an honest and competent government" (Monetary Authority of Singapore 2011b). These "tangible" or "natural" advantages are shared by other IFCs such as Hong Kong and Shanghai. In all three cases, a strategic location facilitated trade, while the availability of cheap labour contributed to manufacturing activities, with the financial services providers often emerging in support of these trade and manufacturing activities.

While Singapore's strategic location and talent pool remain important factors contributing to the republic's growth as an IFC, it is largely through deliberate policy that the government has been able to leverage on and convert these existing advantages into IFC success. This makes Singapore's "strong, stable and proactive government" its core competitive advantage, with the republic's "natural locational advantages of time zone and central position in international trade routes … exploited to the fullest by deliberate government policy" (Lee and Vertinsky 1988). According to MAS Managing Director Ravi Menon, Singapore's "number one value proposition is that we (Singapore) are well regulated and supervised" (Menon 2013b). Singapore's government-sanctioned regulatory and tax benefits have therefore been seen as more important in explaining Singapore's success as an IFC than its naturally occurring competitive advantages of location and time zone (Bryant 1989).

Singapore's success as an IFC is thus driven by its strong fundamentals of "a well-respected regulatory and supervisory regime, a stable domestic economy, a pro-business operating environment and a highly competent financial sector workforce" (Monetary Authority of Singapore 2010a). Aside from its regulatory framework, Singapore's efficient infrastructure and educated workforce are also competitive advantages developed by the government for the purpose of supporting its growth as an IFC, with government investments in areas such as education and telecommunications serving to augment its existing comparative advantages as an IFC (Tan 2006). While Singapore's infrastructure represents the "hardware" of its financial sector, regulations and incentives make up its "software" (Lee 1998a).

Both infrastructural and regulatory factors are therefore competitive advantages that have been developed by the state.

Another important part of the government's role in developing Singapore's competitive advantages is the identification and development of key sectors or niches that eventually grow to become new competitive advantages for Singapore. As Lee and Vertinsky have noted, Singapore's success as an IFC is driven by the government's efforts at "niche creation" (Lee and Vertinsky 1988). Niche creation requires the government to adapt to ever-changing market conditions and therefore possess an inordinate amount of "flexibility in restructuring its economy as particular industrial comparative advantages are eroded by new competitors" (Ho 2009). Niche creation therefore represents an important second dimension of Singapore's competitive advantages as an IFC.

New niches identified and successfully developed through proactive government policy tend to become unique selling points for Singapore's role as an international financial services provider. Reflecting on the government's belief in niche creation, former finance minister and MAS chairman Richard Hu has noted that Singapore needed to "become 'number one' in a particular niche of financial services" in order to fulfil its goals of becoming a successful IFC (Monetary Authority of Singapore 2011b). A recent instance of niche creation is the government's identification of the burgeoning offshore RMB market and the increasingly integrated ASEAN financial markets as key pillars of Singapore's growth as an IFC, which was subsequently followed by the promulgation of polices aimed at enhancing the republic's position in these areas (Menon 2013a; Shanmugaratnam 2013).

In short, niche creation and proactive government policy are Singapore's key sources of competitive advantage. They are also complementary and intertwined factors that drive Singapore's success as an IFC. Proactive government policies give rise to new niches that are further developed to become new competitive advantages. This requires flexible and responsive policy-making that involves close consultation and cooperation with industry actors as well as a willingness to adjust policies to industry needs and changing circumstances. Industry participation in Singapore's financial policy processes and the impacts of the private sector's policy role on policy instrument choice are discussed in a later section on Singapore's financial policy subsystem.

Another competitive advantage enjoyed by Singapore is its status as an independent sovereign state. This is in contrast to Hong Kong and Shanghai, which both remain under the purview of the Chinese central government. Observers have noted how Singapore's strength arises from the fact that it is "similar to Hong Kong but is importantly not Hong Kong", with its independence from China and its strong legal system providing confidence to investors (China Economic Review 2012). Furthermore, Singapore's independence makes the city-state a "gateway to Asia, not China" and is likely to become the IFC of Asia at Hong Kong's expense (China Economic Review 2012). Related to Singapore's sovereign status is its reputation for political stability and good governance, which have "attracted the world's leading commercial banks" (Ngiam 2010).

Along with effective government policy and advanced infrastructure, political and social stability has been identified as one of the most important factors contributing to Singapore's development as a financial centre (Lessard 1994). Furthermore, political stability in Singapore has facilitated the establishment of a stable regulatory regime that establishes and enforces clear and consistent rules, culminating in a "stable and predictable regulatory environment" (Monetary Authority of Singapore 2010b). However, as later sections will show, Singapore's advantage as a sovereign state may be overstated. First, both Hong Kong and Shanghai possess significant autonomy from the central government in the realms of financial and economic policy. Second, financial policies in Singapore are the result of a state–industry policy co-creation process.

Fundamentally, Singapore's competitive advantages as an IFC stem from its proactive and responsive government. Such proactive government policies aimed at developing Singapore as an IFC have further resulted in the creation of two specific layers of competitive advantages. The first layer includes structural advantages such as a sound legal and regulatory infrastructure, competent and educated workforce, and pro-business environment. The second layer comprises the financial market niches which the government has identified and developed into Singapore's strengths, such as forex and wealth management. The significance of governance to Singapore's success as an IFC is further elaborated in the next section of its financial governance.

Financial Governance

Singapore's financial governance model is derived from its state-driven approach to economic policy in general, or what Schein (1996) characterizes as "state-run capitalism". Such an approach requires the government, in the absence of sufficiently large private business actors, to play an entrepreneurial role in terms of establishing and fostering key industries and businesses, particularly through its lead economic development agency, the EDB. Underlying the key role of the EDB in economic governance is the government's ability to create "specialist institutions and agencies tasked with the performance of specific key roles" (Ho 2009). The MAS represents one such agency, by acting as the key policy unit in the realm of finance (Woo 2014).

Financial governance in Singapore also approximates what Schein (1996) has termed "strategic pragmatism", a governance style that originated from Singapore's first finance minister Goh Keng Swee and was subsequently "institutionalised … in the paradigm of the Singapore governance" (Austin 2004). This is a governance style that is "strategic in thinking and pragmatic in execution" (Ngiam 2010), requiring a master vision or strategy and the "practical intelligence" to implement this strategy or vision without compromising it in the process (Schein 1996). Needless to say, this requires "governing capacity" in terms of consistent and transparent policy implementation, which in turn derives from Singapore's moderately Weberian legal–rational public organizations and the various "informal institutions that link public and private spheres" (Hamilton-Hart 2002).

This means that financial policy-making involves both state and private actors. Again, this derives from Singapore's economic policy style, which for historical reasons has evolved to become a collaborative effort between the government, businesses and labour (Schein 1996; Lam 2000). As will be discussed below, this collaborative approach flows into Singapore's financial governance model, with state and industry actors forming strong "policy relations" that facilitate the co-creation of financial policies (Woo 2015a). This melding of state and non-state actors within the governing elite is unique to Singapore. In contrast, the Hong Kong and Shanghai governments have retained full or almost-full control over financial policy-making, with non-state inputs into financial policy generally limited and/or superficial.

In sum, Singapore's financial governance involves an adherence to "strategic pragmatism" that melds long-term strategic planning with flexibility and pragmatism at the implementation level. Linkages between the private and public sector also makes financial governance in Singapore a collaborative affair, manifested in a "governing elite" that comprises a variety of actors socialized and integrated into Singapore's prevailing governing style. The MAS occupies a crucial position within Singapore's financial governance, with former MAS Chairman and current Prime Minister Lee Hsien Loong noting that a "competent MAS is part of the Singapore government" (Monetary Authority of Singapore 2000). The MAS and its position in Singapore's regulatory regime are discussed next.

Regulatory Regime

Singapore's regulatory regime has been crucial to its success as an IFC. As former Prime Minister Lee Kuan Yew has noted, the history of Singapore's financial centre is the "story of how we [the Singapore state] built up credibility as a place of integrity, and developed the officers with the knowledge and skills to regulate and supervise the banks, security houses and other financial institutions so that the risk of systemic failure is minimised" (Lee 2000). The main regulators governing Singapore's financial services sector are the MAS, SGX, Accounting and Corporate Regulatory Authority (ACRA) and Central Provident Fund Board.

The MAS is the overall "integrated regulator and supervisor of financial institutions in Singapore" (Monetary Authority of Singapore 2012d), tasked with regulating financial services associated with the banking, finance, insurance and securities markets (Tan 2011). Its main functions include acting as Singapore's central bank (through the conduct of monetary policy, issuance of currency, oversight of payments systems and acting as a banker to the government), conducting "integrated supervision of financial services and financial stability surveillance", managing the country's official foreign reserves, and developing Singapore as an IFC (Monetary Authority of Singapore 2012a).

In general, the MAS is tasked with ensuring a "sound and progressive financial services sector" through the use of a "full toolkit of regulatory instruments" that includes regulations detailing the responsibilities of financial institutions, risk-based measures, rules of compliance, depositor safety nets, power to intervene when supervisory objectives are not met, and incentives to encourage compliance (Monetary Authority of Singapore 2010b). Given its closed relationship with the financial sector, the MAS also employs moral suasion as a "qualitative method of supervision" (Monetary Authority of Singapore 2011b). Underlying the MAS's work are its four principles of financial supervision: risk-focused, business-friendly, disclosure-based and stakeholder-reliant (Monetary Authority of Singapore 2010b).

The MAS's regulatory style has also taken on a more flexible and systemic perspective over the years. A strategic review conducted by the MAS in 1997 resulted in a shift from "one-size-fits-all prescriptive regulation towards a more flexible risk-focused supervisory approach" (Lee 1997; Chia 2007; Monetary Authority of Singapore 2011b). This tailoring of regulations to an institution's risk profile allows the MAS to "promote greater competition, efficiency and growth in the financial sector without compromising the safety and soundness of institutions or the resilience and stability of the system" (Chia 2007). This facilitates the formulation of high regulatory standards combined with flexible implementation of these standards, or what is known as "Smart Regulation" (Menon 2013a). Aside from the MAS, other institutions are involved in regulating various aspects of Singapore's financial sector.

The SGX was formed in 1999 with the merger of the SES and SIMEX and is a "self-regulatory organization" that performs frontline regulation of the markets and clearing houses that it operates (Singapore Stock Exchange 2011; Tan 2011). Regulatory functions performed by the SGX include issuer regulation, member supervision, market surveillance, enforcement and risk management (Tan 2011). SGX's Risk Management and Regulatory Division is specifically tasked with regulating and monitoring SGX members, including their employees, trading representatives and directors (Tan 2011). Given its dual role as market regulator and profit-maximizing listed company, the SGX is itself supervised by the MAS for Self-Regulatory Organization (SRO) risks (Tan 2011).

Formed in April 2004 with the merger of the Registry of Companies and Businesses and the Public Accountants Board, ACRA regulates business entities and public accountants by monitoring corporate compliance with requirements pertaining to disclosure and regulating public accountants who perform statutory audits (Accounting and Corporate Regulatory Authority 2009; Tan 2011). Lastly, the CPF is a mandatory retirement savings scheme that was set up in 1955 and comprises a wide variety of schemes allowing its members to invest their funds in various financial instruments (Tan 2011). It regulates fund managers handling members' savings through its Investment Guidelines and monitors the performance of the unit trusts which its members have invested in (Tan 2011).

Thus while the MAS occupies a central position within Singapore's financial regulatory regime, it also works with other organizations. Furthermore and as the above discussion has shown, the MAS plays the dual roles of financial regulator and promoter of Singapore's interests as an IFC. More importantly, these dual roles have significant implications for the mix of financial policy instruments that the MAS has at its disposal. These are discussed next.

Financial Policy Mix

Broadly speaking, Bryant (1989) has identified three "paramount characteristics" in Singapore's financial policies. These include encouraging the location of financial intermediaries in Singapore through *preferential regulation and tax incentives*, the maintenance of a *"separating fence"*[1] between domestic and international financial activities, and the preservation of Singapore's sound and resilient financial system through *prudential oversight* by the MAS and other regulatory authorities (Bryant 1989). These three financial policy characteristics in turn underpin the stabilizing, enabling and developmental financial policies which make up Singapore's financial policy mix.

First, prudential oversight and regulatory policy involves the promulgation of stabilizing financial policies that allow the MAS to maintain financial market stability. As Lee and Vertinsky (1988) have noted, the establishment of an "unambiguous, stable legal and regulatory framework" contributed immensely to financial system stability. Similarly, efforts at attracting international financial intermediaries and maintaining a "separating fence" between domestic and international financial activities represent, respectively, enabling policies that establish attractive locational conditions and developmental policies that channel benefits towards a select group of actors, in this case domestic financial institutions, whose survival or success is deemed crucial to IFC development.

The establishment of this "separating fence" has brought Singapore much success in "broadening the economic base through the development of the financial sector and its international content without excessively exposing the domestic economy to external influences" (Lessard 1994). As noted by then-DPM Lee Hsien Loong, the separation of domestic and offshore finance provided protection to Singaporean investors and depositors and ensured market stability amidst the influx of foreign financial firms and rapid regulatory liberalization (Lee 1997). This coexistence of domestic and international financial firms is evident in Singapore's banking sector, with a small number of systematically important domestic banks representing 30 % of total banking assets, while foreign banks represent 65 % of total banking assets (International Monetary Fund 2013).

Aside from these three characteristics, the majority of Singapore's financial policies correspond to the three categories of stabilizing, enabling and developmental financial policy instruments. In fact, Singapore is the only case in this book

[1]This "separating fence" has become more permeable over time, especially with the complete removal of exchange controls in 1978.

that exhibits all three categories of instruments in its financial policy mix. I will now proceed to discuss Singapore's stabilizing, enabling and developmental financial policy instruments in greater detail, situating them within Singapore's overall financial policy mix and discussing their roles in Singapore's development as an IFC.

Like any other financial regulatory agency, the MAS places a significant premium on regulations that ensure market stability. According to MAS Managing Director Ravi Menon, the MAS's most important objective is financial stability, or to "ensure the safety and soundness of our financial institutions and to prevent systemic problems from emerging. That's foremost" (Menon 2013b). According to the MAS, stability in the financial sector is also related to overall economic stability, resilience and growth. This is predicated upon the MAS's belief that a "sound and progressive financial services sector" contributes directly to the GDP, intermediates between borrowers and savers, ensures efficient allocation of financial resources, and "thereby enhances economic growth and job creation" (Chia 2007).

Through its risk-focused supervisory approach, the MAS has shown that sound financial regulation is not an end in itself but a means of "ensuring a stable and efficient financial system to support the growth of the economy with minimum disruption" (Tan 2007). Underlying this focus on financial system stability is the MAS's belief that "the purpose of the financial sector is to facilitate the real economy" (Senior Regulatory Official 2013). As then-Deputy Prime Minister Lee Hsien Loong has noted, Singapore's "emphasis on high prudential standards has allowed us [the Singapore state] to sustain strong financial sector growth over a long period" (Lee 1998b). In such a way, financial regulations that are geared towards market stability contribute to developmental goals as well, particularly through facilitating economic growth and development.

However, this stabilizing aspect of financial regulation tells only half the story. According to Mr. Menon, the MAS's other mandate is "developing the financial centre, which is quite separate, and we have a different team and a different group of people, so there's no conflict of interest" (Menon 2013b). This began in 1998, when the MAS made an official shift from a purely regulatory role to a more promotional role with regard to the financial sector (Hamilton-Hart 2002). It has also been noted that this shift in organizational disposition arose from changes in MAS leadership in 1998 as well as the prevailing influence of free market ideologies, particularly in the form of Thatcherism or Reagonism, which advocated less direct regulation of markets (Former Senior Regulatory Official 2013).

This new leadership included Mr. Koh Yong Guan, who assumed office as MAS Managing Director in January 1998. According to Mr. Koh, the government was then concerned with "positioning Singapore for the next phase of growth as a financial centre; we saw a need to set up a promotional function within the MAS" (Koh 2013b). This promotional function included efforts at stimulating financial sector growth and attracting financial institutions into Singapore, both of which were crucial for the continued growth and positioning of Singapore as an IFC (Koh 2013b). While the EDB typically plays the role of economic promotional agency, the MAS was chosen as the promotional agency for the financial sector due to its strong domain knowledge (Koh 2013b). This makes the MAS a policy-making unit in its own right, although it complements the EDB as both agencies are integral parts of Singapore's policy machinery (Woo 2014).

However, including promotional functions within a regulatory agency may give rise to potential conflicts of interest. In order to prevent this, separate departments were established within the MAS to perform the respective roles of financial supervision and financial centre development (Monetary Authority of Singapore 2004). This means that the MAS's prudential and promotional activities are carried out by different personnel with different reporting structures. The MAS's dual mandates also produce a "creative tension" that is deemed beneficial to the organization (Menon 2013b). Nonetheless, the MAS gives equal priority to both regulatory and promotional or developmental goals, and "in 90 % of the cases, the goals are aligned" (Menon 2013b).

The MAS has since promulgated a vast variety of proactive strategies and regulations that directly promote the development of Singapore's financial markets, enhancing the financial sector's contribution to Singapore's economic growth and development. As noted by a former senior policy-maker who was involved in this drive for development, the Singapore government's efforts at developing its financial sector were predicated upon a need to develop "exportable services" to complement its manufacturing base (Former Senior Policymaker 2013). Given that Singapore's financial sector development has become an integral part of the city-state's overall industrialization journey, financial sector policy is therefore no longer "just about regulation, but promotion as well" (Koh 2013a).

This has resulted in the MAS's inclusion of non-regulatory instruments such as tax incentives, subsidies and provision of funding in Singapore's financial policy mix. Through these instruments, the MAS has sought to "develop the financial markets, introduce new financial instruments to add depth to the market, and to promote stability through timely interventions in the foreign exchange markets" (Tan 2006). Lee and Vertinsky (1988) have also noted the Singapore government's efforts at developing its financial markets by liberalizing regulations for foreign financial institutions, removing exchange controls, providing tax incentives for offshore financial services, introducing new financial instruments and creating new financial markets through "legislation, tax incentives and direct participation using government spending power and its influence on private spending". Public investments in physical, technological, social and institutional infrastructures have also played enabling roles in the development of Singapore as an IFC (Lee and Vertinsky 1988).

These non-regulatory instruments represent enabling and developmental financial policy instruments that either create the conditions necessary for financial sector growth or promulgate policies that facilitate financial sector development, sometimes both. More importantly, these policies allow the MAS to encourage the development of selected financial markets or sectors, further reinforcing its dual functions as regulator and implementor of financial policies (Hamilton-Hart 2002). This requires the MAS to "scan the horizon very carefully, look at long-term trends. Where is the world heading, where are the demand drivers, what are the developments taking place elsewhere? And then we [MAS] ask ourselves, what are our strengths, which can help to match some of these demands" (Menon 2013b). Such efforts at "niche creation" have been discussed above.

Having identified potential growth markets or niches, enabling regulations are then promulgated to create the conditions required for these markets to develop and flourish. An early instance of this was the development of capital markets in the 1980s, with regulations enacted during this period playing "important enabling and promotional roles" (Koh 2013a). Various initiatives were subsequently introduced to promote the development of Singapore's offshore banking, Asian bond, foreign exchange, money and the futures markets (Hamilton-Hart 2002). With regard to the foreign exchange market, the government liberalized currency trading by issuing licences to banks that allowed them to trade currencies (Former Senior Policymaker 2013).

Of particular importance as a developmental instrument are the tax incentives that allow the MAS to promote and develop new emerging markets. These were first used to expand the ADM market and banking sectors and, more recently, offered to fund managers in order to develop Singapore's wealth management industry (Former Senior Regulatory Official 2013). These tax incentives are seen as an "important part of the (MAS's) toolkit" and act as a "sweetener" for fund managers to establish or locate themselves in Singapore (Menon 2013b). Enabling instruments were also used to establish the necessary market and infrastructural conditions in order for wealth management industry to take root and flourish. This involved deliberately growing the Singapore Dollar Bond market, relaxing the Singapore Dollar non-internationalization policy, and engaging private fund managers for the management of government reserves (Koh 2013b).

According to former MAS Managing Director Koh Yong Guan, these policies contributed to the establishment of Singapore's wealth management industry by establishing a market benchmark for the fixed income and securities market and attracting fund managers to Singapore (Koh 2013b). In addition, the MAS also had to enhance Singapore's connectivity to the rest of Asia, maintain the strong presence of many financial institutions and develop a deep talent pool (Menon 2013b). In short, financial policies in Singapore perform all three roles of market stabilization, enablement and development. This entails a "delicate balance" between regulation and promotion (which involves both developmental and enabling instruments) (Monetary Authority of Singapore 2004; Former Senior Regulatory Official 2013), with both regulation and promotion contributing to the ultimate objective of real economic growth and development (Monetary Authority of Singapore 2004).

However, the balance of regulation and promotion in Singapore's financial policy mix also comes with inherent contradictions that require flexibility on the part of the MAS. For instance, Singapore's success as an IFC depends on *both* market stability and the attractiveness of the republic as a destination for the location of financial firms. While the former requires high regulatory standards and stringent supervision, the latter suggests that lower regulatory barriers and taxes will attract more financial intermediation. This has stimulated instances of creative policy-making such as the creation of a tiered banking licensing regime and separating between banks' ACU and DBU accounts (Lessard 1994).

The tiered bank licensing regime and separation between ACU and DBU accounts have allowed the MAS to encourage the entry of foreign banks while at the same time protect the interests of domestic banks. In this way, the MAS has been able to maintain a strong local core to Singapore's banking system while at the same time introducing an element of competition and innovation (Menon 2013b). Moreover, this dual approach also suggests that it may not always be easy to clearly differentiate between different policy instruments, especially when a particular instrument is used to achieve both stabilizing and development-oriented purposes.

In sum, financial policy-making in Singapore ensures the stability of financial markets, provides the enabling conditions for the emergence and development of specific financial market sectors and drives the direct development of financial markets through incentives and provision of resources. This means that financial policy-making in Singapore is much broader and more diverse than that in Hong Kong and Shanghai, in terms of instrument type and choice. This reflects the interests of both state and industry actors, with policy mix design driven by strong state–industry relations. State–industry relations in the form of Singapore's financial policy subsystem are discussed next.

Financial Policy Subsystem

Despite its reputation, particularly in the Western media, as an authoritarian or paternalistic state that dominates both the political and economic spheres (Schiavenza 2015; Tan 2015; Cassidy 2015), the reality is that policy-making in Singapore involves a "mixed sphere that encompasses bureaucratic, political and business actors" (Hamilton-Hart 2002). This commingling of state and industry actors is particularly pronounced in finance, with dense policy relations between state and non-state actors allowing for a co-creation of financial policies (Woo 2015a). This co-sharing of policy responsibilities and economic interests by state and industry is often understated in existing understandings of Singapore's political and policy processes; it also defers markedly from the neoliberal models of financial governance that are more prevalent in Western contexts (Woo 2015b).

This mix of state and private actors in Singapore's governing elite and state–industry "co-creation" of financial policies (Former Senior Regulatory Official 2013) constitutes a unique feature of Singapore's financial policy subsystem. Where such intermixing of state and private actors in financial policy-making have resulted in "regulatory capture" in many other IFCs, this is avoided in Singapore through a set of informal governing institutions that "externalize many of the routines and norms of the formal government sector, such as the commitment to meritocracy, flexibility, performance-based indicators of achievement and an entrenched acceptance of the government's right to govern" (Hamilton-Hart 2002). As a result, the Singaporean state's ideals of transparency and meritocracy are imbibed by the private sector as well.

State influence extends beyond ideational means as well. Individuals are selectively incorporated and socialized into the governing elite through their appointment to senior governing positions in statutory authorities such as the MAS, GLCs like DBS and even the ruling political party (Hamilton-Hart 2002). The appointment of key Singaporeans to the "nominating committees" of local banks, subject to MAS approval, also ensures that these banks "act in a manner consistent with the national interest" (Monetary Authority of Singapore 1999). This gives rise to "norms of interaction" that institutionalize government–business interactions and ensure the private sector's cooperation with regulatory authorities (Hamilton-Hart 2002).

As such, Singapore's financial policy governing elite comprises public and private actors who share common norms and beliefs, forming an advocacy coalition that is based on achieving mutually beneficial policy goals. This advocacy coalition in turn influences policy mix design through an ideational channel that converts these common norms and beliefs into policy instrument choice. Given the governing elite's focus on policy goals and the Singaporean government's reputed pragmatism with regard to choice of policy means, there is weak evidence for the presence of an instruments constituency in Singapore. Singapore's governing elite therefore approximates an advocacy coalition that is formed around ideational factors and which perpetuates itself in a similarly ideational manner. These are discussed at greater length in Chap. 7.

Yet despite the influence of non-state actors in the governing elite, the MAS remains Singapore's key financial policy-maker. It enjoys close linkages to the Singapore government, with Deputy Prime Minister and Minister for Finance Tharman Shanmugaratnam serving as its Chairman, Minister for Trade & Industry Lim Hng Kiang as Deputy Chairman and two other Cabinet Ministers among its Board Member (Monetary Authority of Singapore 2013). This places the MAS at the apex of Singapore's financial policy subsystem and makes it a leading member of Singapore's financial governing elite. This also means that private sector involvement in financial policy-making is guided or led by the MAS, particularly through the Authority's "practice of organized, industry-wide consultation through many committees and formal bodies" (Hamilton-Hart 2002).

As noted by MAS Managing Director Ravi Menon, "[e]very piece of new rule or regulation, almost but not all, almost all new rules or regulations go out for a proscribed period of public consultation. So we put out a document that sets out the policy, we invite feedback, and sometimes we have a second round or we have closed door group meetings. Then we come up with the final set that also goes for consultation, and before legislation" (Menon 2013b). The rationales for public consultation, according to Mr. Menon, are that the MAS does not "want unintended consequences. We don't want policies that are impractical to implement or impose too high a compliance or business cost" (Menon 2013b). Industry and stakeholder consultation forms an integral part of the MAS's practice of "smart regulation" (Menon 2013a).

Beginning in 1985, the private sector has been formally included in the government's policy formulation processes through their membership in various committees (Hamilton-Hart 2002). Further formalization of private sector consultation took place in 1998, with the incorporation of 5 private sector committees into the Financial Sector Review Group (FSRG) chaired by then-Deputy Prime Minister Lee Hsien Loong (Lee 1998c). These committees included the Finance and Banking Competitiveness Sub-Committee, Committee on Banking Disclosure, Corporate Finance Committee, Stock Exchange of Singapore Review Committee and Committee of Governance of Exchanges (Monetary Authority of Singapore 1998c). This was followed by the establishment of the Financial Sector Advisory Council (FSAC) and the International Advisory Panel (IAP) in 1998 (Monetary Authority of Singapore 1998c).

This practice of industry consultation has persisted until today, with the Financial Advisory Industry Review Panel established by the MAS on 2 April 2012 being a more recent example (Financial Advisory Industry Review Panel 2013). As a former senior regulatory official has noted, such consultative committees and industry working groups allow the private sector to "co-create" regulations with the authorities (Former Senior Regulatory Official 2013). However, most of these industry working groups are typically dismantled after the standards have been enforced (Former Senior Regulatory Official 2013). The MAS also consults industry actors through yearly dialogues organized by "sell-side" actors such as banks and fund managers, although a respondent has noted that most of the feedback given at these dialogues tend to reflect the interests of industry actors rather than concerns over national development (Fund Manager with a US Asset Management Firm 2013).

Another important channel through which the MAS consults the private sector is through the publication of consultation papers on its website, which are accessible to the public. The MAS also disseminates such consultation papers to relevant financial institutions in order to collect and assess their feedback prior to the promulgation of a new policy. In general, there are two rounds of consultation. The first round involves gathering feedback on the overall policy framework, followed by a second round of consultation on the text of legislation, which had been drafted based on the first round of consultations (Former Senior Regulatory Official 2013).

Aside from these formal channels of consultation, the MAS also engages and consults the private sector through less formal channels and on a continuous basis (Menon 2013b). Through a "two-way consultation process", both the MAS and private sector can initiate consultation (Senior Regulatory Official 2013). As a senior banker has noted, feedback on regulations is provided to the MAS "as and when needed" (Senior Banker 2013). However, informal consultative processes typically involve issues pertaining to the MAS's IFC development activities, while consultation on prudential rules and regulations is usually carried through formal processes (Menon 2013b). This is largely due to the fact that industry actors find it easier to participate in consultations on rules and regulations that are based on a formal consultation document (Menon 2013b).

The MAS's private sector consultation has generally been seen as "constructive", allowing the MAS to keep its regulations relevant by allowing the industry to "take ownership of regulations" (Former Senior Regulatory Official 2013). Lee and Vertinsky (1988) have found that banking executives working in Singapore value their access to government financial policy decision-makers and their ability to communicate with the MAS. The pervasiveness and effectiveness of private sector consultation is best encapsulated by the fact that most, if not all of the MAS's regulations have been informed and improved by consultation (Menon 2013b). This means that the private sector is highly involved in Singapore's financial policy-making processes, through its role as a significant member of Singapore's financial policy subsystem.

From a regulatory perspective, private sector consultation and the collection of feedback from various non-state stakeholders ensure the relevance and effectiveness of MAS regulations (Monetary Authority of Singapore 2010b; Former Senior Regulatory Official 2013). Industry actors have also noted that MAS consultations allow regulators to understand their businesses better, formulating regulations that allow banks to "serve our customers better" (Senior Banker 2013). More importantly, the direct participation of private sector industry actors in the formulation of financial policies points towards the presence of a development-oriented advocacy coalition which comprises both state and industry actors and influences financial policy mix design by converting such developmental policy beliefs into instruments through an ideational channel.

Other non-state actors involved in the financial subsystem include researchers and academics, through various financial research centres in Singapore's universities, an MAS-sponsored professorship and Eminent Visitor Programme, as well as ad hoc MAS consultations with academics. One participant of such consultations with academics is that of Professor Annie Koh from the Singapore Management University, who chairs the MAS's Asian Bond Fund 2 Supervisory Committee and is tasked with developing the retail ETF market. Professor Koh has found her participation in financial sector policy largely positive, noting that academics provide useful knowledge that can inform and guide policy-making processes (Koh 2013a).

Furthermore, the state itself is not a monolithic unitary actor. While the MAS continues to play a key role as lead organization in spearheading Singapore's IFC strategy, Singapore's success as an IFC has "involved a whole swathe of policy-makers working together, both from within and outside MAS" (Monetary Authority of Singapore 2011b). State institutions such as statutory boards and government-linked companies (GLCs) are often involved in financial policy-making, with the most important of these being the EDB and DBS, respectively(Hamilton-Hart 2002), In particular, DBS has played an important role in financing financial institutions and small local industries (Tan 1999). Similarly, the CPF provides the government with a pool of funds from its members' savings and invests its surplus funds in long-term government securities (Tan 1999). Both the GIC and CPF have been involved in the MAS's strategy to develop the fund management and bond industries in the 1990s (Lee 1998a, d).

Singapore's financial subsystem also includes international actors such as international banks and financial institutions, foreign regulators from other jurisdictions, international organizations and foreign investors. For instance, the MAS has been involved in the Standing Committees of the Financial Stability Board (FSB) and has contributed to international standard-setting bodies such as the Basel Committee on Banking Supervision (BCBS), International Organization of Securities Commissions (IOSC), and International Association of Insurance Supervisors (IAIS) (Monetary Authority of Singapore 2010a). These international organizations may at times influence financial policies in Singapore. For instance, international decision-makers tend to interact with the MAS whenever they arrive in Singapore while international organizations such as the IMF and Basel Committee frequently deploy financial sector experts to examine Singapore's financial stability and its compliance with international regulatory standards (Former Senior Regulatory Official 2013).

In sum, financial policy-making in Singapore relies on the collective efforts of a coalition of government agencies, private industry actors, and other interested non-state actors. While the government remains a powerful driving force in financial sector development, it shares financial policy-making duties with industry actors and other government-related organizations. This is achieved through a "governing elite" made up of both state and private interests. Private sector actors also participate in the financial policy process through the MAS's extensive industry consultations. Singapore's highly open markets and internationalized financial sector further invite the participation of a wide array of international actors in the financial policy subsystem. However, it should be noted that Singapore's financial policy subsystem remains state-led, particularly by the MAS, with private sector industry actors allowed to substantially influence financial policies under the MAS's formal and informal consultative processes.

While other non-state and international actors are also involved in the policy process, they are not as influential as the state or industry. This is due to the significance of industry interests to Singapore's overall economic and financial development. While such non-state and international actors act as a source of knowledge and advice, they possess less influence over policy when compared to industry actors. Although the financial policy subsystems of Hong Kong and Shanghai similarly include industry, non-state and international actors, the participation of these actors in the financial policy processes of these two IFCs is limited and superficial when compared to the state–industry co-creation of financial policies and active participation of non-state actors in financial policy processes which takes place in Singapore.

Conclusion

As this chapter has shown, Singapore's development as an IFC has been largely state-directed with extensive industry participation in financial policy-making and inputs from other non-state actors. This state-led model of financial governance has been in place since Singapore's post-independence drive to develop a financial centre in the late 1960s. This is in contrast to the cases of Hong Kong and Shanghai, where financial policy-making remains very much within the control of the state and non-state participation is limited. As a consequence, Singapore's financial policy subsystem features a strong mix of state, industry, and other non-state actors, with all three sets of actors actively involved in financial policy-making, allowing for a state–industry "co-creation" of financial policies.

In particular, industry and non-state actors are involved in Singapore's financial policy process through the MAS's extensive consultative processes and the participation of select industry and non-state actors in Singapore's governing elite. Given a strong focus on financial market development, Singapore's financial policy subsystem can be characterized as a development-oriented advocacy coalition comprising state and industry actors. This coalition influences financial policy mix design through an ideational channel that converts developmental policy beliefs into policy instrument choice. Hence, enabling and developmental financial policy instruments are chosen to satisfy both the MAS's goal of IFC development and the interests of industry actors seeking to establish a business-friendly environment.

However, financial system stability remains crucial to Singapore's continued success as an IFC. Both the MAS and industry actors thus remain focused on stabilizing goals that ensure a stable business environment, aside from the aforementioned focus on development. This means that the MAS's financial policy mix comprises a judicious mix of stabilizing, enabling and developmental instruments. Importantly, this suggests the lack of a strong instruments constituency and a weak instrumental channel through which policy-makers may influence policy mix design. Rather, policy mix design is determined by the policy beliefs of Singapore's developmental advocacy coalition, with dominant subsystem actors within this coalition influencing policy mix design through a development-oriented ideational channel. This is further discussed in Chap. 7.

References

Accounting and Corporate Regulatory Authority (2009) About us. In: ACRA. http://www.acra.gov.sg/About_ACRA/?indexar=1. Accessed 17 Dec 2012

Austin IP (2004) Goh Keng Swee And Southeast Asian Governance. Marshall Cavendish Academic, Singapore

Bryant RC (1989) The Evolution of Singapore as a Financial centre. In: Sandhu KS, Wheatley P (eds) Management of success: the moulding of modern Singapore. Institute of Southeast Asian Studies, Singapore, pp 337–372

Cassidy J (2015) Can authoritarian capitalism outlive Lee Kuan Yew? New Yorker

Cassis Y (2010) Capitals of capital: The rise and fall of international financial centres 1780–2009. Cambridge University Press, Cambridge

Chia DJ (2007) Objectives and principles of financial supervision in Singapore. Regulation and the limits of competition. SNP International Publishing Pte Ltd, Singapore, pp 44–58

China Economic Review (2012) From offshore to mid-shore. China Econ, Rev

Department of Statistics Singapore (2015) Share of GDP by industry. http://www.singstat.gov.sg/statistics/visualising-data/charts/share-of-gdp-by-industry. Accessed 8 Jun 2015
Financial Advisory Industry Review Panel (2013) Report on the recommendations of the financial advisory industry review panel. Monetary Authority of Singapore, Singapore
Fund Manager with a US Asset Management Firm (2013) Interview
Former Senior Policymaker (2013) Interview
Former Senior Regulatory Official (2013) Interview
Hamilton-Hart N (2002) Asian states, Asian bankers: central banking in Southeast Asia. Cornell University Press, New York
Harrison M (2003) Fund management in Hong Kong and Singapore. Securities and Futures Commission, Hong Kong
Ho KC (2009) Competitive urban economic policies in global cities: Shanghai through the lens of Singapore. In: Chen X (ed) Rising Shanghai: state power and local transformations in a global megacity. University of Minnesota Press, Minneapolis, pp 73–91
Hodjera Z (1978) The Asian currency market: Singapore as a regional financial center (Le marche monetaire d'Asie: Singapour, place financiere regionale) (El mercado monetario de Asia: Singapur como centro financiero regional). Staff Pap—Int Monet Fund 25:221
International Monetary Fund (2013) Singapore: Financial system stability assessment. International Monetary Fund, Washington
Jao YC (1974) Banking and currency in Hong Kong: a study of postwar financial development. Macmillan, London
Jarvis DSL (2011) Race for the money: international financial centres in Asia. J Int Relat Dev 14:60–95
Koh A (2013a) Interview
Koh YG (2013b) Interview
Lam NMK (2000) Government intervention in the economy: a comparative analysis of Singapore and Hong Kong. Public Adm Dev 20:397–421
Lee HL (1997) New approach to regulating and developing Singapore's financial sector
Lee HL (1998a) Improving the hardware and software of the financial sector
Lee HL (1998b) Making Singapore Asia's premier banking centre
Lee HL (1998c) Financial sector review : a round-up and next steps financial sector review group (FSRG) appreciation dinner
Lee HL (1998d) Fund management in Singapore: new directions
Lee KY (2000) From third world to first: the Singapore story: 1965–2000. Times Editions, Singapore
Lee K-H, Vertinsky I (1988) Strategic adjustment of international financial centres (IFCs) in small economies: a comparative study of Hong Kong and Singapore. J Bus Adm 17:151–172
Lessard DR (1994) Singapore as an international financial centre. In: Roberts R (ed) Offshore financial centres. Edward Elgar Publishing Limited, Aldershot, pp 200–235
Low L (2001) The political economy of a city-state: government-made Singapore. Oxford University Press, Oxford
Menon R (2013a) Singapore's financial centre in the new landscape
Menon R (2013b) Interview
Mochizuki N (1985) Growth and development of the Singapore general insurance market and its future outlook. In: Myint S (ed) The Singapore insurance industry: historical perspective, growth and future outlook. Singapore Insurance Training Centre, Singapore
Monetary Authority of Singapore (1998a) MAS' New organisational structure
Monetary Authority of Singapore (1998b) Annual report 1997/1998. Monetary Authority of Singapore, Singapore
Monetary Authority of Singapore (1998c) DPM pays tribute to private sector contribution to financial sector reform
Monetary Authority of Singapore (1999) Liberalising commercial banking and upgrading local banks. Monetary Authority of Singapore, Singapore

Monetary Authority of Singapore (2000) Annual report 1999/2000. Monetary Authority of Singapore, Singapore

Monetary Authority of Singapore (2003) Annual report 2002/2003. Monetary Authority of Singapore, Singapore

Monetary Authority of Singapore (2004) Objectives and principles of financial supervision in Singapore

Monetary Authority of Singapore (2008) Annual report 2007/2008. Monetary Authority of Singapore, Singapore

Monetary Authority of Singapore (2010a) Annual report 2009/2010. Monetary Authority of Singapore, Singapore

Monetary Authority of Singapore (2010b) Tenets of effective regulation. Monetary Authority of Singapore, Singapore

Monetary Authority of Singapore (2011a) Annual report 2010/2011. Monetary Authority of Singapore, Singapore

Monetary Authority of Singapore (2011b) Sustaining stability, serving Singapore. Monetary Authority of Singapore, Singapore

Monetary Authority of Singapore (2012a) Overview of MAS. In: Monetary Authority of Singapore. http://www.mas.gov.sg/en/About-MAS/Overview-of-MAS.aspx. Accessed 2 Dec 2012

Monetary Authority of Singapore (2012b) Wealth management and insurance. In: Monetary Authority of Singapore. http://www.mas.gov.sg/Singapore-Financial-Centre/Overview/Wealth-Management-and-Insurance.aspx. Accessed 2 Jan 2012

Monetary Authority of Singapore (2012c) Commercial banks. In: Monetary Authority of Singapore. http://www.mas.gov.sg/Singapore-Financial-Centre/Types-of-Institutions/Commercial-Banks.aspx. Accessed 25 Dec 2012

Monetary Authority of Singapore (2012d) Regulations and financial stability. In: Monetary Authority of Singapore. http://www.mas.gov.sg/Regulations-and-Financial-Stability.aspx. Accessed 2 Dec 2012

Monetary Authority of Singapore (2013) Board of directors. In: Monetary Authority of Singapore. http://www.mas.gov.sg/About-MAS/Overview-of-MAS/Board-Members.aspx

Monetary Authority of Singapore (2014) Singapore Financial Centre. http://www.mas.gov.sg/singapore-financial-centre/overview.aspx. Accessed 8 Jun 2015

Montes MF (1999) Tokyo, Hong Kong and Singapore as competing financial centres. J Asian Bus 18:153–168

Ngiam TD (2010) Dynamics of the Singapore success story: insights by Ngiam Tong Dow, 1st edn. Cengage Learning Asia, Singapore

Schein EH (1996) Strategic pragmatism: the culture of Singapore's economic development board. The MIT Press, Massachusetts

Schiavenza M (2015) Lee Kuan Yew created the world's least-hated authoritarian state. New Repub

Senior Banker (2013) Interview

Senior Regulatory Official (2013) Interview

Shanmugaratnam T (2013) Key issues in Asian financial markets

Singapore Stock Exchange (2011) Regulation. In: SGX. http://www.sgx.com/wps/portal/sgxweb/home/regulation/overview#panelhead1. Accessed 17 Dec 2012

Tan CH (1982) Singapore as an international financial centre. East Asia dimensions of international business. Prentice Hall, Sydney, pp 29–44

Tan CH (1999) Financial markets and institutions in Singapore, tenth. Singapore University Press, Singapore

Tan CH (2002) Singapore financial and business sourcebook, 2nd edn. Singapore University Press, Singapore

Tan SL (2006) The development of Singapore's financial sector: a review and some thoughts on its future prospects. In: Koh WTH, Mariano RS (eds) The economic prospects of Singapore. Pearson Addison-Wesley, Singapore, pp 246–273

Tan KS (2007) Commentary on promoting competition: the financial sector and competition policy in Singapore. Regulation and the limits of competition. SNP International Publishing Pte Ltd, Singapore, pp 70–74

Tan CH (2011) Financial services and wealth management in Singapore, updated. Singapore University Press, Singapore

Tan C (2015) Lee Kuan Yew leaves a legacy of authoritarian pragmatism. The Guardian

Tee OC (2003) Singapore's policy of non-internationalisation of the Singapore dollar and the Asian dollar market. Bank for international settlements

Woo JJ (2014) Singapore's policy style: statutory boards as policymaking units. J Asian Public Policy 8:120–133

Woo JJ (2015a) Policy relations and policy subsystems: financial policy in Hong Kong and Singapore

Woo JJ (2015b) Beyond the neoliberal orthodoxy: alternative financial policy regimes in Asia's financial centres

Yeandle M (2015) Global financial centres index 17. Z/Yen Group and Qatar Financial Centre Authority, London

Yoon SP (1982) A Comparison of Hong Kong and Singapore as Asian financial centres. In: Grub PD, Tan CH, Kwan K-C, Rott GH (eds) East Asia dimensions of international business. Prentice Hall, Sydney, pp 21–28

Chapter 6
Shanghai

Although it is currently ranked 16th in the latest iteration of the GFCI (Yeandle 2015), Shanghai is one of the most important financial centres to have emerged in Asia. Previously ranked 5th in the world by the GFCI (Yeandle et al. 2011), Shanghai has over the past decade grown to become the "domestic financial hub of mainland China" and a centre for a diverse variety of Chinese financial activities (Laurenceson and Tang 2005). As the main financial centre for the largest economy in Asia, Shanghai is expected to take on an even-greater role in regional and global finance. It aims to become a full-fledged IFC by 2020 (Balis 2012) and a global centre for RMB trading by 2015 (Bloomberg 2012). Shanghai also plays a leading role in China's overall market liberalization process by being a key site for Chinese financial policy experimentation (Xu 1998).

As such, Shanghai's development as an IFC is a state-driven process that is inextricably linked to overall national economic development. Its emergence and development as an IFC was in fact part of a "state strategy" aimed at promoting China's role in global financial markets (Xiao 2012), with the state "determining the timing, pace and economic and spatial configuration of Shanghai's development" (Lai 2006b). This makes financial policy-making in Shanghai highly state-centred, carried out under the aegis and guidance of both the central and municipal governments (Chen 2009). State monopoly over financial policy-making is complemented by the dominance of state-owned banks and financial institutions in Shanghai's financial markets.

This makes Shanghai's financial policy subsystem state-dominated, with government agencies from both central and local levels and state-owned financial institutions forming an advocacy coalition around state ideologies and developmental policy beliefs. Non-state actors such as foreign financial institutions and independent experts play limited roles in financial policy-making. Such a state-dominated and development-oriented advocacy coalition also serves to influence policy mix design through a development-oriented ideational channel that converts state developmental policy beliefs into Shanghai's financial policy instrument mix. As a consequence, Shanghai's financial policy mix largely comprises enabling and developmental financial policy instruments that are geared towards developmental policy outputs.

J.J. Woo, *Business and Politics in Asia's Key Financial Centres*,
DOI 10.1007/978-981-287-985-1_6

This state dominance of Shanghai's financial policy subsystem and the central government's interest in its development as an IFC derives from the city's historical significance as a centre for trading and financial activities. Shanghai has been described as the "birthplace of China's modern financial industry" (Ji 2008). It has, from the start, been a key driver of national economic growth and financial sector development, and it continues to occupy a central position in China's national economic development. The origins of Shanghai's financial sector can be traced back to the mid-Ming Dynasty era (1368-1664 C.E.), when money houses had first been set up to support Shanghai's role as a trading centre in the booming Yangtze River Delta area (Ji 2008). By the mid-1930s, Shanghai already had the makings of an IFC, such as markets for securities, gold, foreign exchange, silver bullion, internal remittances and inter-bank financing (Jao 2003).

However, both the Japanese occupation and the subsequent commencement of communist rule in Shanghai by the Communist Party of China (CPC) served to disrupt financial sector development and caused an outflow of financial institutions into Hong Kong (Ji 2008). This decline of Shanghai's financial sector was exacerbated by a spate of "financial repression" by the Chinese government; this involved driving out foreign financial institutions and banks, nationalizing private Chinese banks and the closure of all financial markets (Jao 2003). As McCauley and Chan (2009) have noted, "policy drove practically all international banks out of Shanghai in the years after the founding of the People's Republic".

It was only with the economic reforms of the late 1970s that Shanghai re-emerged as an IFC. Specifically, China's 1979 economic reforms sparked off a shift towards a market economy model, featuring "an open-door policy towards trade, financial flows and foreign investments" (Zhang 2000). The story of Shanghai's development as a modern IFC therefore only begins from this period, when the 1979 reforms planted the seeds of its gradual economic liberalization and, more importantly, the internationalization of its financial markets. However, economic liberalization and financial internationalization would only take form at a much later stage; both processes are arguably still ongoing today.

At the beginning of Shanghai's emergence as an IFC, it was local financial institutions that took centre stage, with many of them serving developmental purposes for the local government (Wang 1999). Apart from driving economic development, the local government was also instrumental in driving political changes that would favour Shanghai's development as an IFC. For instance, the powerful officials who were transferred from Beijing to Shanghai, such as Jiang Zemin in 1985 and Zhu Rongji in 1987, lobbied aggressively and successfully for Shanghai to obtain a financial contract system similar to those enjoyed by Guangdong and Fujian, effectively allowing the Shanghai government to keep all revenues above an agreed amount (Yatsko 2001). This provided the Shanghai municipal government with both fiscal independence and policy autonomy, in the realms of economic and financial policy at least.

Yet despite the economic policy autonomy enjoyed by its municipal government, it is undeniable that Shanghai's post-reform re-emergence as an IFC in the late twentieth century was driven by deliberate strategic planning at the national level.

As is the case with many other aspects of Chinese economic development, Shanghai's redevelopment as an IFC was a "major strategic decision made by the CPC Central Committee and the State Council" (Ji 2008). This began in the 1990s, with China's reformist leader Deng Xiaoping stating in 1991 that the government needed to develop Shanghai into an IFC in order to boost China's status in international financial markets (Hong Kong Legislative Council Secretariat 2011).

According to Ji (2008), China's state strategy with regard to Shanghai's development as an IFC was carried out in three stages: (i) China's conversion to an open market economy from 1984 to 1992 ("exploring the state strategy"), (ii) the development of Shanghai into China's domestic financial centre from 1992 to 2002 ("laying a foundation for the state strategy") and after 2002, (iii) its emergence as a successful IFC ("implementing the state strategy"). From the 1990s, this state strategy involved the implementation of a "slew of preferential policies" at the central government level, including approval for the establishment of a Pudong New Area, permission to set up new service industries, attract foreign banks and establish a free trade zone in Shanghai (Yatsko 2001).

Such "Shanghai-leaning" policies also included the establishment of several major exchanges (上海市《迈向21世紀的上海》課题领导小组编 Shanghai City <Shanghai in the 21st Century> Discussion Group Editorial Group 1995). These included the establishment of the Shanghai Stock Exchange (SSE) in 1990, the China Foreign Exchange Trade System (CFETS) in 1994, National Interbank Funding Centre (NIFC) and National Bond Trading Centre in 1997, Shanghai Futures Exchange in 1999, Shanghai Gold Exchange in 2002, Note Market Service Centre in 2003, Shanghai Petroleum Futures Market and China Financial Futures Exchange in 2006, Shanghai Financial Arbitration Court in 2007, and Shanghai Clearing House in 2009 (Yang et al. 2010; Subacchi et al. 2012).

From the beginning, the central government's intentions to transform Shanghai into an IFC were clear. Aside from Deng Xiaoping's comments, then President Jiang Zemin also articulated the government's desire to "make Shanghai one of the international economic, financial and trade centres as soon as possible and to bring about a new leap in economic development in the Yangtze River Delta and the whole Yangtze River basin" during the 14th Party Congress of the CPC in 1992 (Beijing Review 1992). This was to be achieved by opening up China's markets to foreign investments, providing foreign investors with adequate legal protection and maintaining an environment that is conducive for investments. Under the leadership of Jiang Zemin, the central government channelled large amounts of grants an loans into Shanghai, effectively stimulating the influx of FDIs into the city (Li 2009).

In particular, the central government focused on concentrating financial activities within the Pudong area. Specifically, 18 "super-special" policies were implemented with the aim of enhancing Pudong's development by granting permission for foreign banks in Pudong to conduct local currency business, granting all Pudong-area projects the status of "priority national projects" and allocating 700 million Yuan of loans annually to the Pudong government (Yatsko 2001). These initiatives were complemented by the official establishment of the Pudong New Area in 1993

(Pudong New Area Government 2012) and the introduction of accompanying incentives geared towards attracting foreign banks and financial institutions, promoting offshore banking businesses and increasing trade in currencies and B- shares within the New Area (Liu 2008).

Pudong's Lujiazui district was subsequently developed into Shanghai's key financial district, with foreign banks and insurance companies allowed to set up representative offices, branches and sub-branches in the district (Yatsko 2001). The development of the Pudong New Area and the Lujiazui financial district attracted a "mad rush of foreign investment into the city", with many major international financial institutions such as Citibank, Goldman Sachs, Merrill Lynch and Morgan Stanley setting up or expanding operations in Shanghai (Yatsko 2001). More importantly, the establishment of the Pudong New Area prompted the central government to grant the Shanghai municipal government greater autonomy in enacting policies and regulations promoting trade, finance and industry within the New Area (Liu 2008). This further served to consolidate the Shanghai municipal government's economic policy autonomy.

Nonetheless, the central government continued to assert its authority over China's financial system. First, it sought to centralize its regulation and control of the financial system and "ensure vertical leadership of the financial system" by setting up the Central Financial Work Commission (CFWC) after the AFC (Wang 1999). This was accompanied by the establishment of national regulatory authorities for the banking, securities and insurance sectors. However, the CFWC was only able to supervise and control national financial institutions, with provincial, municipal and local banks as well as other financial institutions falling outside of its influence (Heilmann 2005a). Given the inefficiency of such centralized regulation, the task of financial regulation and supervision fell to local governments, with cooperation and coordination between central regulators and local government bodies taking place at the local level (Heilmann 2005a).

Local governments subsequently reinstated their control and influence over their financial sectors with the formation of municipal financial work bodies and "Financial Safety Zones" that served the functions of "supervising local financial institutions, linking up [*goutong*] with central government regulatory, contributing to the reduction of non-performing loans, guarding against financial risks, fighting financial crime, preventing asset stripping and capital flight" (Heilmann 2005a). From the mid-1990s, the Shanghai municipal government stepped up its efforts at attracting domestic and foreign financial companies and encouraging them to set up their head offices in Shanghai (Heilmann 2005a). The Shanghai municipal government further concentrated its influence over financial sector development with the formation of the Shanghai Municipal Financial Work Party Committee (FWPC) in 2000.

The FWPC acts directly under the direct purview of the Shanghai Municipal CCP Committee, meaning that the CFWC had "no organizational hierarchical control over the Shanghai FWPC but merely exercised general policy guidance [*zhidao*] through issuing documents and holding occasional joint work conferences" (Heilmann 2005a). The CFWC would subsequently be dissolved in 2002 due to its perceived inefficacy in managing local financial institutions, with most of its functions and responsibilities transferred to national regulatory bodies. The Shanghai Municipal Financial Service Office (FSO) was also set up in the same year as an administrative body overseeing the regulation and development of Shanghai's financial sector, to compliment the FWPC's role as a political body. However, the distribution of functions and responsibilities between the two remains unclear.

Even as Shanghai's local government consolidated control and management of its financial sector, the central government has managed to retain a significant measure of influence. This was achieved through the establishment of the CSRC Shanghai Bureau in 1993, the CIRC Shanghai Bureau in 2000, the CBRC Shanghai Bureau in 2003 and the PBOC Shanghai Head Office in 2005 (Ji 2008). The establishment of these state organization branches in Shanghai has allowed the central government to perform central banking, regulatory and supervisory functions in the municipality. The FSO works closely with these central regulatory institutions in the implementation of its laws, rules and policies; it has also established regular "3 + 2" meetings between the FSO, PBOC Shanghai Head Office and the three state financial regulatory authorities (Ji 2008). As discussed below, such central–local government dynamics define Shanghai's financial policy subsystem.

Regardless of the extent and nature of state intervention, financial liberalization and internationalization are crucial to any IFC's success. Shanghai is no exception. Financial reform and internationalization in the municipality were sparked off by China's entry into the World Trade Organization (WTO) in 2001, with Shanghai experiencing greater international cooperation in its financial markets and attracting the establishment of 326 foreign-funded and Sino-foreign joint-venture financial institutions by 2005 (Ji 2008). The opening up of China's financial markets therefore stimulated Shanghai's rapid internationalization through an increase in the number of foreign financial institutions that established themselves in the city. A government pilot programme that sought to reform the foreign exchange and offshore banking sectors further attracted foreign financial institutions, with many of these foreign firms acquiring stakes in Chinese financial institutions (Ji 2008).

The introduction of the Qualified Foreign Institutional Investor (QFII) scheme in 2003 and the Qualified Domestic Institutional Investor (QDII) scheme in 2006 further encouraged the inflow of foreign funds and the expansion of Yuan-denominated trading activities, liberalizing trade on the SSE (Yang et al. 2010). Financial liberalization and internationalization in Shanghai were therefore state-driven processes that hinged upon the central government's economic and regulatory reforms. As such, the central government continued to play an active role in developing Shanghai as an IFC. These were expressed in the government's 11th Five-Year Plan, which aimed to build Shanghai into a successful IFC by 2010 through the establishment of a financial market system, strengthening of financial institutions, tightening of regulations, introduction of reforms and innovations, and maintenance of a favourable financial environment (Pan 2006; Hong Kong Legislative Council Secretariat 2011).

Further endorsement from the central government came in March 2009, when the Chinese State Council announced plans to turn Shanghai into a major IFC on par with London, Hong Kong and Singapore by 2020 (Yang et al. 2010). In particular, the 2020 plan aimed to develop in Shanghai: a multifunctional and internationalized financial market system, internationally competitive financial institutions and financial professionals, and a compatible system of taxation, credit, regulation and law (Leung and Yim 2009). These plans were accompanied by policy initiatives such as tax incentives, measures promoting market liberalization and gradual convertibility of the RMB (Li 2009). Significantly, Shanghai received permission from the central government in April 2009 to use RMB in overseas trade settlements (Li 2009).

The central government's plans for Shanghai's development as an IFC were complemented by the key role of the municipal government in establishing the conditions necessary for financial sector development. For instance, housing and healthcare benefits were introduced by Shanghai city officials to attract financial sector professionals (Tong 2009). Liu (2008) has also noted that China's central and local governments share the same goals of turning Shanghai into Asia's leading IFC, surpassing even Hong Kong. China's national strategy of establishing Shanghai as an IFC was formally enacted as the "Regulations on Promoting the Development of an International Financial Centre in the Shanghai Municipality" (Shanghai Municipal Commission of Commerce 2010), signifying a progression of this strategy from policy to legislation (Hong Kong Legislative Council Secretariat 2011).

While the regulations placed the Shanghai municipal government in charge of financial industry development, this was to be carried out under the "unified arrangement of the State" (Shanghai Municipal Commission of Commerce 2010). The Shanghai municipal government was also tasked with fostering greater cooperation with Hong Kong SAR and other cities from the Yangtze River Delta area and fostering stronger exchange with other major IFC's, in accordance with the "strategic positioning and labour division determined by the State" (Shanghai Municipal Commission of Commerce 2010). More policy measures aimed at encouraging financial liberalization and innovation were unveiled in the State Council's "Opinions on Accelerating Shanghai's developing its Modern Service and Advanced Manufacturing Industries, and its development into an International Financial Centre and an International Shipping Centre" (Hong Kong Legislative Council Secretariat 2011).

The central government's ambitions for accelerating the development of Shanghai as an IFC were further enunciated in its 12th Five-Year Plan in 2011 (People's Bank of China et al. 2011), 4th National Financial Work Conference in 2012 (Lan 2012a; Subacchi et al. 2012), as well as plans announced by the National Development and Reform Commission (NDRC) in 2012 to make Shanghai a "global centre of renminbi product innovation, trading, clearing and pricing" by 2015 (Lan 2012b). These plans culminated in the launch of the Shanghai Free Trade Zone (FTZ) on 29 September 2013, an initiative that allows the Chinese government to test significant financial and economic reforms such as loosening restrictions on foreign investments and introducing full RMB convertibility (BBC News 2013). Other major financial reforms within the FTZ include allowing foreign banks to be established in the zone, allowing foreign financial institutions to set up joint-venture banks and allowing qualified domestic banks to engage in offshore business (Palmioli and Heal 2014).

While Shanghai's financial sector was gradually liberalized in line with its ambition to become a leading IFC and its municipal government has obtained significant autonomy to do so, Shanghai's financial sector growth is still controlled or at times constrained by the authority wielded by the central government and regulators over the introduction of new financial products and exchanges (Tong 2009). Intuitively, this suggests that the Shanghai government is in charge of formulation and implementation of financial policies, while the central government decides on the overall IFC development strategy. This is further discussed in the sections on financial governance and policy subsystem. Regardless, state-leadership and support from both the central and local governments has enabled Shanghai establish several key sources of competitive advantage. These are discussed next.

Determinants of Competitive Advantage

As China's main financial centre and top port-city, Shanghai's competitive advantages as an IFC are derived from its political and economic position within Asia's largest economy. Laurenceson and Tang (2005) have identified Shanghai's high rate of economic growth, international orientation, strategic access to key markets, low business input costs, as well as its rapidly improving physical and human capital stocks as the city's strengths as an IFC. These advantages reflect China's rapidly growing economy, its increasing open markets, as well its abundance of labour and resources.

However, Shanghai's prior history as a hub for trade and finance also factor into its current success. These include a "financial culture" that emerged from the city's historical position as a financial centre and the diverse financial markets that have been present since (上海市《迈向 21世紀的上海》課题领导小组编 Shanghai City <Shanghai in the 21st Century> Discussion Group Editorial Group 1995; Hong Kong Legislative Council Secretariat 2011). More importantly and like many other IFCs, Shanghai's strategic geographical location in the Yangtze River Delta region and its favourable time zone are crucial in its initial development as an IFC and port-city. These have allowed it to interact and cooperate directly with foreign investors and international financial institutions (Liu 2008).

Aside from its strategic location and availability of skilled workers, Shanghai's prospects as an IFC have also benefited immensely from national policies that were favourable to its development (Zhang 2000). Representing a unique advantage enjoyed by Shanghai, favourable national policies arise from Shanghai's economic and political proximity to China. Furthermore, the Chinese central government views Shanghai as its "trump card" in the global economy and has thus provided

Shanghai with incentives and resources that far exceed those offered to other SEZ's (Liu 2008). As such, Shanghai's proximity to the rapidly expanding Chinese economy and the availability of strong political support from the central government represents a key competitive advantage for the Chinese IFC, providing a measure of policy and political stability (DBS Bank Singapore Economic Research Department 1996; Yatsko 2001; Leung and Yim 2009).

Political support from the central government is aided by the presence of former Shanghai leaders (known as the "Shanghai Clique") in key state institutions such as the Politburo (DBS Bank Singapore Economic Research Department 1996). Specifically, Shanghai's financial sector benefits from the "favourable policies" enjoyed by the Pudong New Area as well as other "Shanghai-leaning" policies promulgated by the central government (上海市《迈向 21 世紀的上海》課题领导小组编 Shanghai City <Shanghai in the 21st Century> Discussion Group Editorial Group 1995). A more recent instance of such strong state political support can be found in Premier Li Keqiang's backing of the recently established Shanghai free trade zone despite the opposition from various financial regulators (Chen 2013).

This strong role of the state gives rise to political stability, policy efficiency, predictable planned development, and advantages enjoyed by Singapore as well (Ho 2009). It is also important to note that this "strong state" factor underpinning Shanghai's financial success includes both the central and municipal governments. As later sections will show, municipal government agencies play a significant role in regulating and developing Shanghai's financial sector, working under the purview of and in tandem with central government agencies. Shanghai's status as an IFC is also aided by its strong and well-diversified real economy, which provides an additional engine to the growth of the financial sector (Jao 2003).

Two distinct sets of competitive advantages can thus be discerned, separated by China's 1979 economic reforms. The first set comprises pre-existing advantages such as strategic location and time zone, availability of human capital and an existing financial sector; these existed before the 1979 reforms and can be seen as relatively "natural-occurring". These advantages were related to Shanghai's initial role as a trade entrepot. The second set of competitive advantages includes Shanghai's participation in a rapidly expanding Chinese economy and strong political support from the central government in terms of favourable policies. This second set of advantages is essentially state-driven and the result of deliberate policy design.

While these key factors have driven Shanghai's rise to prominence, several competitive *disadvantages* continue to hinder the city's development. First, China's inconvertible RMB continues to act as a stumbling block to Shanghai's development and prospects as an IFC (Leung and Yim 2009). As Tong (2009) has noted, Shanghai's future as a leading IFC hinges on the convertibility of the RMB, with partial or no RMB convertibility restricting Shanghai's role to domestic financial centre rather than a full-fledged IFC. Furthermore, Shanghai's lack of capital mobility and RMB convertibility stands in stark contrast to the full currency convertibility and capital mobility that underpin Hong Kong's success as an IFC (Jao 2003).

Jao (2003) further notes that Shanghai continues to lag behind Hong Kong in terms of its inability to grant "national treatment" to foreign banks and financial institutions, the highly interventionist and restrictive nature of its financial governance mode, weak prudential supervision, complex and onerous tax system, and its ineffective legal system. Due to such shortcomings, Shanghai is far less attractive as a location for regional headquarters when compared to Hong Kong (Laurenceson and Tang 2005). However, the recent establishment of the Shanghai free trade zone seeks to ameliorate some these weaknesses, by allowing the government to experiment with and progressively introduce full RMB convertibility, liberalize interest rates and allow greater participation of foreign financial institutions within the area.

It has also been noted that Shanghai lacks the "software" of a successful IFC, such as strong rule of law, good accounting systems, financial sector talent, an attractive tax system, access to accurate information, market-oriented corporate incentives and an English-speaking environment (Yatsko 2001; Chong 2013). This lack of the necessary legal, regulatory, and human capital-related infrastructure reflects an under-representation of stabilizing policy instruments that would have aided in the establishment of such infrastructure. Instead, China's development-focused government relies on developmental and enabling instruments to stimulate financial sector development. This is discussed in a later section on Shanghai's financial policy mix.

Shanghai's future as an IFC therefore hinges on the development of these "software" factors, albeit with much resistance, given that the development of these factors may require a reduction in the Party's power and influence over Shanghai's financial markets (Yatsko 2001). In contrast, such "software" is readily available in Hong Kong and Singapore and has become entrenched as part of these two IFC's key competitive advantages, particularly the presence of robust and reliable legal and regulatory infrastructures in both IFCs (Chong 2013; Tsang 2013). In response to these disadvantages, the Chinese government's Fourth National Financial Work Conference in 2012 identified improving corporate governance, reinforcing financial infrastructure and strengthening financial regulation and supervision as key areas of financial reform for the next five years (Lan 2012a; Subacchi et al. 2012).

Regardless, Shanghai's emergence and development as an IFC will impact regional and international financial markets, providing both challenges and potential for cooperation to other IFCs. Shanghai's rise as an IFC poses direct challenges to Hong Kong by attracting project financing, syndication loans, potential stock listings and debt issues away from the SAR by virtue of its proximity to booming Chinese industries (DBS Bank Singapore Economic Research Department 1996). In contrast, Singapore's comparative advantage in serving the South-east Asian region shields the republic from competitive pressures arising from Shanghai's rise to prominence (DBS Bank Singapore Economic Research Department 1996).

However, Shanghai also benefits from close cooperation with other IFCs in the region. This is related to its strategic locational advantages. For instance, the establishment of the Mainland Market Data Collaboration Programme between the HKEx Information Services Limited and SSE Infonet Limited in 2008 and the signing of the Closer Cooperation Agreement the HKEx and SSE in 2009 have ensured greater cooperation and coordination between Shanghai and Hong Kong (Subacchi et al. 2012). This reflects "functional complementarity" between the two competing centres, given that Shanghai provides investors with strong access to China's domestic markets, while Hong Kong offers good international exposure and diversity (Jao 2003; Karreman and van der Knaap 2012). Similarly, Lai (2012) positions Shanghai as a commercial centre operating within China's "financial centre network" that also includes Beijing as the political centre and Hong Kong as offshore financial centre.

In sum, Shanghai's key comparative advantages as an IFC stem from its proximity to China's burgeoning national economy as well as strong support from the central government. Support from the central government also means access to economic and political resources, as is evident from the recent establishment of the Shanghai free trade zone. Nonetheless, Shanghai is comparatively disadvantaged due to its weak rule of law and lack of the necessary "software" that typically drive other successful IFC's such as Hong Kong and Singapore. Both these limitations and its state-driven competitive advantages feature heavily in Shanghai's model of financial governance. This is discussed next.

Financial Governance

As the above discussion has shown, financial sector development in Shanghai has from the start been seen as a means for promoting economic development at the national level. As Jarvis (2011) has noted, "Shanghai's financial sector development is not its own but reflects a national development strategy substantially controlled by Beijing". This also means that "financial policies must be subsumed under economic policies" (Yang et al. 2010). As a consequence of this linkage between local financial sector development and national economic policy, the state features heavily in Shanghai's model of financial governance.

Financial governance in Shanghai has been also described as "state-managed capitalism" (Karmel 1994), with the state determining the nature and pace of financial sector development and reform. However, the Chinese state is far from a monolithic unified entity. Rather, both the central and local governments, as well as a slew of state-owned enterprises and other state-related institutions, are heavily involved in Shanghai's financial governance. This bears some similarity to the case of Singapore, particularly in terms of the use of specialized state agencies and government flexibility in identifying and exploiting new opportunities (Ho 2009). However, the difference lies in the greater complexity and larger number of actors in Shanghai's political and policy landscape.

The most important actor in Shanghai's financial governance is its municipal government. As the municipality's main policy implementer, the Shanghai municipal government is in charge of directing financial policy and economic governance in Shanghai (Heilmann 2005a; Chen and Orum 2009). It has also on occasion been able to influence the formulation of central government policies (Li 1997). As discussed above, this is largely due to the significance of Shanghai's financial sector to national economic development, as well as the presence of influential officials within the Shanghai municipal government. However, the Shanghai municipal government remains by and large focused on financial governance at the local level, with the central government providing guidance through its various agencies and SOEs. This is discussed in greater depth below.

At the this local level of the municipality, strategic decisions involving the financial sector are generally made by the Municipal CCP committee or its Standing Committee. By virtue of their membership in the Standing Committee and their positions within the Core Party Group of the municipal government, the Shanghai Mayor and Vice-Mayor in charge of financial sector policy are effectively the key decision-makers in Shanghai's financial policy-making process (Heilmann 2005a). Shanghai Mayors also tend to possess high levels of influence in the CCP or the central government, with several former individuals moving on to key Party positions after their tenures as Shanghai Mayor (Liu 2008).

Aside from the Mayor and Vice-Mayor, another important figure in Shanghai's financial governance is a deputy chief of staff within the General Office of the Municipal Government who is tasked with overseeing the financial sector and who serves a concurrent appointment as head of Municipal Financial Services Offices (FSO) (Heilmann 2005a). Another key financial policy-maker is the secretary of the Shanghai Financial Work Party Committee (FWPC), who also serves as deputy director of the FSO; the director of the FSO serves as deputy secretary of the FWPC (Heilmann 2005a). This inverse ranking between the FWPC and FSO was introduced in 2002 and allows for a clearer division of responsibilities and functions between the Party secretary and administrative head for financial work bodies (Heilmann 2005a).

As a political organization overseeing financial sector development, the FWPC is a unique aspect of Shanghai's financial governance. Formed in 2000, the FWPC acts directly under the purview of the Shanghai Municipal CCP Committee and provides municipal political leaders with a means through which they can direct and oversee Shanghai's financial industry, particularly through deciding the appointment of senior executives and top managers of local financial institutions in Shanghai (Heilmann 2005a). Even in privately held financial institutions, the FWPC is able to influence executive appointments through the CCP cadre membership system (Heilmann 2005a). Furthermore, the FWPC is also able to indirectly exert its influence over Shanghai's financial markets by holding shares in major local financial institutions. This allows the local government to use local financial institutions "as a policy tool… to support economic growth", making the FWPC a "major political player in Shanghai's financial business" (Heilmann 2005a).

Given the secretive nature of the FWPC and its inaccessibility to foreign investors and other non-party actors, the Municipal FSO was established in 2002 and was tasked with enforcing national regulations, minimizing systemic risks, planning Shanghai's medium to long-term development as an IFC and coordinating the allocation of financial resources (Heilmann 2005a). The FSO therefore represents the non-political and outward-oriented face of Shanghai's financial governing milieu. However, the FSO was from the start led by officials who were involved in the FWPC, leading to views that the FSO was merely "an organizational extension and … state facade organization of the FWPC" (Heilmann 2005a). This means that both the FWPC and FSO are organizations or channels through which the Shanghai municipal government facilitates and directs financial sector development, although the FSO is remains more accessible to non-party and non-state actors.

Given the role of the Shanghai municipal government in financial sector development, Heilmann (2005a) has noted that communication and coordination between financial policy-makers in Shanghai and their counterparts in the central government remain weak, with exchanges between Shanghai's financial work bodies and central regulatory commissions as well as Shanghai branches of the central bank carried out through informal personal connections. As such, central government bodies are seen as "outsiders" to Shanghai's financial sector policy-making process, resulting in "grave deficiencies" arising from the "lack of effective coordination between central government regulators and municipal financial administrators" (Heilmann 2005a). However, such a view ignores the indirect channels through which the central government is able to influence or direct Shanghai's economic and financial development.

For instance, China's "policy banks", namely the "China Development Bank, the Import and Export Bank of China and the Agricultural Development Bank of China", established branches in Shanghai during the mid-1990s and have since become "a leading force in the economic development of Shanghai" (Ji 2008). State-owned commercial banks play a similar role, with their Shanghai branches becoming "a leading force in promoting Shanghai's economic development with their abundant resources, perfect functions, superior services and advanced technology" (Ji 2008). Through these state-owned banks, the central government is able to determine Shanghai's financial sector growth and development.

Importantly, Shanghai's status as a Special Economic Zone (SEZ) allows the melding of central and local government interests and influence in the city's development as an IFC. This reflects an interactive and mutually constitutive relationship between the central and local governments (Li 1997). Beginning with the economic reforms of Deng Xiaoping, China's SEZ model has been used as a strategy for economic development, allowing a constructive combination of top-down Party-driven central government control with bottom-up local influence from local leaders and administrators (Liu 2008). The Chinese government also often treats these SEZ's as "experiments" in market liberalization and development, applying different combinations of capitalist and socialist economic governance principles within SEZ's (Liu 2008).

In sum, Shanghai's model of financial governance is highly state-centred. Through various government agencies, state-owned financial institutions and Party-related organisations, both the central and municipal governments are heavily involved in the governance and development of Shanghai's financial sector.

The state's strong interest in Shanghai's success as an IFC is based on the importance of Shanghai's financial sector development as a key driver of economic development at the national level. This complexity in Shanghai's multi-level and multi-actor financial governance model is somewhat replicated in its regulatory regime. The next section provides a brief overview of the regulatory regime in Shanghai, discussing the agencies and institutions that are involved in financial policy-making in the municipality.

Regulatory Regime

Reflecting China's multi-level system of government, Shanghai's regulatory regime is made up of two levels: national and municipal. At the national level, China's financial regulatory framework operates on the "One-Bank, Three-Commissions" model, with the PBC playing a central leading role as the nation's central bank and the three commissions (the CBRC, CSRC and CIRC) overseeing and regulating their respective financial sectors (Subacchi et al. 2012). All four organizations report directly to the State Council, which is in charge of formulating regulatory and monetary policies as well as implementing financial reform strategies (Subacchi et al. 2012). The PBC, CBRC, CSRC and CIRC have all established branches in Shanghai and play significant roles in regulating the respective financial sectors in Shanghai through these branches.

At the municipal level, the FSO is tasked with the implementation of financial regulations, laws, policies and guidelines, in cooperation with central regulatory authorities (Shanghai Municipal People's Government 2002). Importantly, the FSO "play(s) a key inside role in the local financial sector" that involves supervising local financial institutions and maintaining financial system stability (Heilmann 2005a). This makes the FSO Shanghai's key financial policy-maker at the local level. Given the various central and municipal government regulatory agencies present, financial policy-making in Shanghai is highly complex and often bifurcated along central-municipal lines. While central-level regulatory agencies generally formulate financial policies, municipal-level agencies are tasked with implementing these policies.

Financial policy-making is further imbued with an additional level of complexity in Shanghai's securities market. The Shanghai Securities Regulatory Bureau (SSRB) is the key regulatory agency of Shanghai's securities markets, operating as the Shanghai branch of the CSRC (China Securities Regulatory Commission 2008). However, the Shanghai Stock Exchange (SSE) also plays a role in regulating and supervising the securities market, operating a "self-regulatory framework with a focus on supervision of listed companies, SSE members and the securities market" (Shanghai Stock Exchange 2010a). Nonetheless, the SSE remains governed under the purview of the CSRC (Shanghai Stock Exchange 2010b). This suggests a multi-level nested aspect to securities regulation in Shanghai, with the SSE existing as a regulator in its own right and at the same time, regulated by the CSRC.

The complementary roles played by the SSRB and SSE in Shanghai's securities regulation is highlighted by the fact that firms issuing and listing securities in Shanghai are required to submit applications to both the SSRB and SSE (Nottle 1993). At the national level, the Securities Association of China (SAC) facilitates self-regulation of the securities industry under the guidance and supervision of the CSRC and Ministry of Civil Affairs of China (Securities Association of China 2012). In other words, the governance and regulation of Shanghai's securities markets is highly complex and involves the CSRC, SSRB, SSE and SAC operating within nested relations of inter-regulation.

Importantly, the separation of central and local regulatory authority in Shanghai has resulted in a "lack of specificity" that allows local branches of national regulatory authorities to adapt laws and regulations to local needs (Lai 2012). As such, local regulatory authorities in Shanghai possess significant autonomy to interpret and implement laws formulated at the national level (Lai 2012). However, such a "lack of specificity" has its drawbacks as well. Jurisdictional overlaps among regulatory agencies and continuously evolving mandates have also resulted in "regulatory confusion" or even obfuscation (Jarvis 2011). However and as discussed above, this perceived regulatory complexity or confusion is in reality balanced by the overarching authority of the central government, through its agencies, state-owned institutions and Party organizations.

The ability of the central government to retain some measure of influence over financial policy and regulation in Shanghai, as well as the alignment of local-level officials and institutions with national goals of economic development, is reflected in Shanghai's development-oriented financial policy mix, which is discussed next. Nonetheless and as will be discussed below, central–local dynamics continue to impact Shanghai's financial policy mix and policy subsystem.

Financial Policy Mix

With China's burgeoning trade and high savings rate, the financial sector has been seen as a key means through which the central government can exercise national economic governance or control (上海市《迈向 21 世紀的上海》課题领导小组编 Shanghai City <Shanghai in the 21st Century> Discussion Group Editorial Group 1995). The development of Shanghai as an IFC therefore constitutes a key part of the Chinese central government's "state strategy" of enhancing the role of China's financial sector as a key driver of economic growth and revenue (Xiao 2012). However and as discussed above, the Shanghai municipal government remains the city's main implementor of financial policies. This gives it significance autonomy over the interpretation of policies and even a certain extent of influence of policy formulation.

This means a dominant and varied role of the state in driving Shanghai's development as an IFC that involves distributing financial policy roles across central and municipal government agencies. Such a distribution of financial policy roles is reflected in Shanghai's focus on financial innovation and new markets, while Beijing plays a larger role in financial regulation and macro-policy (Lai 2012). As such, Shanghai is "tasked with testing new products, developing new markets and financial innovation" (Lai 2012). Along with Shanghai's importance to national economic development, such a focus on financial innovation and new market development suggests a heavy reliance on development-oriented financial policy instruments. This section discusses Shanghai's heavily development-oriented financial policy mix and the role of the state in designing and implementing such a policy mix.

As Wei and Leung have noted, the Chinese state is involved in Shanghai's development as "a planner, a reformer and a developer/entrepreneur", with the local state acting specifically as "developer and financier" (Wei and Leung 2005). Financial sector development is thus not an end in itself, but a means through which overall economic development and governance can be achieved or enhanced. The attainment of this development-oriented financial sector growth is greatly aided by the use of developmental policy instruments. At the most basic level, developmental financial policy instruments have been used to generate revenue for the state directly. As Gordon and Li (2003) have noted, the Chinese government behaves as a "discriminating monopolist", in selecting regulations that maximize its revenue income from both foreign and domestic investors.

This is most clearly reflected in the Shanghai government's bank finance policies during the 1980s, which had discriminated against private enterprises in an effort to accrue revenues to the state (Li 1997). State control over interest rates and credit allocation has also served to ensure cheap access to capital for SOEs, while private enterprizes remain credit-constrained (Palmioli and Heal 2014). This means that financial policies and regulations have been used by the Shanghai government to *extract rents*, representing a direct but crude way in which financial policies can be used to attain developmental goals of increasing government revenues. Such developmental policy instruments differ from those employed in Hong Kong and Singapore. While developmental financial policy instruments in Hong Kong and Singapore serve to develop specific financial markets or sectors by attracting investments and channelling resources to these sectors, Shanghai's extractive financial regulations serve to directly obtain government revenues with less focus on developing markets per se.

Given Shanghai's relatively weak legal and regulatory infrastructure, there is little evidence of financial regulation playing a stabilizing function in the municipality. As noted in an earlier section, the lack of a robust and transparent regulatory framework is a comparative disadvantage or weakness that continues to hamper Shanghai's prospects as an IFC. However, this is likely to change as Shanghai improves its regulatory infrastructure and seeks to comply with international standards in order to attract more foreign investment and enhance its development as an IFC. As noted by Mr. Andrew Sheng, who has served on Shanghai's International Financial Advisory Council, financial regulations in Shanghai are moving towards international standards, particularly in the areas of clearing and payments system and logistical issues (Sheng 2013).

The PBC Shanghai Head Office has also started pilot programmes in financial consumer protection (People's Bank of China 2012). This means that the Shanghai government is beginning to include stabilizing financial policy instruments such as establishing an efficient and transparent clearing and payments system in its financial policy mix. Furthermore, the establishment of the Shanghai FTZ suggests a desire to attract more foreign investment and invite the participation of foreign financial institutions in the city. This will inevitably require Shanghai to implement more stabilizing policy instruments that ensure investor protection and systemic stability, both of which are key points of attraction for Hong Kong and Singapore.

Nonetheless, financial policies in Shanghai remain heavily skewed towards enablement and development for now, with Shanghai's development as an IFC replete with examples of the government's use of development-oriented financial policies. For instance, regulatory authorities directed enterprise bond issuances in 1991 towards industries in foreign trade, textiles and electronics, in a bid to develop and expand these industries (Xu 1998). The developmental role of financial policy in Shanghai is also well-understood and practiced by its regulatory agencies. For instance, the CSRC is tasked with both "developing" and "regulating" China's capital markets and is "expected to do both well" (Wang 2004). Aside from regulating Shanghai's financial sector, the FSO is also tasked with promoting financial development as well as financial sector reform and innovation, albeit in accordance with national developmental plans and financial policies (Shanghai Municipal People's Government 2002).

In particular, the FSO promotes the financial services sector to serve local economic and social development goals (Shanghai Municipal Government 2010). The FSO is further responsible for restructuring municipal assets held in financial companies; this includes initiating mergers among financial companies under the control of the Shanghai government to improve the competitiveness of these financial companies and Shanghai's financial sector in general (Heilmann 2005a). Similar to the state-engineered consolidation of local banks in the 1980s Singapore, such mergers can be seen as an important developmental instrument used by the FSO in developing and increasing the competitiveness of Shanghai's financial sector. Furthermore, the FSO provides administrative support to Non-Shanghainese financial companies, encouraging them to set up their headquarters in Shanghai (Heilmann 2005a).

Importantly, the FSO is able to regulate and promote Shanghai's financial sector to both Chinese and foreign financial institutions as a non-Party institution, although foreign financial institutions generally prefer to deal with the national regulatory bodies (Heilmann 2005a). For instance, central government banking regulators played a major role in supporting the Shanghai's efforts at encouraging Citigroup to invest in Pudong Development Bank and HSBC in the Bank of Shanghai in 2003 (Heilmann 2005a). The two foreign banks eventually agreed to the deals after they were allowed to issue dual currency credit cards in Shanghai, a service that was hitherto not available in China and hence required special permission from national banking regulators (Heilmann 2005a). The PBC has also sought to promote Shanghai's development as an IFC through its various initiatives aimed at attracting foreign financial institutions and increasing cross-border RMB business (People's Bank of China 2012).

In sum, Shanghai's financial policy mix is comprised largely of developmental and enabling financial policy instruments. These instruments allow direct government intervention in the promotion and development of Shanghai's financial sector. Developmental instruments also allow the government to extract revenues through the use of financial regulations. However, both central and municipal governments have recently placed more attention on stabilizing financial policy instruments, in a bid to improve investor confidence in Shanghai and hence contribute to Shanghai's development as an IFC. This is exemplified in the Shanghai FTZ and other efforts at introducing transparency to regulatory and payments systems in the city.

Financial Policy Subsystem

In contrast to both Hong Kong and Singapore, Shanghai's financial policy subsystem is heavily dominated by state actors from both the central and municipal governments and features very limited participation by non-state and industry actors. Combined with its focus on national economic development, this state dominance has resulted in the formation of an advocacy coalition comprising state and state-related actors, formed around developmental policy beliefs. This has allowed state actors acting through this coalition to influence policy mix through an ideational channel that converts such developmental beliefs into a preference for enabling and developmental financial policy instruments.

Financial policy-making in Shanghai involves both central- and municipal-level government actors. As discussed above, the Shanghai municipal government has maintained a significant level of autonomy in economic and financial policy-making (Wu 2000; Lai 2006a), making it a dominant policy actor in Shanghai's financial policy subsystem. In particular, the highly influential Shanghai municipal government has driven Shanghai's development as an IFC through two main organizations: the FWPC and FSO. Both organizations and their roles have been discussed in earlier sections. While Shanghai's municipal government retains significant autonomy in governing the city's financial sector, the central government has also been able to exert a significant amount of influence by establishing branches of key state financial institutions in the city.

For instance, the PBC had set up its headquarters in Shanghai in 2005, establishing a "significant interactive relationship" between the central and municipal governments (Hong Kong Legislative Council Secretariat 2011). The PBC has since established itself as a significant policy actor in Shanghai's financial policy subsystem through its Shanghai Head Office (People's Bank of China 2012). The establishment of the CSRC Shanghai Bureau in 1993, the CIRC Shanghai Bureau in 2000 and the CBRC Shanghai Bureau in 2003 (Ji 2008) also means that state regulatory authorities continue to play a key role in the promulgation and implementation of rules and regulations governing Shanghai's financial sector. Aside from local branches of central government agencies, the central government also influences financial sector development in Shanghai by enacting preferential policies and channelling resources towards the municipality's development (Wei and Leung 2005).

However, the simultaneous presence of central and municipal government agencies has also been seen as a source of regulatory uncertainty, given competing political interests and jurisdictional overlaps among agencies from both levels (Jarvis 2011). In particular, the central government's more protectionist "centralizing tendencies" has been seen as an important cause of the aforementioned deficiencies in Shanghai's "software" or "soft-institutional capacities" (Jarvis 2011). Nonetheless, these differences between the central and municipal governments may easily be overstated, given that the central government retains control and influence over municipal government officials through the Party cadre system (Heilmann 2005a, b).

Another channel through which the central government influences and supports Shanghai's development as an IFC is through its state-owned banks and other financial institutions, which have established a strong presence in Shanghai. China's three policy banks, namely the China Development Bank, the Import and Export Bank of China and the Agricultural Development Bank of China, have been operating branches in Shanghai since the mid-1990s. State-owned commercial banks have also been used as "mechanisms" of economic governance and control in Shanghai by the central government (陈 1993), especially through their provision of special development loans (Wei and Leung 2005). This is similar to the early role played by DBS in Singapore and to some extent, HSBC in Hong Kong. While such practices have largely declined in Hong Kong and Singapore, state-owned banks continue to play a major role in Shanghai's financial policy subsystem.

More importantly, state-owned banks and financial institutions are able to dominate Shanghai's financial policy subsystem by virtue of their strong political connections (Chong 2013). Such political connections act as an effective barrier to entry, given the unwillingness of local financial institutions to face the political consequences of competing directly with well-connected state-owned firms (Chong 2013). Furthermore, firms in China generally require political connections in order to gain access to loans and capital (Yu and Pan 2008; Duan and bin Chik 2012). Aside from the "big four" state-owned banks that include the Bank of China, the China Construction Bank, the Agricultural Bank of China, and the Industrial and Commercial Bank of China and the policy banks identified above, other smaller commercial banks are also strongly involved in Shanghai's development as an IFC.

For instance, a key goal of the Shanghai Pudong Development Bank is to build itself into a "financial flagship that fits the needs of Shanghai international financial centre", having from its inception "actively supported and promoted Shanghai's economic revitalization and development of the domestic economy" (Shanghai Pudong Development Bank 2010). While the Shanghai Pudong Development Bank is technically a joint-stock commercial bank, 8 of its 11 Board Directors are CCP Party members (Shanghai Pudong Development Bank 2010). Majority owned by the Shanghai Municipal Government, the Bank of Shanghai also serves to "support the development of Shanghai into an international financial centre" (Bank of Shanghai 2012). Whether through direct government ownership or Party linkages, commercial banks in Shanghai are an important part of the municipality's financial policy-making process.

The state's influence on Shanghai's financial markets also extends beyond the banking sector, with listings on Shanghai's stock market dominated by state-owned companies (Laurenceson and Tang 2005). Given that the government is involved in Shanghai's financial markets through its agencies, authorities and state-owned banks, state actors in Shanghai's financial policy subsystem play both the roles of regulator and market participant, effectively dominating the subsystem. More importantly, a cooperative set of relations have emerged between central and local government bodies that are geared towards the shared goal of developing Shanghai into a successful IFC. For instance, the concept of a "Financial Safety Zone" was introduced in the early 2000s, providing a platform for "intensive and regular cooperation between central regulators and local government bodies" (Heilmann 2005a.)

Furthermore, the key duties of the FSO also require it "to cooperate with the central supervisory institutes of the central government in implementing national finance-related guidelines, policies, laws and regulations" and "be responsible for the contact between the local government and the financial institutes of the central government and their financial agencies in Shanghai" (Shanghai Municipal People's Government 2002). In this regard, the FSO has established regular "3 + 2" meetings between the FSO, PBOC Shanghai Head Office and the three state financial regulatory authorities (Ji 2008). While non-state actors are also involved in Shanghai's financial policy subsystem, their influence over financial policy-making is typically limited.

Examples of major non-state actors include the Shanghai Banking Association (SBA), a professional, non-profit trade association that represents the interests of Shanghai's banks and financial institutions; members include commercial banks, policy banks, foreign-funded banks, asset management companies and representative offices of foreign financial institutions (Shanghai Banking Association 2012). The Securities Association of China (SAC) performs a similar role for the securities industry at the national level, complimenting the Shanghai Stock Exchange. The interests of the asset management industry are represented by the Asset Management Association of China (AMAC). However, there is little evidence of these associations being able to influence financial policies, whether at the local or central level.

As is the case with most IFCs, international actors are present in Shanghai's financial policy subsystem as well, although their presence and role remain determined by the state. The Shanghai government has established an International Financial Advisory Committee that advises the Shanghai mayor on Shanghai's development as an IFC, based on the input of mostly foreign committee members, which has included the City of London's Policy Chairman (City of London 2013; Sheng 2013). The Mayor is further advised by an International Business Leaders Advisory Council comprising enterprisers from major transnational corporations.

Through this Council, business leaders such as Junichi Ujiie, senior adviser to the board of directors of Nomura Holdings, Inc, and Michael Diekmann, chairman of the board of directors of Allianz S.E., have suggested increasing the participation of foreign financial institutions and liberalization of the RMB in order to boost Shanghai's development as an IFC (Foreign Affairs Office of Shanghai Municipality 2009).

At the central level, the CBRC has established a similar international advisory committee. Such international consultation allows China to learn from international experience and collect policy advice from international experts; it also allows China to anticipate and understand the response of international and foreign actors to its financial policies (Sheng 2013). Yet despite such efforts at incorporating the views of domestic and international non-state actors in Shanghai's financial policymaking process, the continued dominance of state-owned banks and financial institutions suggests an overwhelmingly state-dominated financial policy subsystem in Shanghai.

Importantly, foreign banks and financial institutions are severely under-represented in Shanghai's financial policy subsystem. This is due to government restrictions on foreign bank participation and the scope of their financial activities in Shanghai (Yusuf and Wu 2002). While it has been noted that foreign banks hold the most potential of challenging Chinese state-owned financial institutions by virtue of their immunity from the political consequences of doing so (Chong 2013), they have shown neither interest nor capacity to increase their influence over financial policy-making in Shanghai, choosing instead to further their business interests within Shanghai's existing financial policy subsystem configuration.

While the establishment of the Shanghai free trade zone provides much promise for greater foreign bank participation in its financial markets, the only foreign banks which have been able to operate relatively smoothly in the zone are Citigroup and DBS (Rabinovitch 2013). In contrast to the large number of foreign financial institutions in Hong Kong and Singapore and the strong influence of these institutions in Singapore's financial policy processes, Shanghai's financial policy subsystem features foreign financial institutions to a much lesser extent. In contrast to the ability of banks in Singapore to inform or influence financial policy, foreign financial institutions in Shanghai wield negligible influence over financial policy.

Conclusion

This chapter has discussed Shanghai's development as an IFC, placing particular focus on its historical development, comparative advantages, financial governance model, regulatory regime, the financial policy mix it has used for IFC development, and the financial policy subsystem within which financial policies are formulated and implemented. These discussions have shown that Shanghai's development as an IFC has largely been a state-dominated process that involves both central and local government agencies as well as state-owned financial institutions. Non-state actors play a very limited role in Shanghai's financial governance. This differs markedly from Hong Kong's laissez-faire financial governance approach and Singapore's extensive inclusion of industry actors in its financial policy process.

Financial policies are generally formulated by central government agencies such as the PBC, CBRC, CSRC and CIRC, while the implementation of these policies is carried out by municipal-level government agencies such as the FSO and the Shanghai branches of the four central government regulators. The central government also exerts a significant influence on Shanghai's development as an IFC through its policy banks and state-owned enterprises. While the recently established Shanghai FTZ promises to liberalize foreign entry requirements, the results of this policy move remain to be seen. State-owned banks continue to dominate the free trade zone.

While future developments are likely to involve the entry of more foreign financial institutions, Shanghai's financial policy subsystem is likely to remain state-dominated and development-focused, in the near future at least. This also means that state actors in Shanghai's financial policy subsystem make up a development-oriented advocacy coalition that affects policy mix design by expressing developmental policy beliefs through an ideational channel. As a consequence, Shanghai's financial policy mix is largely comprised of enabling and developmental policy instruments. This is further discussed in the next chapter.

While this necessarily provides a developmental slant to Shanghai's development as an IFC, fledgling steps have been made to introduce more stabilizing policy instruments to the mix, in a bid to improve Shanghai's legal and regulatory infrastructure. However, the impacts of such efforts remain to be seen. Shanghai's financial policy mix largely retains a development orientation, and its financial policy subsystem remains mostly state-dominated.

References

Balis R (2012) The road to Shanghai 2020. American Chamber of Commerce, Shanghai

Bank of Shanghai (2012) 2012 Annual report. Shanghai

BBC News (2013) Shanghai free-trade zone launched. BBC

Beijing Review (1992) Full text of Jiang Zemin's report at 14th Party Congress. In: Beijing Review. http://www.bjreview.com.cn/document/txt/2011-03/29/content_363504.htm. Accessed 21 Jan 2013

Bloomberg (2012) Shanghai aims to become global Yuan Trading Center by 2015. Bloomberg News

Chen X (ed) (2009) Shanghai rising: state power and local transformations in a global megacity. University of Minnesota Press, Minneapolis

Chen G (2013) Li Keqiang fought strong opposition for Shanghai free-trade zone plan. South China Morning Post

Chen X, Orum AM (2009) Shanghai as a new global(izing) city: lessons for and from Shanghai. In: Chen X (ed) Shanghai rising: state power and local transformations in a global megacity. University of Minnesota Press, Minneapolis, pp 237–249

China Securities Regulatory Commission (2008) Shanghai branch. In: China Securities Regulatory Commission Website. http://www.csrc.gov.cn/pub/csrc_en/about/organ/Regionaloffices/200811/t20081122_95860.htm. Accessed 4 Mar 2013

Chong TL (2013) Interview

City of London (2013) Priority areas of focus. In: City London Website. http://www.cityoflondon.gov.uk/business/support-promotion-and-advice/promoting-the-city-internationally/china/Pages/Priority-areas-of-focus.aspx. Accessed 4 Dec 2013

DBS Bank Singapore Economic Research Department (1996) Development of Shanghai as a financial centre: implications for Hong Kong and Singapore. Development Bank of Singapore, Singapore

Duan H, bin Chik AR (2012) Institutional environment, political connection and financial constraints—evidence from private enterprise in China. Bus Manage Res 1:133–140

Foreign Affairs Office of Shanghai Municipality (2009) At the meeting of the International Business Leaders Advisory Council to the Mayor of Shanghai, International think tankers make suggestions for Shanghai strengthening the construction of market system. Shanghai

Gordon RH, Li W (2003) Government as a discriminating monopolist in the financial market: the case of China. J Public Econ 87:283–312

Heilmann S (2005a) Policy-making and political supervision in Shanghai's Financial Industry. J Contemp China 14:643–668

Heilmann S (2005b) Regulatory innovation by Leninist means: Communist Party supervision in China's Financial Industry. China Q 181:1–21

Ho KC (2009) Competitive urban economic policies in global cities: Shanghai through the lens of Singapore. In: Chen X (ed) Rising Shanghai: state power and local transformations in a global megacity. University of Minnesota Press, Minneapolis, pp 73–91

Hong Kong Legislative Council Secretariat (2011) The development of Shanghai as an International Financial Centre. Hong Kong Legislative Council, Hong Kong

Jao YC (2003) Shanghai and Hong Kong as International Financial Centres: historical perspective and contemporary analysis

Jarvis DSL (2011) Race for the money: International Financial Centres in Asia. J Int Relat Dev 14:60–95

Ji X (2008) Shanghai Finance. Thomson Learning

Karmel SM (1994) Emerging securities markets in China: capitalism with Chinese characteristics. China Q 140:1105–1120

Karreman B, van der Knaap B (2012) The geography of equity listing and financial centre competition in mainland China and Hong Kong. J Econ Geogr 12:899–922

Lai H (2006a) Reform and the non-state economy in China: the political economy of liberalization strategies. Palgrave Macmillan, New York

Lai K (2006b) Developing Shanghai as an International Financial Centre: progress and prospects

Lai K (2012) Differentiated markets: Shanghai, Beijing and Hong Kong in China's Financial Centre Network. Urban Stud 49:1275–1296

Lan X (2012a) Setting financial tones: China's financial industry focuses on serving the real economy. Beijing Rev

Lan X (2012b) Money Hub. Beijing Rev

Laurenceson J, Tang KK (2005) Shanghai's development as an International Financial Center. Rev Pac Basin Financ Mark Policies RPBFMP 8:147–166

Leung B, Yim J (2009) Shanghai's future as an International Financial Centre. Hang Seng Bank, Hong Kong

Li LC (1997) Provincial discretion and national power: investment policy in Guangdong and Shanghai, 1978–93. China Q 152:778–804

Li C (2009) Reclaiming the "Head of the Dragon": Shanghai as China's Center for International Finance and Shipping

Liu H (2008) 中国经济特区: 从深圳到上海的特区政策变迁与现代化新路径 China's special economic zones: from Shenzhen to Shanghai: a new path to industrialization, urbanization, globalization and modernization. Shanghai People's Publishing House, Shanghai

McCauley RN, Chan E (2009) Hong Kong and Shanghai: yesterday, today and tomorrow. In: Ito T, Rose AK (eds) Financial sector development in the Pacific Rim. University of Chicago Press, Chicago, pp 13–37

Nottle R (1993) The development of securities markets in China in the 1990s

Palmioli G, Heal A (2014) Structural economic reform in China: the role of the Shanghai free trade zone. UNESCAP, Washington, D.C

Pan L (2006) Shanghai issues 11th Five Year Plan for financial sector. In: Gov.cn. http://english.gov.cn/2006-11/27/content_454961.htm. Accessed 21 Jan 2013

People's Bank of China (2012) 2012 Annual report. Beijing

People's Bank of China, China Banking Regulatory Commission, China Securities Regulatory Commission et al (2011) The 12th Five-year Plan for the Development and Reform of the Financial Industry

Pudong New Area Government (2012) History. In: E-Pudong. http://english.pudong.gov.cn/html/pden/pden_ap_oop_history/List/list_0.htm. Accessed 7 Mar 2013

Rabinovitch S (2013) Global banks cautious on Shanghai free-trade zone. Financ Times

Securities Association of China (2012) Introduction to SAC. In: Securities Association of China Website. http://www.sac.net.cn/en/About_US/Introduction_to_SAC/. Accessed 4 Mar 2013

Shanghai Banking Association (2012) About SBA. In: Shanghai Banking Association Website. http://www.sbacn.org/En/ComDetail.aspx?st=00010001. Accessed 25 Feb 2013

Shanghai Municipal Commission of Commerce (2010) Regulations on promoting the development of an International Financial Centre in the Shanghai Municipality. In: Shanghai Municipal Commission of Commerce Website. http://www.scofcom.gov.cn/engb/227375.htm. Accessed 21 Jan 2013

Shanghai Municipal Government (2010) Shanghai Municipal Office of Finance Service. In: Shanghai Municipal People's Government Website. http://www.shanghai.gov.cn/shanghai/node2718/node27386/node27400/node27848/userobject22ai38993.html

Shanghai Municipal People's Government (2002) Notice of the General Office of Shanghai Municipal People's Government about printing and distributing The "Provisions on the Allotment of Functions, the Set-up of Internal Structure, and The Manning Quotas of Shanghai Municipal Financial Service Office". Shanghai Municipal People's Government, Shanghai

Shanghai Pudong Development Bank (2010) 2010 Annual report. Shanghai

Shanghai Stock Exchange (2010a) Historical review. In: Shanghai Stock Exchange Website. http://edu.sse.com.cn/sseportal/en/c01/c05/c02/p1110/c15010502_p1110.shtml. Accessed 24 Feb 2013

Shanghai Stock Exchange (2010b) Brief Introduction. In: Shanghai Stock Exchange Website. http://edu.sse.com.cn/sseportal/en/c01/p996/c1501_p996.shtml. Accessed 24 Feb 2013

Sheng A (2013) Interview

Subacchi P, Huang H, Molajoni A, Varghese R (2012) Shifting capital: the rise of Financial Centres in Greater China. Chatham House, London

Tong S (2009) Shanghai: aspirations and reality, and implications for Hong Kong

Tsang D (2013) Interview

Wang H (1999) The Asian financial crisis and financial reforms in China. Pac Rev 12:537–556

Wang J (2004) Dancing with Wolves: regulation and deregulation of foreign investment in China's stock market. Asia-Pac Law Policy J 5:1–61

Wei YD, Leung CK (2005) Development zones, foreign investment, and global city formation in Shanghai. Growth Change 36:16–40

Wu F (2000) The global and local dimensions of place-making: remaking Shanghai as a world city. Urban Stud 37:1359–1377

Xiao L (2012) 金融战略与财经论衡: 迈向国际金融中心的上海之路 Financial strategy and economic forum: Shanghai road to International Financial Centre. Shanghai People's Publishing House, Shanghai

Xu X (1998) China's financial system under transition. Macmillan Press Ltd, London

Yang M, Heng MS-H, Lim TS (2010) Shanghai as an International Financial Centre: problems and prospects. East Asian Institute, Singapore

Yatsko P (2001) New Shanghai: the rocky rebirth of China's legendary city, 1st edn. Wiley, New York

Yeandle M (2015) Global Financial Centres Index 17. Z/Yen Group and Qatar Financial Centre Authority, London, UK

Yeandle M, Horne J, Danev N (2011) The Global Financial Centres Index 9. Long Finance, London

Yu M, Pan H (2008) The relationship between politics, institutional environments and private enterprises' access to bank loans

Yusuf S, Wu W (2002) Pathways to a world city: Shanghai rising in an era of globalisation. Urban Stud 39:1213–1240

Zhang W-B (2000) Shanghai: a gateway to China's economic modernization. In: Andersson AE, Andersson DE (eds) Gateways to the global economy. Edward Elgar Publishing Limited, Cheltenham, pp 254–268

上海市《迈向21世紀的上海》課题领导小组编 Shanghai City <Shanghai in the 21st Century> Discussion Group Editorial Group (1995) 迈向 21世紀的上海: 1996–2010年上海经济、社会发展战略研究 Shanghai in the 21st Century: Shanghai's economic and social development strategies in 1996–2010. Shanghai People's Publishing House, Shanghai

陈伟恕 (1993) 论我国银行主体角色的转变 Changes in the general role of China's banks. In: 张恩照, 冯国荣 (eds) "复关'与上海金融 GATT and Shanghai Finance. Shanghai People's Publishing House, Shanghai, pp 40–46

Chapter 7
Comparisons and Analysis

Having discussed the cases of Hong Kong, Singapore and Shanghai, this chapter will provide a comparative analysis of the three IFCs. This comparative analysis aims to take a structured approach to assessing the similarities and differences across the three cases, in the process delineating and addressing some of the structural and causal explanations for these differences and similarities. This is followed by an application of the nested instrumental approach to the three cases. As I have discussed in earlier chapters, existing IFC studies often lack an awareness and sensitivity to the sociopolitical context. I seek to address such limitations through an application of the nested instrumental approach in the second part of this chapter. But first, I will begin with the comparative analysis.

In line with the descriptive metrics applied in Chaps. 4, 5 and 6, this chapter compares the three IFCs across the areas of comparative advantages, financial governance models, regulatory agencies, financial policy instrument mixes and financial policy subsystems. As I will further elaborate below, the results of the comparative analysis can be condensed into a two-by-two matrix, with the three cases occupying one cell each. The matrix is formed by two axes: (1) extent of state intervention in financial markets; (2) influence of industry actors in financial policy. These two axes provide an operationalizable way of measuring and describing policy subsystem configurations in the three cases and categorizing the types of financial policy mixes that arise from different subsystem configurations.

The matrix represents a summary of the comparative analysis and is presented in Table 7.1. As Table 7.1 shows, the three IFCs reflect different extents of state and industry involvement in financial sector development and financial policy, respectively. This is due to each IFC's unique financial policy mix and subsystem configuration, which will be discussed later in this chapter. Table 7.1 also includes the case of London, which is often seen as representative of the neoliberal model of IFC development that is dominant in many Western developed economies. Taken together, London, Hong Kong, Singapore and Shanghai represent four distinct "policy regimes" of financial sector development and governance (Woo 2015b). Before delving into the comparative analysis, it is useful to provide a brief overview of the four regimes identified in Table 7.1.

J.J. Woo, *Business and Politics in Asia's Key Financial Centres*,
DOI 10.1007/978-981-287-985-1_7

Table 7.1 Summary of comparative analysis

	Low state intervention	High state intervention
Industry actors influential in financial policy	**London**	**Singapore**
	Industry interest groups dominant	State-industry "co-creation"
	Stabilizing and industry-centred policy mix	Stabilizing and development-oriented policy mix
Industry actors not influential in financial policy	**Hong Kong**	**Shanghai**
	Limited government intervention; limited industry influence	State-dominated
	Stabilizing policy mix	Development-oriented policy mix

First and in the lower-left cell of Table 7.1, Hong Kong's laissez faire approach of non-interventionist financial governance indicates low state intervention in its financial markets. However, as discussed in Chap. 5, state dominance of Hong Kong's financial policy subsystem means that industry actors are not influential in financial policy-making. This results in a financial policy mix that is largely comprised of stabilizing financial policy instruments, reflecting the HKMA's focus on maintaining financial market stability and its reluctance towards market intervention. This reflects the SAR's commitment to a "big markets, small government" doctrine of financial governance.

In contrast, Singapore's financial policy subsystem is marked by strong state intervention along with heavy involvement of industry actors in financial policy-making. While financial sector development has been a state-led endeavour from the start, industry actors have also been able to influence financial policies through their participation in MAS consultations and membership in a less formal financial governing elite. Such high state intervention in financial markets and strong industry influence over financial policies have resulted in a collaborative "co-creation" of financial policies, the result of which is a financial policy mix that includes the full spectrum of stabilizing, enabling and developmental policy instruments. This reflects the developmental and business interests of both state and industry actors.

While Shanghai's financial policy subsystem similarly exhibits strong state intervention, industry actors in the municipality possess little or no influence over financial policy-making. Given this dominance of state actors and the government's overarching focus on financial and economic development, Shanghai's financial policy mix is largely made up of enabling and developmental policy instruments. Instances where stabilizing policy instruments have been implemented, such as the recent FTZ, are also based on a desire to stimulate financial sector development, in this case attracting foreign investors and financial institutions through improving regulatory stability.

Lastly, low state intervention and strong industry influence on policy-making describe the financial policy subsystem of London, as well as many other Western IFCs which subscribe to a neoliberal model of financial governance. In these IFCs, a fundamental belief in the free market has resulted in a financial policy mix that is largely comprised of stabilizing policy instruments. However, industry actors such as banks and financial conglomerates are highly influential and hence able to influence policy mix design towards their own interests through what is known as "regulatory capture" (Baker 2010). However, I will not focus on London or the neoliberal model of financial governance in this book, having addressed these to some extent elsewhere (Woo 2015b).

Having provided a brief summary of the three cases, I will now proceed with the comparative analysis. The following sections will compare and analyse Hong Kong, Singapore and Shanghai across the areas of comparative advantages, financial governance, regulatory agencies, financial policy mixes and financial policy subsystem configurations. These areas of comparison represent the variables which underpin the comparative analysis provided in Table 7.1, having been condensed into the two comparative metrics of state intervention in financial markets and industry influence over financial policies. What follows below is therefore a more in-depth explication of the comparative analysis results presented in Table 7.1, beginning with a comparison of the three IFCs' comparative advantages.

Comparative Advantages

The three IFCs occupy different niches and play different roles in the global financial markets, although there are some overlaps. Hong Kong is well-established as a loan syndication centre and a gateway into China through its role as leading offshore RMB centre. Singapore has established itself as a leading centre for wealth management and foreign exchange; it has also recently sought to establish itself as an offshore RMB centre and a commodities hub. Shanghai has attained pre-eminence as China's national financial centre, serving domestic business and trading interests. With the recent establishment of a Shanghai free trade zone, Shanghai is also seeking to establish itself as a full-fledged IFC rivalling Hong Kong.

The different roles played by the three IFCs' stem from differences in their comparative advantages. While all three IFCs share similar "natural" or "external" advantages arising from favourable geographical locations and time zones as well as similar histories as colonial port cities, differences in the political systems and developmental strategies or policies across the three IFCs mean that each IFC is characterized by its own unique set of "internal" comparative advantages. They are listed in Table 7.2.

Table 7.2 Comparative advantages

	Hong Kong	Singapore	Shanghai
Robust regulatory infrastructure	X	X	
Rule of law	X	X	
Political and economic stability	X	X	
Sovereign independent state		X	
Deep talent pool	X	X	
Proximity to China	X		X
English as working language	X	X	
Support from Chinese government			X
Strength of domestic economy	X	X	X

As Table 7.2 shows, Hong Kong and Singapore share many similar comparative advantages. Both have established robust and trusted regulatory systems along with a strong commitment to the rule of law, based on similar common law systems derived from their respective British colonial histories. Furthermore, both cities are known for their high levels of political and economic stability. In both cases, such stability is underscored by the longevity and autonomy of the governing regime.

Given its lack of universal suffrage, the Hong Kong government is effectively appointed by the Chinese government and a core group of local elites and granted economic policy autonomy by the Chinese government. While elections are held as part of Singapore's parliamentary system, the ruling People's Action Party has been in the power since independence. Through its dominance over parliament as majority ruling party, the Party possesses significant policy autonomy. This means a firm establishment of the government as a significant and enduring subsystem actor in both cases, as will be discussed in a later section. Lastly, both Hong Kong and Singapore boast a deep pool of financial sector talent and the use of English as an official working languagc.

However, the two IFCs differ on one significant score. Given its geographical location and its position as a Chinese SAR, Hong Kong enjoys close geographical and political proximity to China. Not only does this proximity make Hong Kong the gateway into China's burgeoning markets, it has also contributed to Beijing's decision to grant Hong Kong a head start in its development as leading RMB offshore centre. In contrast, Singapore is an independent sovereign state, granting it "safe haven" status and allowing it to become established as a successful wealth management centre (Koh 2013b). In contrast, Hong Kong's proximity to China and its potential vulnerability to Chinese interference tend to deter fund managers (Fund Manager with a US Asset Management Firm 2013). Given its political distance from China, Singapore does not face this problem.

In contrast to Hong Kong and Singapore, Shanghai is comparatively disadvantaged in terms of its weak rule of law and less established regulatory infrastructure. However, Shanghai possesses a key advantage in terms of its proximity to and strong support from the Chinese central government. As a municipality located within China, Shanghai is firmly situated within China's political regime and economic development. This means that Shanghai's proximity to China both economically and politically surpass that of Hong Kong. While both Hong Kong and Shanghai are technically Chinese IFCs, Shanghai represents a "domestic market engine" focused largely on its internal market while Hong Kong is an "international market engine" by virtue of its convertible currency and highly liberalized financial markets (Tsang 2013).

Nonetheless, all three IFCs enjoy high rates of domestic economic growth, which contributes to the health of each IFC's financial sector. It is important to note that these differences in comparative advantages arise from differences in each IFC's model of financial governance and regulatory agencies. These are discussed in the next section.

Financial Governance and Regulatory Agencies

While financial governance in Hong Kong, Singapore and Shanghai represents three distinct models that involve varying extents of state intervention, differences between the how the regulatory agencies of the three are set up tend to be less stark. Table 7.3 details the financial governance models and regulatory agencies of the three IFCs.

Hong Kong's "big market, small government" approach to financial governance involves minimal government intervention, with any intervention limited to instances of necessity such as crises or market failures. This allows industry actors to drive financial sector development, albeit within the limits of state regulation. In contrast, Singapore's model of financial governance is essentially state-driven with strong industry participation in financial policy processes. Financial policies are jointly "co-created" by the MAS and its industry partners through the latter's involvement in the MAS's consultative processes.

Differences between Hong Kong's and Singapore's financial governance models stem from differences in their philosophies of management, which were in turn historically derived. Hong Kong's laissez faire approach can be traced to its

Table 7.3 Financial governance models and regulatory agencies

	Hong Kong	Singapore	Shanghai
Financial governance	State-facilitated, industry-driven: "big market, small government"	State-led with heavy industry involvement: "policy co-creation"	State-dominated
Regulatory agencies	Single regulator: HKMA	Single regulator: MAS	Multiple regulators: PBC, CSRC, CBRC, CIRC, municipal level regulatory agencies

colonial history and early efforts by the British government to indirectly benefit its own companies operating in the territory, while Singapore's state-driven approach derives from its post-independence focus on ensuring that economic gains accrue to the state (Independent Expert 2013). As a consequence, private entrepreneurs in Hong Kong tend to accumulate economic profits and rents, while such profits tend to accrue to the state in Singapore (Independent Expert 2013).

Hong Kong and Singapore are also characterized by their different underlying "political engines", with the Singaporean government playing the role of a "leader" with its strong central state institutions and the Hong Kong government's role as a "facilitator" enabling the formation of a strong society that is able to adjust and adapt with little government intervention (Pauly 2011). Given that Singapore lacks many of the natural advantages which Hong Kong enjoys, it also had to develop "artificial advantages" through heavy government interventions in order to thrive as an IFC (Topping 2013). As discussed in earlier chapters, this involved state efforts at "niche-creation".

In Shanghai, financial governance is driven by the heavy hand of the state and involves both central and local governments. While the Shanghai municipal government is highly autonomous in economic and financial policy-making, it also receives strong support from the Chinese central government, which has expressed its drive to develop Shanghai as an IFC. However, given its position as a Chinese municipality Shanghai may also need to on occasion "submit to the will of the state (i.e. central government)" (Independent Expert 2013). Shanghai's financial markets are also largely dominated by the politically connected state-owned banks (Chong 2013). This means state dominance in both financial policy-making and financial market participation.

In sum, financial governance across the three cases involves varying degrees of state intervention. Hong Kong's laissez faire model of financial governance requires minimal government intervention, with the state merely facilitating or supporting financial sector development. In contrast, the Singapore state plays a more significant role in leading financial sector development, although financial policies are co-created with industry actors through their extensive involvement in the financial policy process. Shanghai's model of financial governance involves an even greater extent of state intervention, with the state effectively dominating the financial sector through both government agencies and state-owned enterprises.

Differences in the set-up and operations of regulatory agencies across the three cases are more subtle. While Hong Kong's and Singapore's financial sector regulatory activities are each carried out by a single chief regulatory agency, the HKMA and MAS, respectively, the two agencies differ in terms of policy instrument preferences, as discussed in the next section. In contrast, financial sector regulation in Shanghai involves a plethora of regulatory agencies associated with central and local levels of government. Such differences in financial governance models and regulatory agencies have an impact on financial policy mixes and policy subsystem configurations across the three IFCs. The different financial policy mixes used by the governments the three IFCs are discussed next.

Financial Policy Mix

Due to the varying extents of state intervention in financial sector development, as reflected in their differing financial governance models and subsystem configurations, the financial policy mixes of the three IFCs differ in composition and design across the three cases. This means varying weightages of stabilizing, enabling and developmental policy instruments across the three IFCs. More importantly, each IFC's financial policy mix is characterized by a *dominant* type or class of policy instruments that reflects the interests and instrument preferences of dominant subsystem actors.

This means that while a policy mix may feature instances of all three types of instruments in varying weightage, the policy mix itself may be geared towards either financial market stabilization, enablement or development, depending on the type(s) of instruments that are dominant within the policy mix. Each IFC's financial policy mix can therefore be characterized as either stabilizing, enabling and developmental, or various combinations of the three. This is illustrated in Table 7.4.

Given Hong Kong's laissez faire approach to financial governance that limits direct government intervention in markets, the HKMA relies largely on stabilizing financial policies to maintain market stability as well as protect investors and depositors. While enabling financial policies has occasionally been used to encourage the formation of new markets, offshore RMB businesses being the most recent case in point, the HKMA's financial policy mix remains largely comprised of stabilizing policy instruments that enhance Hong Kong's key advantages of stability and reliability. These instruments include developing the financial infrastructure and strict supervision of financial institutions.

In contrast, Singapore's financial policy mix comprises all three types of financial policy instruments. Like Hong Kong, Singapore is renowned for its transparent and reliable regulatory infrastructure as well as its strong rule of law. These are maintained through the MAS's stabilizing policy instruments that involve strict regulation and supervision of financial institutions. However, the government has also employed enabling and developmental policy instruments in order to develop the financial sector. As discussed in Chap. 5, these include establishing the necessary conditions and incentives for new growth markets to emerge, providing direct incentives to existing financial institutions, and encouraging mergers and consolidation among domestic financial institutions.

However, differences between Hong Kong's and Singapore's financial policy mixes can sometimes be subtle. This is particularly so when similar policy instruments are used for different purposes. A key policy instrument used by both

Table 7.4 Financial policy mixes

	Hong Kong	Singapore	Shanghai
Stabilizing	X	X	
Enabling		X	X
Developmental		X	X

Hong Kong and Singapore for the purpose of IFC development is the establishment of tiered bank licensing systems. Hong Kong had established its tiered bank licensing system in response to an increase in the number of unlicensed DTCs, with the aim of ensuring financial market stability and investor protection through the licensing and regulation of these DTCs. In contrast, the Singapore government established its tiered bank licensing system in order to attract foreign banks and at the same time protect or even advance the interests of domestic banks. As such, the tiered bank licensing system is used by the HKMA as a stabilizing policy instrument and by the MAS as an enabling and developmental policy instrument.

Lastly, Shanghai's financial policy mix is largely comprised of enabling and developmental policy instruments. Given Shanghai's role as a key driver of China's economic growth, both the Shanghai municipal government and the Chinese central government have used developmental policies in order to direct financial sector development towards generating national revenues. Enabling policy instruments have also been used to promote the development of specific markets in order to drive Shanghai's overall development as an IFC, with the Shanghai FTZ being a recent example. However, stabilizing policy instruments do not factor heavily in Shanghai's financial policy mix. This has led to perceived weaknesses in Shanghai's legal and regulatory infrastructure.

Importantly, differences in financial policy mix stem from the different policy subsystem configurations that are found in the three cases. As discussed in Chap. 3, dominant subsystem actors tend to influence and affect policy mix design through instrumental and ideational channels, by virtue of their membership in instruments constituencies and advocacy coalitions, respectively. While this causal linkage between subsystem configuration and policy mix design is discussed in greater detail below, the next section provides a comparative analysis of the policy subsystem configurations within each IFC.

Financial Policy Subsystem

Policy subsystems can be characterized by their level of complexity. Complex subsystems are typically made up of a large set of actors, with their membership in the subsystem fluid and changing. Such high turnover of subsystem actors also reflects their limited influence over policy. In contrast, a simple subsystem is characterized by the enduring presence of a small but often influential group of dominant actors. Furthermore, as discussed earlier, dominant actors in a subsystem often exercise their influence over policy through their membership in advocacy coalitions or instruments constituencies. Table 7.5 provides an overview of the financial policy subsystems of the three IFCs.

Given its commitment to a laissez faire model of financial governance and limited government intervention in markets, Hong Kong's financial policy subsystem displays a high degree of complexity. This is reflected in its large number of

Table 7.5 Financial policy subsystems

Dimensions	Hong Kong	Singapore	Shanghai
Number of members	Large	Moderate	Small
Homogeneity of membership	Low	Moderate	High
Influence of non-state actors on financial policy	Low	High	Low
State dominance over financial policy	High	Moderate	High

subsystem actors. Furthermore, homogeneity of subsystem membership is low, with subsystem actors including a wide array of state, private sector and other non-state actors. Yet paradoxically, financial policy-making in Hong Kong is dominated by the HKMA. This means that industry and non-state actors possess little influence over financial policies, with their presence in Hong Kong's financial policy subsystem dependent upon the availability of business opportunities.

While the HKMA does engage in industry consultation, these are largely seen as more of a mechanism for the dissemination of policy information rather than a means through which industry actors may actually influence financial policies (Topping 2013; Chong 2013). This reflects Hong Kong's centralized and state-dominated policy process, with policy-makers insulated from political and societal influence (Harris 1988; Scott 1989; Painter 2005). This arguably lowers the risk of regulatory capture, although this state dominance over financial policy is not always obvious, given the Hong Kong government's commitment to laissez faire approaches to financial governance. This leaves industry actors with a significant amount of space and leeway to develop their business interests, in the process driving financial sector development through their participation in Hong Kong's free and open markets.

Furthermore, the HKMA's almost exclusive preference for stabilizing instruments suggests the presence of an instruments constituency that advocates the use of stabilizing financial policy instruments. Similarly, the Hong Kong government's adherence to free market principles derives from the presence of an advocacy coalition formed around such principles. Specifically, free market principles make up the coalition's policy core beliefs while the belief that stabilizing instruments will allow these policy core beliefs to be fulfilled make up the coalition's secondary beliefs. Hong Kong's dominant state actors are thus simultaneously members of a stabilizing instruments constituency and an advocacy coalition based on a belief in free market principles.

In contrast to Hong Kong, Singapore's financial subsystem features less actors but comprises a less homogenous or more diverse mix of actors formed around an enduring "governing elite". Importantly, both state and non-state actors are influential in financial policy-making. While the MAS leads financial sector development with its full array of stabilizing, enabling and developmental financial policy instruments, private sector industry actors are also heavily involved in financial policy-making through the MAS's extensive consultative processes. Given the MAS's concerns with the implementability of its financial policies and its focus on financial sector development, state and industry policy objectives are closely aligned. This allows a "co-creation" of financial policies by the MAS, its various non-state and industry partners, through formal and informal consultative mechanisms.

As such, Singapore's financial policy subsystem involves the state, industry and other non-state actors, with all three sets of actors involved financially in policy "co-creation", although the state retains its leadership over financial policy-making under the aegis of the MAS. Given that the MAS employs a wide array of stabilizing, enabling and developmental financial policy instruments in its regulation and promotion of Singapore's financial markets, there is no identifiable instruments constituency in Singapore. Rather, instruments are selected based on their efficacy in attaining desired policy outputs. In the case of Singapore, these policy outputs include both financial sector development and market stability.

Given this focus on financial market development and stability, dominant subsystem actors in Singapore, both state and non-state, belong to an advocacy coalition formed around development-oriented policy core beliefs, with secondary beliefs predicated upon the efficacy of stabilizing and development-oriented instruments in attaining developmental goals. As later sections will show, this has resulted in the design of a diverse and varied financial policy mix that includes a wide array of stabilizing, enabling, and developmental financial policy instruments, reflecting the interests and instruments preferences of both state and non-state actors in Singapore's "governing elite".

In contrast to the highly internationalized financial markets in Hong Kong and Singapore, Shanghai's financial markets are by and large dominated by state-owned institutions. This is due to the significance of Shanghai's financial sector as a key driver for overall national economic development. Indeed, the central government sees Shanghai's financial markets as a means for "propelling domestic economic growth" (Pauly 2011). As a consequence, both central and local governments have a strong interest in ensuring Shanghai's success as an IFC. More importantly, this dominance of state actors means that Shanghai's financial policy subsystem comprises fewer members and a higher degree of actor homogeneity when compared to Hong Kong and Singapore.

Aside from its limited and homogenous subsystem membership, the limited role of the private sector in financial policy-making also makes Shanghai's financial policy subsystem relatively simpler, as compared to both Hong Kong and Singapore. While financial policies are formulated and implemented by state actors including the various financial regulatory agencies, state-owned financial institutions dominate Shanghai's financial markets by virtue of their political connections (Chong 2013). However, the Shanghai government has on occasion consulted external and internal experts through various consultative and advisory committees (Sheng 2013; Independent Expert 2013).

Having said that, Shanghai's financial policy subsystem has recently become slightly more complex, with the implementation of the Shanghai FTZ. Under the FTZ, restrictions on foreign participation in Shanghai's financial sector have been liberalized, bringing forth an influx of foreign financial institutions. However, these foreign financial institutions do not possess any influence over the state's financial policy-making processes. Given the dominance of state actors in Shanghai's financial policy subsystem and the state's overarching focus on financial sector growth and national economic development, developmental and enabling instruments are often selected based on policy-makers' interest and desire to fulfil developmental goals. Yet as the recent establishment of the Shanghai FTZ has shown, the state is not averse to implementing stabilizing policy instruments, so long as these are shown to be beneficial for Shanghai's development as an IFC.

This focus on development and the consequent selection of instruments based on a need to fulfil developmental goals suggests the absence of a strong instruments constituency in Shanghai. Rather, the focus of Shanghai's dominant state actors on financial sector growth and national economic development suggests the presence of an advocacy coalition, with developmental and state ideologies making up its policy core beliefs. Secondary beliefs are thus predicated upon the perceived efficacy of particular instruments in the pursuit of developmental and state objectives. Given the dominance of state actors in Shanghai's financial policy subsystem, such a coalition comprises government agencies of all levels as well as state-owned enterprises.

In sum, Hong Kong, Singapore and Shanghai differ across the areas of comparative advantages, financial governance model and regulatory agencies, financial policy mix and financial policy subsystem. Furthermore, each IFC's unique policy subsystem configuration affects the policy mix developed and used by its government in attaining specified policy outputs. These linkages between policy subsystem configuration and policy mix design are further explored in the next section, which applies the nested instrumental approach introduced in Chap. 3 to the three cases.

Application of the Nested Instrumental Approach

As discussed in earlier chapters, the existing IFC literature does not sufficiently address the causal linkages between the political economic context and financial policy design. While public policy theory provides the foundation for such studies, in the form of the policy subsystems and policy instruments approaches, the separate development of such approaches within their individual silos does not lend easily to conceptual integration. Such integration is necessary in order that the impacts of context on policy, and vice versa, can be studied. The nested instrumental approach presents a useful framework that combines the subsystems and instruments approach for such integrative studies.

While the nested instrumental approach has been discussed in Chap. 3, the remainder of this chapter will focus on applying it to the three cases. This entails studying the case material through the lens of the nested instrumental approach, providing a structured and nuanced understanding of IFC development and success. This in turn contributes to the explanatory strength of the approach, contributing to its potential as a theoretically driven framework for analysis. In doing so, the nested instrumental approach aims to provide an integrated approach to understanding IFC development that accounts for both political context and policy considerations in financial policy. An illustrated overview of the nested instrumental approach is reproduced in Fig. 7.1.

To recapitulate from Chap. 3, policy subsystem configurations define policy mix design, with dominant actors shaping a policy mix around their preferences, interests and beliefs. Policy mixes in turn determine the achievement of policy outputs through the application of policy instruments to a policy issue. This means that causal linkages exist between policy subsystem configuration and policy mix design, as well as between policy mix design and policy output. Policy subsystem configurations influence and affect policy mix design through the actions of dominant subsystem actors, exercised through instrumental and ideational channels that involve varying levels of participation in instruments constituencies and advocacy coalitions.

Policy mix design in turn determines the successful attainment of desired policy outputs. Policy mixes are designed to comprise stabilizing, enabling or developmental financial policy instruments in varying weightage, with instruments choice related to the type of policy output which dominant subsystem actors choose to pursue, in this case either financial stability or IFC development. Hence, both causal linkages are driven by a logic of "nested instrumentality", with the use of policy instruments centring the study of policy around a means-ends dichotomy and policy subsystem configurations serving to "nest" policy instruments within the wider political economic context.

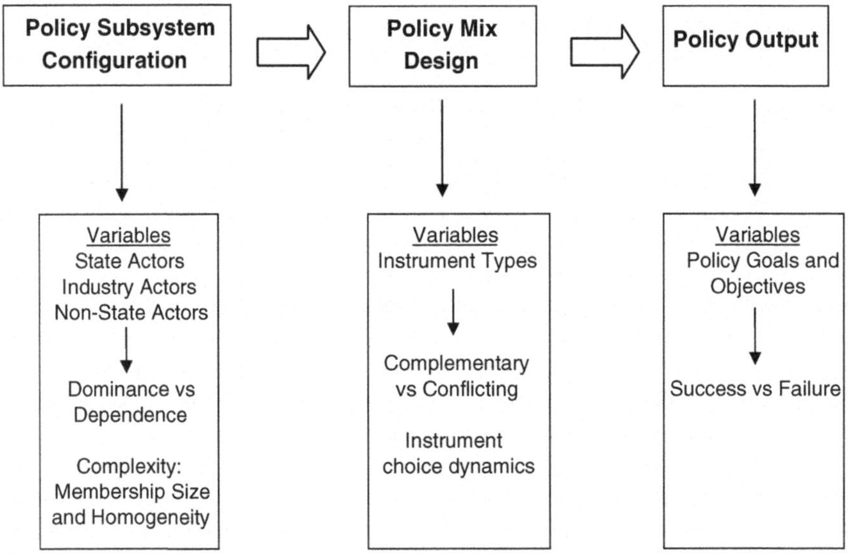

Fig. 7.1 Nested instrumental approach

According to the nested instrumental approach, an IFC's policy subsystem configuration results in the design of a unique policy mix that reflects and caters to the political economic context of that subsystem, with the implementation of such nested policy mixes geared towards the attainment of a desired policy output. In the cases of Hong Kong, Singapore and Shanghai, policy outputs are relatively clear and homogenous: all three cities are focused on attaining IFC success, and all three have attained comparable levels of success. However, the three cases differ in terms of their political systems and economic conditions, as reflected in their different policy subsystem configurations. There is therefore a need for clearer explication of how the political economic context of an IFC impacts policy success.

As I will discuss below, IFC success in all three cases is dependent upon the successful design and implementation of financial policy mixes, which in turn depends on existing subsystem configurations. In other words, different subsystem configurations across the three cases shape or determine the design of different policy mixes, in terms of the balance of stabilizing, developmental and enabling financial policy instruments. It is the core argument of this book that the nested instrumentality that defines causal linkages between subsystem configuration and policy mix design determines IFC success. The remainder of this chapter applies the nested instrumental approach to the three cases. Conclusions and implications for public policy theoretical development will then be discussed.

Hong Kong

Financial policy in Hong Kong is characterized by the government's "big markets, small government" doctrine that involves limited government intervention and as a consequence, a financial policy mix that is largely comprised of stabilizing policy instruments. Enabling and developmental instruments that typically reflect significant government intervention do not factor heavily in Hong Kong's financial policy mix. Given the government's predisposition towards laissez faire approaches, financial policy-making in Hong Kong is geared towards achieving the policy outputs of financial sector stability and investor protection. Figure 7.2 provides an overview of Hong Kong's IFC development through the lens of the nested instrumental approach.

As discussed in Chap. 4, financial policy-making in Hong Kong lies within the sole province of the government. While the HKMA carries out consultations and other interactions with industry actors, such consultations have been seen to represent a channel through which the government informs industry of impending policies rather than as a means of collecting industry feedback and policy inputs. Government agencies, specifically the HKMA, remain the dominant subsystem actors in financial policy-making. While industry actors remain important driving financial sector development, they typically operate within the regulatory boundaries established by the HKMA and possess very limited influence over financial policy-making. Other non-state actors such as experts and academics are

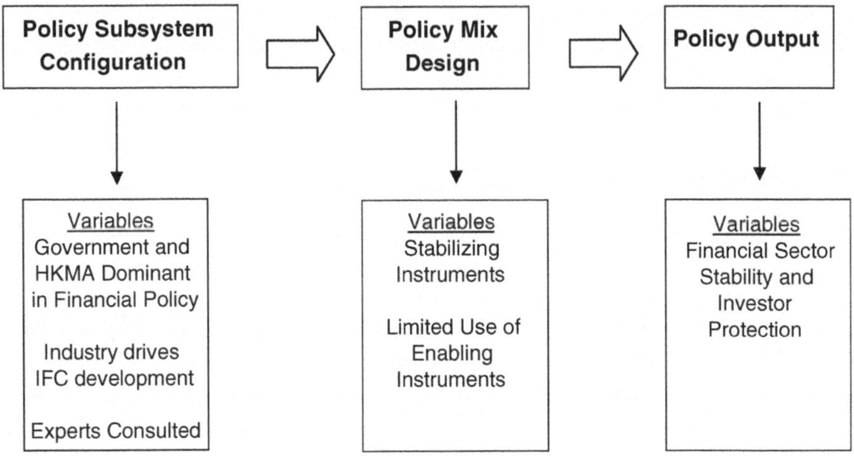

Fig. 7.2 Hong Kong's nested instrumental framework

occasionally consulted by the government and the HKMA, although their influence over financial policy is also limited.

Given the government's predisposition towards laissez faire approaches and its commitment to the "big market, small government" doctrine, Hong Kong's financial policy mix largely comprises stabilizing instruments that aim to maintain financial system stability and investor protection, thereby providing the fundamental "software" necessary for financial sector development (Chong 2013). This focus on providing the infrastructure or environmental conditions necessary for financial market stability stands in contrast to Singapore's and Shanghai's developmental and enabling policies that aim to channel resources or advantages to specific markets or sectors.

While enabling instruments have on occasion been used to stimulate the development of new markets, such as the government's more recent efforts to establish the necessary infrastructure and conditions for the establishment of offshore RMB business in Hong Kong, government intervention in financial markets remains largely limited to instances of market failure. Furthermore, past HKMA interventions in the market have also been justified as means to ensure systemic stability and do not contradict with the government's commitment to laissez faire (Sheng 2013.) In short, Hong Kong's financial policy mix is largely skewed towards stabilizing policy instruments.

The government's dominance over financial policy-making and the limited influence of industry and other non-state actors over policy also serves to reinforce the stabilizing character of Hong Kong's financial policy mix. With industry actors possessing limited influence over financial policy-making, Hong Kong's financial policy mix does not reflect or cater to specific industry interests. As shown in the case of Singapore, enabling and developmental instruments tend to reflect the demands of industry for financial policies that contribute to their business interests

(Former Senior Policy-maker 2013) or minimize costs of regulatory compliance (Menon 2013b). The dominance of stabilizing instruments and relative under-representation of enabling and developmental instruments in Hong Kong's financial policy mix thus reflects a lack of input or influence from the private sector.

In sum, the dominance of the state in Hong Kong's financial policy subsystem and the focus of these dominant state actors on laissez faire approaches have resulted in a policy subsystem configured around the government's chief role as regulator and the industry as drivers of financial sector development within the regulatory purview of the state. As a consequence of this stability-focused and regulation-based subsystem configuration, Hong Kong's financial policy mix predominantly comprises stabilizing instruments and excludes more "industry-friendly" enabling and developmental instruments. This has allowed it to achieve a high level of financial market stability and investor protection.

Singapore

In contrast to Hong Kong, financial policy-making in Singapore involves a greater of state intervention. However, state intervention is complemented by industry participation in financial policy-making. Industry and other non-state actors are highly involved in financial policy-making through various channels of formal and informal consultative processes. This "co-creation" of policy by state and industry actors reflects the presence of a "governing elite" comprising state and non-state actors. Reflecting the interest of both state and non-state actors, Singapore's financial policy mix comprises a full array of stabilizing, enabling and developmental financial policy instruments that aims to achieve both financial sector stability and IFC development or industry growth.

This "nesting" of Singapore financial policy mix and its policy outputs within the context of its policy subsystem is illustrated in Fig. 7.3.

As Singapore's lead agency for financial sector policy and development, the MAS has consistently involved industry actors in its financial policies through various formal and informal consultative processes. These include consultative and advisory committees as well as informal interactions between regulators and financial sector professionals. Other non-state actors such as academics have also been included in many of these consultative processes. These were discussed in Chap. 5. More importantly, this diverse array of policy actors has resulted in the co-dominance of Singapore's financial policy subsystem by state and industry actors. As a consequence, state and industry actors tend to "co-create" financial polices. Inputs from other non-state actors such as academics are often also solicited and factored into the MAS's policies.

The MAS's financial policy mix is reflective of the interests and needs of both state and industry. While the MAS's overriding mandate or goal is that of financial sector stability, it is also tasked with developing or promoting Singapore as an IFC (Menon 2013b). In order to attain its dual goals of stability and development,

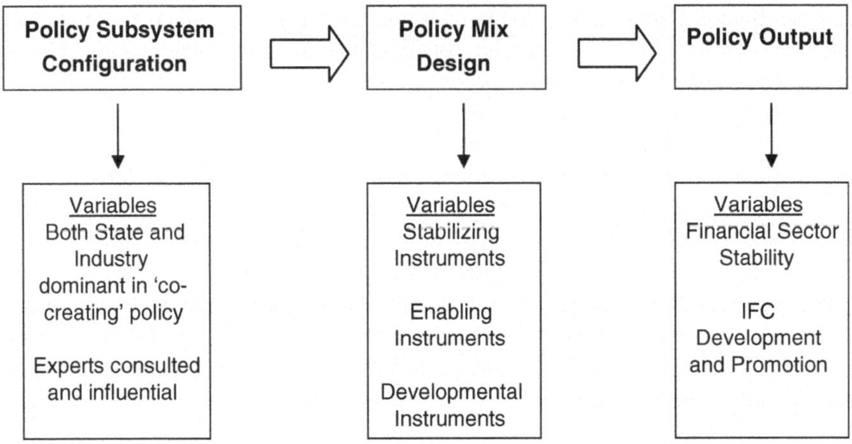

Fig. 7.3 Singapore's nested instrumental framework

Singapore's financial policy mix comprises a full spectrum stabilizing, enabling and developmental financial policy instruments. While stabilizing instruments are typical of most IFCs seeking to ensure financial sector stability and investor protection, enabling and developmental instruments are reflective of both state developmental goals and industry needs.

More importantly, Singapore's financial policy mix reflects the co-dominance of state and industry actors in the financial policy subsystem, with the state focused on providing suitable incentives and environmental factors for the maintenance of a thriving financial system and the industry in turn providing inputs on the form and substance of financial policies that are necessary for financial institutions to contribute to Singapore's continued success as an IFC. In particular, industry actors tend to recommend and promote policies that enhance their business prospects (Former Senior Policy-maker 2013; Koh 2013b) or minimize costs of regulatory compliance (Senior Banker 2013; Menon 2013b).

However, the MAS's desired policy outputs of financial sector stability and IFC development remain defined by the state (Former Senior Policy-maker 2013; Koh 2013b; Menon 2013b). This means that the co-dominance of state and industry in financial policy-making and its inherent "co-creation" of policy is deliberately designed by the state for the purpose of achieving state developmental goals. However, this does not reduce the industry's influence over or contributions to financial policies. Financial policy co-creation remains driven by the coinciding goals of state and industry, with both desiring greater financial sector stability and development for their respective aims of national economic development and business continuity.

In short, Singapore's policy subsystem is configured around a "governing elite" made up of state and industry actors. Such a subsystem configuration has resulted in the design of a financial policy mix that comprises stabilizing, enabling and developmental instruments, reflecting the goals and interests of both state and industry actors. However, industry participation or involvement is deliberately designed into the MAS's consultative processes. Hence, the government retains overall influence over the formation of Singapore's subsystem configuration through its inclusion of industry actors into its policy deliberations and its key role in defining the belief structure and norms underpinning this subsystem. Nonetheless, state and industry goals often coincide, which facilitates financial policy co-creation.

Shanghai

Compared to Singapore, financial policy-making in Shanghai is even more state-centric, with the municipality's financial policy subsystem largely dominated by state actors. However, conceptions of the state in Shanghai are necessarily more complex than both Singapore and Hong Kong, given the presence of both central and local level governmental actors. With the State Council aiming to turn Shanghai into a leading trade, finance and shipping hub by 2020, central government involvement in Shanghai's financial sector development is predicated upon the municipality's contribution to national economic development. Shanghai's financial policy mix reflects these developmental concerns by including enabling and developmental instruments that aim to develop and promote Shanghai as an IFC.

However, stabilizing instruments remain weakly represented in the mix, with Shanghai's rule of law and regulatory infrastructure perceived to be relatively weak. Nonetheless, the government has more recently shown a greater interest in improving Shanghai's regulatory infrastructure and its compliance to international regulatory standards (Sheng 2013). Despite such fledgling efforts at incorporating stabilizing instruments into Shanghai's financial policy mix, enabling and developmental instruments remain dominant in Shanghai's financial policy mix. Figure 7.4 provides an illustration of a nested instrumental approach to understanding Shanghai's development as an IFC.

Shanghai's financial policy subsystem is configured around the dominance of the state, with both central and local level government actors heavily involved in its development as an IFC. This is due to the significance of Shanghai's role in China's economic development and reform process (Wall 1993; Tian 1996). The recent establishment of a free trade zone in Shanghai, along with the expected liberalization of the RMB and interest rates, reinforces Shanghai's leading role in China's economic reform and experimentations with new reform measures. Given Shanghai's central position in national economic development, both the central and municipal governments are highly involved in developing Shanghai as an IFC. Furthermore, state-owned financial institutions exert a near-monopoly over Shanghai's financial markets (Chong 2013).

Given this prevailing presence of government agencies and state-owned firms, Shanghai's financial policy subsystem is essentially state-dominated. Both

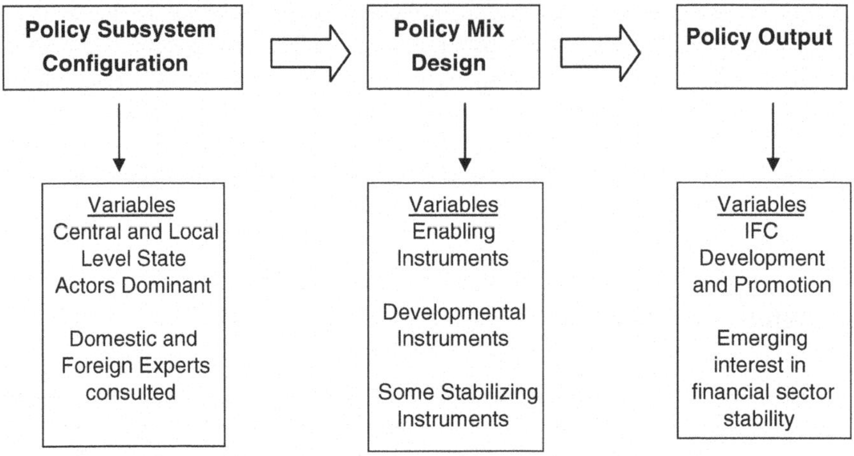

Fig. 7.4 Shanghai's nested instrumental framework

government agencies and state-owned financial institutions are highly influential over financial policy-making through their roles as dominant subsystem actors. While the government has introduced various consultative and advisory committees that aim to collect feedback and inputs from domestic and foreign experts, the influence of these experts on financial policy-making in Shanghai remains limited. Private sector actors, whether domestic or foreign, also exercise negligible influence over financial policy-making in Shanghai. Rather, industry actors tend to be dependent upon state policy for their ability to operate or thrive in Shanghai's financial markets.

As a result of the state-dominated and development-oriented aspects of Shanghai's financial policy subsystem, Shanghai's financial policy mix is highly development-oriented. This means that Shanghai's financial policy mix largely comprises enabling and developmental policy instruments geared towards the development of Shanghai's financial markets. Enabling and developmental instruments are favoured by the government, as these allow the state to directly determine or influence the growth and development of Shanghai's financial sector. An instance of this is the recent establishment of the Shanghai free trade zone, with the associated promulgation of various enabling and developmental instruments such as the liberalization of interest rates and the lowering of entry requirements for foreign banks and financial institutions.

However, Shanghai is perceived to be relatively weak in its rule of law and regulatory infrastructure (Chong 2013). This is reflected in the relative under-representation of stabilizing policy instruments in Shanghai's financial policy mix. Nonetheless, the Shanghai government has recently taken up an interest in enhancing its regulatory framework and improving compliance to international regulatory standards (Sheng 2013). This means that stabilizing policy instruments are beginning to be incorporated into Shanghai's financial policy mix. Despite this emerging interest in stabilizing instruments, Shanghai's financial policy mix still remains largely dominated by enabling and developmental instruments. This is reinforced by the government's desired policy outputs of IFC development and promotion, albeit with an emerging interest in ensuring financial sector stability. Like Shanghai's financial policy mix, these policy outputs are also state-determined.

In sum, Shanghai's state-dominated financial policy subsystem configuration has resulted in a highly development-oriented financial policy mix that comprises mostly enabling and developmental instruments. This is due to the central and municipal governments' desires to develop Shanghai into a leading IFC by 2020 through active state interventions in the form of enabling and developmental financial policies. Given the dominance of state actors in Shanghai's financial policy subsystem, the design of its financial policy mix is reflective of the state's goals and ambitions for Shanghai as an IFC, with its policy output essentially focused on IFC development.

Conclusion

This chapter has provided a comparative analysis of Hong Kong, Singapore and Shanghai. It has also developed an in-depth application of the nested instrumental approach to the three cases. The comparative analysis has shown how the three IFCs differ across the areas of comparative advantages, financial governance model, policy subsystem configuration and financial policy mix. As shown in Table 7.1, these differences stem from differing extents of state and industry involvement in financial policy-making, which means different combinations of dominant subsystem actors across the three cases. This has necessitated an application of the nested instrumental approach to the three cases, in order to derive a clearer understanding of the impacts and influence of policy subsystem configuration, as defined by dominance–dependence relations between subsystem actors, on policy mix design.

This chapter's application of the nested instrumental approach to the three cases has served two important purposes. First, it has provided empirical backing to the nested instrumental approach, ensuring that this approach is practicable as a useful tool or framework for policy analysis. Second, applying the nested instrumental approach to the three cases has allowed for a deeper and more structured analysis of the three cases. The nested instrumental approach has therefore proven to be a useful framework for analysis, around which case data can be structured and comparative analysis carried out. Importantly, it has combined the insights of the policy instruments and policy subsystems approaches. This allows it to draw on the insights of both approaches and at the same time, address their individual limitations and shortcomings.

In combining the context-sensitivity of the subsystems approach with the instruments approach's focus on policy tools and means, the nested instrumental approach provides a more accurate understanding of the policy and politics of IFC development. Hopefully, this helps address the limitations and gaps in the existing IFC literature, as discussed in Chap. 2. More importantly, the nested instrumental approach presents a useful way of thinking about how policy and politics are intertwined. Understanding the policy process devoid of politics and vice versa presents a danger of omitted variable bias and more fundamentally, results in contextually sterile analyses that may not be relevant to real-world public policy practitioners.

By melding policy and politics, the nested instrumental approach provides an analytical framework that ensures relevance in its analysis and provides policy practitioners with a more structured way of understanding policy-making and policy design within the political economic context of the policy subsystem. In doing so, it encourages policy-makers and policy designers to be cognizant of the political economic context within which they operate. This will encourage the development of a financial policy process that is more attuned to political economic realities and nuances on the ground. The nested instrumental approach also provides policy scholars with a potentially useful tool for policy analysis. More importantly, it provides a useful first step towards further developments in public policy theory.

References

Baker A (2010) Restraining regulatory capture? Anglo-America, crisis politics and trajectories of change in global financial governance. Int Aff 86:647–663

Chong TL (2013) Interview

Fund Manager with a US Asset Management Firm (2013) Interview

Former Senior Policymaker (2013) Interview

Harris PB (1988) Hong Kong: a study in bureaucratic politics. Macmillan, Hong Kong

Independent Expert (2013) Interview

Koh YG (2013b) Interview

Menon R (2013b) Interview

Painter M (2005) Transforming the administrative state: reform in Hong Kong and the future of the developmental state. Public Adm Rev 65:335–346

Pauly LW (2011) Hong Kong's international financial centre: retrospect and prospect. Savantas Policy Institute, Hong Kong

Scott I (1989) Administration in a small capitalist state: the Hong Kong experience. Public Adm Dev 9:185–199

Senior Banker (2013) Interview

Sheng A (2013) Interview

Tian G (1996) Shanghai's role in the economic development of China: reform of foreign trade and investment. Praeger, Westport

Topping S (2013) Interview

Tsang D (2013) Interview

Wall D (1993) China's economic reform and opening-up process: the role of the special economic zones. Dev Policy Rev 11:243–260

Woo JJ (2015b) Beyond the neoliberal orthodoxy: alternative financial policy regimes in Asia's financial centres

Chapter 8
Conclusions

This book had set out to understand how Hong Kong, Singapore and Shanghai have achieved their individual successes as IFCs. In Chap. 1, two research questions were posed, the first question is how have Hong Kong, Singapore and Shanghai achieved their current levels of success as IFCs, and the second question relates to how these three IFCs managed to attain their comparable levels of success despite differences in their political-economic conditions. These two questions have driven the research behind this book.

This book has sought to answer both questions through the nested instrumental approach. This involved drawing on the theoretical insights of the policy subsystems and policy instruments approaches, the result of which was a more integrative framework of analysis which was then applied to the analysis of the three IFCs. This application of the nested instrumental approach has allowed me to articulate the core argument of this book. Specifically, I have found that relations of dominance and dependence among actors within a policy subsystem configuration influence policy mix design, with policy mixes reflecting and catering to the interests and instrument preferences of dominance subsystem actors. I will provide a more in-depth recapitulation of this book's findings below.

In the process of answering these two research questions, several significant limitations in the existing literature were also encountered. Specifically, the existing IFC literature continues to place an intellectual premium on structural economic factors and does not sufficiently address the sociopolitical context within which IFCs exist. This has further resulted in an over-statement of an assumed convergence in models or modes of IFC development and financial governance. On the theoretical side of things, this book has shown how the policy subsystems approach lacks specificity in its understanding of policy means, choosing to base its analysis on a broader systemic level. What the policy instruments approach makes up for in specificity and depth, it lacks in contextual sensitivity and breadth.

This book was motivated by these gaps in the existing empirical (IFCs) and theoretical (policy subsystems and policy instruments) literatures. By introducing and applying the nested instrumental approach, I have sought to provide a closer analysis of the politics and policy of IFC development in the three cities. The approach also provides a useful foundation for further theoretical development, with the aim of developing more integrative and contextually nuanced frameworks

J.J. Woo, *Business and Politics in Asia's Key Financial Centres*,
DOI 10.1007/978-981-287-985-1_8

of policy analysis. The remainder of this chapter provides a summary of this book's findings, its implications for policy-makers, contributions to the existing IFC and public policy literature, as well as issues for further research.

Summary of Findings

Based on primary and secondary data collected and an application of the nested instrumental approach to the case material, I argue that differences in policy subsystem configurations across the three cases have resulted in the formulation and design of policy mixes comprising stabilizing, developmental and enabling policies in varying weightages. Each policy mix reflects the interests and instrument preferences of its dominant subsystem actors, given their influence on policy mix design. Policy mixes are in turn applied to the attainment of policy outputs, which are also defined by dominant subsystem actors.

In other words, the ways in which dominant actors are arrayed within a subsystem configuration result in the design of policy mixes that reflect the interests and instrument preferences of these dominant actors. Importantly, the interaction of interests and instrument preferences impacts policy mix design. For instance, both Hong Kong and Shanghai exhibit state dominance over financial policy-making. However, state dominance is filtered through the Hong Kong government's laissez faire approach and the Shanghai government's development orientation to result in Hong Kong's stabilizing policy mix and Shanghai's development-oriented policy mix, respectively.

The formulation of these three different financial policy mixes suggests that three different processes of financial policy are at work. This stems from differences in the three IFCs' policy subsystem configurations, manifesting in different policy mixes that reflect and are tailored to the political-economic context of each IFC's policy subsystem. Differences in subsystem configuration are also reflected in a focus on different policy outputs across the three IFCs. While all three IFCs have been deemed successful by IFC rankings and hierarchies (Poon 2003; Poon et al. 2004; Yeandle and Dranev 2013), it is important to note that models of IFC development and desired policy outputs vary across the three cases.

First, Hong Kong operates on a financial governance system of "big markets, small government" that involves a laissez faire approach to financial governance, with government interventions limited to instances of necessity or market failure. Paradoxically, the government's commitment to laissez faire also instates its dominance over financial policy-making, given that such a laissez faire approach requires policy-makers to be impartial to industry demands and influence. As such, Hong Kong's financial policy subsystem is dominated by government agencies such as the HKMA. While industry actors play an important role in driving Hong Kong's financial sector development, their activities remain subsumed within the regulatory overview of the state. Other non-state actors possess limited influence over financial policy-making.

In other words, Hong Kong's financial policy subsystem is configured around a dominant state that is committed to free market principles and a laissez faire model of financial governance. This has resulted in the design of a financial policy mix that largely comprises stabilizing policy instruments, with little or no inclusion of enabling and developmental instruments that would usually involve more extensive government intervention in markets and reflect specific industry interests. Given this focus on stabilizing instruments and laissez faire principles, the Hong Kong government is mostly focused on attaining the policy outputs of financial market stability and investor protection. This focus on financial market stability and the consequent use of stabilizing instruments have been the basis of Hong Kong's key comparative advantages as an IFC, namely its robust legal and regulatory infrastructure as well as political and economic stability, both of which are underpinned by a strong rule of law.

In contrast, IFC development in Singapore involves a larger extent of state intervention; Singapore's initial formation as an IFC was essentially a state-driven initiative. However, industry and other non-state actors have since achieved strong involvement in financial policy-making through the MAS's various consultative channels as well as the participation of select industry and non-state actors in Singapore's "governing elite". By the MAS's own reckoning, financial policy-making involves a "co-creation" (Former Senior Regulatory Official 2013) of policy by state and industry actors. This means that Singapore's financial policy subsystem is configured around the co-dominance of state and industry actors, with other non-state actors such as experts and academics providing significant inputs to financial policies.

However, it is important to note that this state-industry co-dominance of financial policy-making does not necessarily mean equal levels of authority or status among actors. Financial policy-making in Singapore remains state-led, with the MAS continuing to occupy a peak position in Singapore's financial policy subsystem. As a consequence of this collaboration of state and industry actors in financial policy-making, Singapore's financial policy mix comprises a wide array of stabilizing, enabling and developmental policy instruments. This reflects the MAS's dual goals of financial market stabilization and IFC development. Furthermore, the inclusion of enabling and developmental policy instruments can also be seen as a consequence of industry involvement in policy-making, given that these policies are particularly beneficial to the interests of industry and hence reflect their inputs.

As interviews have shown, it is in fact the deliberate design of the MAS that its policies should include the inputs of industry and hence provide the conditions deemed necessary by industry actors for their success, which in turn contributes to Singapore's overall success as an IFC (Former Senior Regulatory Official 2013; Koh 2013b; Menon 2013b). As a result of industry input in financial policy-making and the MAS's dual goals of stabilization and development, financial policy-makers in Singapore are focused on achieving the two policy outputs of financial market stability and IFC development.

Relative to Singapore, financial governance in Shanghai involves an even larger extent of state involvement. Given the Chinese government's ambitions of developing Shanghai into a full-fledged IFC by 2020, both central and municipal governments are involved in developing Shanghai as an IFC. Furthermore, Shanghai's financial markets are largely dominated by state-owned enterprises, while foreign participation remains limited. However, the recent establishment of a free trade zone in Shanghai portends a loosening of these restrictions and the entry of more foreign financial institutions. Nonetheless, both the Chinese central government and the Shanghai municipal government have continued to maintain their control over financial policy-making.

As a consequence, Shanghai's financial policy subsystem is configured around this state dominance, with dominant state actors including both central and municipal governments, their related regulatory agencies, as well as state-owned enterprises that include the "big four" state-owned commercial banks and three main policy banks. Given this dominance of the state over financial policy-making and that of state-owned enterprises in the financial markets, private sector industry players possess little influence over policy. Rather, they are dependent upon the state's financial policies for their survival. While other non-state actors such as experts and academics have been involved in the government's various advisory committees both at the central and municipal level, their actual influence over policy has also been found to be limited.

Shanghai's state-driven financial policy subsystem as well as the Chinese central government's focus on developing Shanghai as an IFC and maintaining its contribution to China's overall economic development means that Shanghai's financial policy mix is necessarily development-oriented, comprising mostly enabling and developmental policies. Stabilizing policies remain under-represented, as reflected in Shanghai's relatively weak rule of law and under-developed regulatory infrastructure, although policy-makers have more recently begun focusing on improving Shanghai's regulatory system and ensuring compliance to international regulatory rules. Despite these efforts, Shanghai's financial policy mix remains largely dominated by enabling and developmental instruments, geared towards the central and municipal governments' desired policy output of IFC development.

As such, IFC development across the three cases is characterized by a high degree of diversity and variegation. Yet such diversity has not prevented the three IFCs from attaining comparable levels of success. Rather, the three IFCs have attained success through policy design processes that are cognizant and reflective of the extant political-economic context, and based on the actions and influence of dominant subsystem actors who are focused on attaining IFC success. By "nesting" policy mix design within policy subsystem configuration, Hong Kong, Singapore and Shanghai have each been able to achieve their individual successes as IFCs. The findings of this book go against conventional thinking on IFC convergence and expectations of an increasing homogeneity of financial policy mixes across different IFCs. Furthermore, this book has also made several contributions to the IFC literature and public policy theory. These are discussed next.

Contributions to Literature and Theory

As Chap. 2 has shown, the existing literature on IFCs and financial policy tends to overstate the impacts of structural economic variables on IFC success, with the consequence being an assumed convergence of IFC development models around the development of these variables. In reality, IFCs exhibit a vast diversity in terms of the financial activities which take place within them, the financial policies formulated and implemented by policy-makers in their development, and the political-economic contexts within which they exist. More importantly, as this book has shown, IFC success is dependent on the adaptation of policy mix design to the unique political-economic context of the IFC's policy subsystem.

However, existing public policy theoretical approaches do not provide the tools necessary for a deeper understanding of this interplay between policy mix design and subsystem configuration. As shown in Chap. 3, extant shortcomings in the policy subsystems and policy instruments approaches present an incomplete picture of IFC development when these two approaches are individually applied to the study of IFCs. This has necessitated the establishment of the nested instrumental approach, which draws upon and combines the policy subsystems and instruments approaches into an integrated analytical framework. The application of this approach has brought forth empirical and theoretical contributions.

First, the application of the nested instrumental approach to the three cases has served to provide a deeper and more nuanced understanding of IFC development, by accounting for policy subsystem configurations and their impacts on financial policy mix design. This inclusion of contextual subsystem data is a significant empirical contribution, given the existing literature's bias towards quantitative understandings of IFC success that do not sufficiently address the political-economic context within which IFCs exist and succeed. The use of case study and qualitative methods in this book has proven particularly useful in providing such an in-depth understanding of how the political-economic context affects IFC development and financial policy instrument choices.

Furthermore, the nested instrumental approach presents a useful structure around which case data can be organized, allowing for a more integrated understanding of how financial policy mix design is determined by its subsystem configuration, leading to the attainment of desired policy outputs. Given the above-mentioned neglect of political context in the existing IFC literature, this melding of policy and politics in the nested instrumental approach contributes significantly to the existing literature and provides a useful new analytical framework for studying the politics of finance.

Secondly, the development and introduction of the nested instrumental approach in this book contributes directly to public policy theory. As Chap. 3 has shown, shortcomings in the policy subsystems and policy instruments approaches suggest that the subsystems' approach tends to be overly broad and does not sufficiently explicate the policy instruments through which policies are made while the instruments approach downplays the influence of context in its focus on instruments design and implementation processes. In combining the two approaches, the nested instrumental approach allows for a melding of key insights from both the subsystems and the instruments approaches and a simultaneous negation of their individual shortcomings.

As such, the nested instrumental approach represents a unique and theoretically driven analytical framework that both addresses the political-economic context and examines policies as instruments or means applied in the attainment of defined ends. Through the facilitation of a more integrative approach to understanding policy processes, the nested instrumental approach presents a potentially useful tool for policy analysis. In particular, a greater understanding of policy mix design, coupled with a deeper appreciation of the political-economic context and its influence on policy-making, will allow for a policy design process that is more attuned to political-economic context and political realities. This facilitates a contextually nuanced understanding of the politics and policy of finance.

Implications for Policy-Makers

The findings of this book also present important implications for policy-makers. First, this book has shown how Hong Kong, Singapore and Shanghai have attained comparative success as IFCs despite differences in their political systems and the types of financial activities they specialize in. Much of this has to do with ensuring that financial policy mixes are designed to complement the IFC's policy subsystem configuration. Extrapolating from these findings, a case can be made that there are different paths to success for different IFCs.

This means that policy-makers need to re-evaluate preconceived notions or expectations of IFC convergence and instead become more cognizant of their political-economic contexts. This in turn requires a deeper awareness of the ways in which context has shaped policy in order to bring about financial sector development and success. This requires policy-makers to take on what Wu et al. have termed a "political perspective" and develop related competencies in "policy acumen" (Wu et al. 2010). Policy-makers and policy designers therefore need to build up deep extensive knowledge of inter-actor relations and dynamics within their respective IFCs, with the policy design process factoring in such relations and dynamics. This also means achieving a deeper understanding of the relations of dominance and dependence among major subsystem actors which define and shape policy subsystem configurations.

Singapore presents a positive instance of such contextual understanding on the part of its policy-makers, with financial policy-making processes driven by a strong appreciation of nested instrumentality. Specifically, Singapore's financial policy-makers have exhibited a strong understanding of the city–state's policy subsystem configuration as an IFC and correspondingly designed their policies in accordance with this configuration, allowing for the attainment of both prudential regulatory goals and industry ambitions. This has been largely achieved through the MAS's extensive consultative processes, which have imbued regulatory officials with a keen understanding of industry interests and allowed for the inclusion of industry actors in the drafting of rules and regulations.

Policies that are reflective or representative of the political context are likely to benefit from increased compliance and greater public support, since such policies are able to cater to the interests and benefits of both policy-makers and financial institutions that are often targets of these policies. More importantly, policy-makers who develop a closer understanding of the political-economic context within which they operate and are then able to establish closer working relations with their industry counterparts will contribute to a regulatory "compact" between the state and the industry that facilitates mutual understanding and policy co-creation. However, mechanisms must be in place to ensure that "regulatory capture" does not take place.

Aside from accounting for its policy subsystem configuration, policy mix design should also be attuned to desired policy outputs. In other words, policy mixes should comprise instruments that are more efficiently targeted towards the attainment of policy outputs through processes or pathways which are clear and well-understood by policy-makers. While the policy instruments literature has made significant advances in this respect, there remains a need to understand how policy outputs themselves are defined by policy subsystem configurations, with a set of desired policy outputs typically defined or set in place by dominant subsystem actors. In the context of IFCs, these policy outputs are also related to the type of financial centre that policy-makers wish to establish (such as an investment safe haven with a strong wealth management industry, loan syndication centre with deep capital markets, or an international banking centre with strong international linkages and compliance with international regulations).

As this book has shown, Hong Kong's policy-makers have chosen to focus on policy outputs of financial market stability and investor protection based on their commitment to free market principles. In contrast, policy-makers in Singapore and Shanghai view financial markets as a significant contributor to national economic development, with the result being a focus on IFC promotion and development, although Singapore has retained its desired policy output of financial market stability as well. This has resulted in the design of financial policy mixes that are geared towards the attainment of policy outputs which the respective dominant subsystem actors of the three IFCs have chosen to pursue.

In tying policy mix design to the interests and aspirations of senior policy-makers and the IFC's existing advantages, financial policy instruments can be designed to be more effective in achieving targeted or desired policy outputs, whether in terms of financial market stabilization or IFC development and promotion. In short, policy mix design needs to take into account policy subsystem configurations and as a corollary, the policy outputs deemed desirable by dominant policy actors, which also flow from the subsystem configuration. This means that there is a need to align the three components of policy-making which the nested instrumental approach has laid out, namely policy subsystem configurations, policy mix design and policy outputs.

Going Forward

Given constraints of space and scope, this book has not been able to address all issues related to IFC development. Rather, I have chosen to take a more targetted and focused approach in focusing on Hong Kong, Singapore and Shanghai. There are invariably issues which may lie beyond the scope of this book. Nonetheless, these issues provide potential avenues for future research, with this book providing a useful foundation for future research on IFCs and nested instrumentality. For instance, future research could address IFC development in other Asian cities as well as second-tiered financial centres. These may include Shenzhen, Dubai and Kuala Lumpur.

Related to these less successful IFCs is the issue of IFC failure. IFCs which have failed to attain success remain understudied. While this book has focused on IFC success, its findings can just as easily be applied to the study of IFC failure. Failure, after all, is the flipside of success. However, it should also be noted that definitions of failure are subjective and contentious. Policy-makers of less successful IFC's may well argue that they have not failed, but more time is needed before their cities can take off as IFCs. Regardless, there is still a need to understand why or how less successful IFCs have not been able to attain the levels of financial sector development and success which the three IFCs studied in this book have achieved.

This book has enumerated and discussed the various factors which have contributed to the success of the three IFCs. It then goes without saying that the lack of these factors is likely to contribute to failure or at the very least, raise the barriers of entry to success. Furthermore, the nested instrumental approach that was introduced and applied in this book suggests that IFC success is very much dependent on ensuring that financial policy mixes and policy-makers are attuned to the political-economic realities of the subsystem. Correspondingly, failure to address subsystem configurations is also likely to lead to IFC failure. However, further research on failed IFCs is required, in order to achieve a clearer understanding of why these IFCs have failed.

Regardless, this book has provided a useful empirical and theoretical starting point for future IFC studies. It has sought to better incorporate political-economic contextual variables into the study of IFCs and financial policy. From a theoretical perspective, it has made attempts at delineating and understanding the linkages between context (subsystem configuration) and policy (policy mix design). At the very least, it has provided a useful account of how Hong Kong, Singapore and Shanghai have emerged and continued to reign as Asia's top financial centres. This is an account that other financial centres will continue to watch closely, as competition between cities to become the leading financial hub heats up.

References

Former Senior Regulatory Official (2013) Interview. 22 May 2013, Singapore
Koh YG (2013b) Interview. 7 August 2013, Singapore
Menon R (2013b) Interview. 16 September 2013, Singapore

Poon JPH (2003) Hierarchical tendencies of capital markets among international financial centers. Growth Change 34:135–156
Poon JPH, Eldredge B, Yeung D (2004) Rank size distribution of international financial centers. Int Reg Sci Rev 27:411–430
Wu X, Ramesh M, Howlett M, Fritzen SA (2010) The public policy primer. Routledge, London
Yeandle M, Dranev N (2013) The global financial centres index 14. Z/Yen Group and Qatar Financial Centre Authority, London

The manufacturer's authorised representative in the EU is Springer Nature Customer Service Centre GmbH, Europaplatz 3, 69115 Heidelberg, Germany. If you have any concerns regarding our products, please contact ProductSafety@springernature.com

Printed and bound by CPI Group (UK) Ltd, Croydon, CR0 4YY
01/10/2026
02226499-0001